NONE OF YOUR BUSINESS

Government Secrecy in America

NONE OF YOUR

BUSINESS

Edited by Norman Dorsen and Stephen Gillers
With an Introduction by Anthony Lewis

A BOOK OF THE COMMITTEE FOR PUBLIC JUSTICE

The Viking Press New York

First published in 1974 by The Viking Press, Inc.
625 Madison Avenue, New York, N.Y. 10022
Published simultaneously in Canada by
The Macmillan Company of Canada Limited
SBN 670-51500-0
Library of Congress catalog card number: 73-17685
Printed in U.S.A. by Vail-Ballou Press, Inc.

This book is based on the proceedings of a conference on government secrecy held in New York on May 18–19, 1973, sponsored jointly by the Committee for Public Justice and the Arthur Garfield Hays Civil Liberties Program at New York University School of Law.

Foreword

Bacon said, "All governments are obscure and invisible." His dictum reflects a long tradition of government secrecy, here and abroad. It stands to reason that a person disposing of weighty and controversial issues gets through the day more easily when his decisions are shrouded from view, particularly from the eyes of those most affected by them. This is true whether the decision-maker is a corporate executive or union leader, an academic administrator or government official. But government officials conduct public business. Secrecy and deviousness, often unjustified in other contexts, are intolerable when national interests of high importance are involved.

Although the Constitution does not expressly guarantee American citizens a right to know what their government is doing, the Supreme Court on several occasions has recognized the "right to know" as a general proposition. For example, it has stated that "the Constitution protects the right to receive information and ideas" and that, as far as radio and tv are concerned, "it is the right of the viewers and listeners, not the right of the broadcasters, which is paramount."

But government secrecy and public access to information are not primarily legal questions. They are rather political issues of basic importance to democratic government. They were so recognized from the beginning of the nation. Henry Steele Commager, the noted historian, has written: "The generation that made the nation thought secrecy in government one of the instruments of Old World tyranny and committed itself to the principle that a democracy cannot function unless the people are permitted to know what their government is up to."

Anthony Lewis points out in his Introduction that Vietnam and Watergate are the twin events—he rightly calls them earthquakes—which have focused unprecedented attention on the misuse of executive power and on the secrecy which facilitated these abuses. We have since endured a third earthquake—the disclosure of the illegal financial dealings of Vice President Spiro Agnew, leading to his resignation. And a fourth earthquake may be coming—impeachment of the President.

The Vietnam misadventure alone was sufficient to impel the Committee for Public Justice and the Arthur Garfield Hays Civil Liberties Program to convene a conference of historians, lawyers, journalists, scientists and public officials to discuss the dangers and limits of government secrecy. Watergate broke while the conference was being planned, and the Agnew conviction and resignation came afterward.

Neither the organizers of the conference nor the editors of this volume believe that all government business must take place in a fish bowl. There are situations in which secrecy is permissible, even desirable. Thus, a government should be able to protect certain military and diplomatic information of potential value to enemies; to safeguard the process of decision-making by protecting confidences in order to encourage frank discussion; and to assure that private information about people is not widely disseminated.

The precise boundaries of these and perhaps other exceptions to the general requirement of open government are an important subject of this book. Not all the participants agree on what these boundaries should be. But we should candidly state that the perception of public policy shared by many of the contributors to this volume leads them to favor open government and to define the exceptions narrowly. They are likely to agree, in other words, with the premise of the House Committee on Government Operations, which approved the Freedom of Information Act in 1966:

> A democratic society requires an informed, intelligent electorate, and the intelligence of the electorate varies as the quantity and quality of its information varies. A danger signal to our democratic society in the United States is the fact that such a truism needs repeating. . . .

Norman Dorsen
Stephen Gillers

NEW YORK CITY
JANUARY 1974

Acknowledgments

There are many people whose efforts made the conference on government secrecy successful. Charles Goodell served as chairman of the conference, and Leon Friedman helped to plan and organize the proceedings with the assistance of Leslie Harman and Rochelle Korman. Other members of the Committee for Public Justice who provided substantial assistance prior to and at the conference were Blair Clark, Elinor Gordon, Burke Marshall, and Telford Taylor.

In addition to the contributors to this volume, Sam Archibald, Ben Bagdikian, Richard Barnet, Lawrence Baskir, Senator Lawton Chiles, Michael Green, Nat Hentoff, James Kronfeld, Ralph Lapp, Ellen Lurie, Representative John Moss, James Ridgeway, Reuben Robertson, A. M. Rosenthal, and Leon Ulman provided valuable assistance in the planning of the conference.

Finally, we wish to thank Sheila Rossi and Dorothy Waleski for their help in the preparation of the manuscript of this book.

Contents

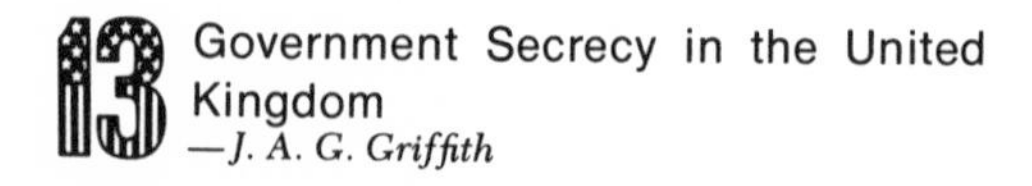

Contributors to the Conference on Government Secrecy

Norman Dorsen, a professor at the New York University Law School, is General Counsel of the American Civil Liberties Union and author and editor of many books, including *The Rights of Americans.*

Daniel Ellsberg is the author of *Papers on the War* and other books. He was a defendant in the government's unsuccessful prosecution arising out of the release of the Pentagon Papers.

Ernest Fitzgerald is an industrial engineer and author of *The High Priests of Waste.* He is former Deputy for Management Systems, Office of the Secretary for the Air Force. He was fired for exposing cost overruns but was subsequently reinstated.

Stanley Futterman is an associate professor at New York University Law School and a former Assistant Legal Adviser at the State Department.

Albert Gore is a former United States Senator from Tennessee. He is now Chairman of the Island Creek Coal Company of Cleveland.

J. A. G. Griffith is senior professor of law at the London School of Economics and the author of books on administrative law, local government, and public administration in England.

Morton H. Halperin is a Senior Fellow at The Brookings Institution. He is a former staff member of the National Security Council and a former Deputy Assistant Secretary of Defense.

Anthony Lewis is a columnist for *The New York Times.*

William Phillips is Staff Director of the House Government Information and Foreign Operations Subcommittee.

Robert Saloschin is a senior staff attorney with the Justice Department and Chairman of the Justice Department's Freedom of Information Committee.

John Shattuck is staff counsel in charge of the American Civil Liberties Union's privacy and government secrecy litigation.

M. L. Stein is a professor at the New York University School of Journalism and has written for *The Nation, World,* and *The New York Times.* His books include *When Presidents Meet the Press* and *Freedom of the Press.*

Jeremy Stone is Director of the Federation of American Scientists and a long-term commentator on national-security and arms control problems.

Harrison Wellford is legislative assistant to Senator Philip Hart and former senior staff counsel for the Center for the Study of Responsive Law. He is author of *Sowing the Wind.*

Alan Westin is a professor of public law at Columbia University and the author of *Data Banks in a Free Society* and *Privacy and Freedom.*

David Wise is a political writer based in Washington and coauthor of *The Invisible Government.* His latest book is *The Politics of Lying.*

Participants

Robert A. Black, Jr., has been a Fellow in international studies at Columbia University.

Earl Callen is a professor of physics at American University.

Blair Clark, a former newspaper and broadcasting correspondent and general manager of CBS news, is Vice Chairman of the Committee for Public Justice.

Thomas Emerson is professor of law at Yale University and the author of many books, including *The System of Freedom of Expression.*

Leon Friedman is Executive Director of the Committee for Public Justice.

Stephen Gillers, a New York lawyer, is former Executive Director of the Committee for Public Justice, author of *Getting Justice: The Rights of People,* and an editor of *Investigating the FBI.*

Ira Glasser is Executive Director of the New York Civil Liberties Union.

Charles E. Goodell is a former United States Senator from New York and author of *Political Prisoners in America.* He is Chairman of the Committee for Public Justice.

Frederick Holborn teaches at the School for Advanced International Studies at Johns Hopkins University.

Herman Kahn is Assistant Librarian at Yale University.

Edward Koch is a United States Congressman from New York.

James Kronfeld is counsel to the House Government Information and Foreign Operations Subcommittee.

Andreas Lowenfeld is a professor at New York University Law School and former Deputy Legal Adviser at the State Department.

Irene Margolis is a lawyer on the staff of the United States Senate Constitutional Rights Subcommittee.

Burke Marshall is Deputy Dean of the Yale Law School and a former Assistant Attorney General.

David Martin is a special assistant to the Secretary of Health, Education, and Welfare.

Aryeh Neier is Executive Director of the American Civil Liberties Union.

Ronald Plesser is a staff attorney for the Center for the Study of Responsive Law.

Christopher Pyle is a journalist and was responsible for uncovering information about the Army's domestic surveillance program.

Harry Ransom is professor of political science at Vanderbilt University and author of *Central Intelligence and National Security.*

Bernard Schwartz is a professor at New York University Law School and author of many books, including *The Bill of Rights: A Documentary History.*

Arthur Sylvester is former Assistant Secretary of Defense for Public Affairs.

Telford Taylor is a professor at Columbia University Law School and the author of many books on legal subjects, including *Nuremberg and Vietnam.*

Jerome Wiesner is President of M.I.T. and former Science Adviser to President Kennedy.

NONE OF YOUR BUSINESS

Introduction

—by Anthony Lewis

A popular Government, without popular information, or the means of acquiring it, is but the Prologue to a Farce or a Tragedy; or, perhaps both. Knowledge will forever govern ignorance: And a people who mean to be their own Governors, must arm themselves with the power which knowledge gives.

— JAMES MADISON

For eighty-nine days in the winter and spring of 1973, Daniel Ellsberg and Anthony J. Russo, Jr., were tried on criminal charges of espionage, theft, and conspiracy in the publication of the Pentagon Papers. After the judge dismissed the case because of the prosecution's misconduct, some of the jurors spoke about how their feelings had changed in the prior months. What had changed most was their attitude toward the secret behavior of the United States government.

"I was a typical apathetic American" before the trial, said Mrs. Joan B. Duhigg, a housewife. "But this has awakened me to what is going on. I'm going to read" from now on, she said, adding that she "might even march" against government policies.

Mrs. Cora C. Neal said it was "rather surprising" to learn from the trial testimony that the government often did one thing in Vietnam while telling the public it was doing another. Mrs. Darlene Y. Arneaud told reporters that she had favored the prosecution during the trial. But after it was over, she read the newspapers for the first time in four months and learned about the misconduct that had led the judge to dismiss the case—especially the burglary planned by White House agents to get Ellsberg's files from his psychiatrist's office. "There has to be a change in the government," Mrs. Arneaud said, "there's no doubt about it. The power is overwhelming. I'm just a little guy. I just want our country to survive."

The Ellsberg-Russo trial happened to bring together, in one forum, the two outstanding contemporary American symbols of government secrecy: Vietnam and Watergate. Those two great series of events—we might better call them earthquakes—changed the feelings of millions of Americans toward their institutions.

Vietnam, it is often said, marked the end of American innocence. We learned that our government, like others, tells lies and commits crimes; in the name of freedom it can support tyranny and brutal repression. And it can do these things, we discovered, without consulting or even advising the people or their representatives in Congress: It can govern in secret. It even carried on secret wars, we belatedly learned—bombing Laos from 1965 to 1969 and running a mercenary ground force there, and bombing Cambodia in 1969–1970, all without any authority from Congress.

Watergate taught Americans that secrecy may similarly lead to the perversion of democracy at home. We learned that the President of the United States had in 1970 sought to establish a secret police system in this country, authorizing burglary, electronic eavesdropping, and other measures in the name of internal security despite explicit advice that they were illegal. We learned that members of Richard Nixon's White House made lists of "enemies"—American citizens who were to be "screwed" by pressure on their tax returns and other means. We learned that that White House had joined in a massive attempt to cover up the crimes of Watergate and obstruct justice, even going so far as involving the Central Intelligence Agency and, during the Ellsberg trial, offering the trial judge, Matthew Byrne, Jr., the equivalent of a bribe: the directorship of the Federal Bureau of Investigation.

All that was done in secret. Watergate became the political

earthquake it was when the press, the courts, and the Congress stripped away the secrecy.

It was against the background of Vietnam and Watergate that a conference on government secrecy was held in New York on May 18 and 19, 1973. The sponsors were the Committee for Public Justice and the Arthur Garfield Hays Civil Liberties Program at New York University Law School, where the meeting took place. The participants included lawyers, journalists, present and former members of Congress, and other public officials.

Conferences can be tame affairs, treating public issues in the abstract. This one was something else. It met during events not envisaged when it was planned, events that made its subject extraordinarily urgent. The Select Senate Committee under Senator Sam Ervin had started its hearings just that week; after frantic months of effort to conceal the Nixon reelection committee's involvement in the burglary at Democratic headquarters, the Watergate facts were emerging from the shadows. The Vietnam war had been officially "settled," four bloody years after the promise of peace, and now American planes were bombing Cambodia without any authority in law. Just a week earlier, the Ellsberg-Russo trial had ended.

The dramatic events that provided a setting for the conference made clear that secrecy in government is not a mere abstraction, a subject for theoretical debate by philosophers or lawyer defenders of civil liberty: it is a matter of power. In the last century Lord Acton warned that power corrupts. In our century, when man has achieved the scientific techniques to destroy his world or enslave his fellows, the new danger is secrecy. For secrecy shields the abuse of office that endangers freedom and peace. Knowledge is power, in the familiar phrase. But secret knowledge is greater. It is the key to absolute power.

That became the theme of the conference: secrecy as a means of power—and the defenses against it.

I

"Secrecy in government is as American as apple pie." So said Herman Kahn of Yale University, provoking his fellow conferees with that echo of Rap Brown's famous comment, "Violence is as American as cherry pie." Kahn's point was that secrecy is not something invented by the Nixon administration. It has never been the rule in the United States that public life is carried on at all times in a goldfish bowl. At the founding moment of the nation, privacy of deliberation was assured: the Constitutional Convention of 1787 began with a decision by the delegates to close their meetings to the public and publish no official journal of their debates. So anxious were they to insulate themselves from the distractions of the outside world, Justice Felix Frankfurter reminded us, that they had the streets outside their hall in Philadelphia covered with straw to muffle the sound of horses and carriages.

In considering the political dangers of official secrecy, it is important to remember the balancing value of privacy. Even the most ardent advocate of open government, for example, might hesitate at a rule that allowed anyone to root around in the files of the Federal Bureau of Investigation, to look over the collected gossip and poison-pen accusations against individuals. In matters in which private reputations can be unfairly damaged, confidentiality is desirable.

There is also a case for confidentiality in those situations where public interest requires the most unembarrassed advice and discussion. Nearly everyone would concede that a President is ordinarily entitled to ask the private advice of intimates about, say, the character of possible appointees or the political outlook for some policy—without having to publish the text of their conversation the next week. The nine Justices of the Supreme Court could not do their difficult job if they could not confer among themselves in assured privacy.

Albert Gore, the former Senator from Tennessee, argued at the conference for a limited degree of secrecy for Congress. He said Senators and Members of the House sometimes have to educate themselves in closed meetings prior to public ones, lest they be overwhelmed by better-informed witnesses. He noted, for example, that the public sessions of the Senate Watergate Committee were preceded by private interrogation of the witnesses—just as lawyers would prepare for a public trial. He drew on his own experience with the example of the Johnson administration's proposal to deploy antiballistic missiles. He and others wanted hearings, he said, "but we did not know what questions to ask. . . . It required an executive hearing in which we could expose our ignorance, so to speak. . . . An overwhelming majority of this subcommittee became convinced during the executive session that deployment of the ABM was wholly in error. We determined to take the issue to the people."

But all these arguments for confidentiality contain their own dangers. The secrecy of FBI and other personal files, for example, led during the 1950s to the grotesque injustice of American citizens being dismissed from government service or denied industrial employment as "security risks" on the basis of political charges by unnamed accusers. If a talk with the President of the United States may have involved discussion of high crimes, the public interest requires that appropriate authorities—either legislative or prosecutorial—be able to pierce the protective veil of privacy.

Senator Gore's example raises the question: what if the scientists with whom he and other Senators were able to discuss the ABM candidly in closed meetings had been less capable, less wise, less informed? Suppose, in short, that they had misadvised the Senators? One great purpose of openness in public life is to expose policy arguments to the clear light of public discussion. That is the theory of democracy, and at the conference Senator Gore recalled the most terrible example of the price that can be paid for departing from it. That was, of course, Vietnam. The Foreign Relations Committee, of which he was a member, held innumerable executive sessions over the decade of Vietnam to get the highly classified "facts" from the Pentagon, the State Department, and other agencies. But the intelligence reports they received turned out to be faked or distorted or just wrong. Looking back at it all, Senator Gore said he was "convinced now that the public would have been better served had all these sessions been public."

It is not possible, in a general introduction to the complex subject of this book, to touch on the many suggested grounds for permitting degrees of secrecy in government; they are analyzed in the chapters and in the conference discussions. But it can be said—it should be said—that any such argument should always be scrutinized with a skeptical eye. The reason is simple: those who argue for secrecy, however sophisticated their explanation, may really have in mind their own convenience. Life is simpler for those who govern if they do not have to worry about explaining their actions. And so, very often, the arguments for secrecy, however strenuously and sincerely pressed, fade away if openness is demanded. Professor Bernard Schwartz of the NYU Law School reminded the conference that not only its committee sessions but the meetings of the United States Senate itself were once closed to the public. And when the proposal was made to open them, Senators asked, how can you do this, how can we conduct our business and have our debates in public, how can we speak freely?

The other general observation to be made is that in considering these claims of a public interest in secrecy, there is a tremendous difference between informal advice and the making of decisions, between discussion and action, between the beginning of a governmental process and the end. To put it graphically, there is a difference between a President getting intelligence advice in secret on the situation in Laos and his secret decision to wage a war there.

That is the real point to be drawn from the way the Constitution was framed. The Philadelphia Convention was held behind closed doors. But the document it produced was adopted as the foundation of a new republic only after the most exhaustive public debate. Within a year, twelve of the states held ratifying conventions. The draft was argued in the Federalist Papers and in dozens of other pamphlets. The people of America were involved in the decision to adopt that Constitution to an extent perhaps unparalleled in political history. And we should not forget that the promoters of the new system had to accept changes in their charter in order to secure ratification. They had to promise a Bill of Rights, which was shortly proposed and ratified as the first ten amendments. Those amendments confirmed the commitment to an open political process. Most significant was the First, with what Justice Oliver Wendel Holmes called its "sweeping command": "Congress shall make no law . . . abridging the freedom of speech, or of the press." Holmes recognized that those principles of free thought would always seem uncomfortable to many. But he wrote in 1919: "When men have realized that time has upset many fighting faiths, they may come to believe, even more than they believe the very foundations of their own conduct, that the ultimate good desired is better reached by free trade in ideas—that the best test of truth is the power of the thought to get itself accepted in the competition of the market. . . . That, at any rate, is the theory of our Constitution. It is an experiment, as all life is an experiment."

In the deeper sense, then, the constitutional sense, secrecy in government is *not* as American as apple pie. It has occurred, it may be defended in particular circumstances, but it must always be regarded as an exception. From the beginning, government in the United States has been philosophically committed to an open system, to inclusion of the public in its decisional process. Anyone who has compared attitudes in America with those in almost any European country knows that the assumptions are quite different. A British journalist who knows Washington well, David Watt of the *Financial Times*, London, has put it: "In America the onus of proof that any particular piece of secrecy is necessary lies with the person who is imposing the restriction. In Britain it is assumed that unless you can establish a clear right ot know, it is better that you should not."

The contrast between British and American attitudes is revealing. Professor J. A. G. Griffith of the Law Department, London School of Economics, spoke to the conference about the penchant of the British government—all governments, of all parties—to make policy in private. To prevent tyranny, he said, the system really relies on social understandings that certain things are just not done. There is a close-knit Establishment, tied together by school, university, class or, indeed, membership in the House of Commons. It informally decides whether government has acted within the proprieties. So few are the voices that dissent out loud, Professor Griffith said, that he sometimes thinks all really challenging criticism of government could be ended by suppressing fifty people.

Britain has no written constitution limiting the government's authority to specified powers. The government of the day, in theory, has total power through its parliamentary majority. If Parliament so willed, it could order all left-handed men executed at dawn of a particular day. At least no higher law would stop it, because there is no higher law than what a majority of Parliament decides from time to time. What would stop it is the unwritten understanding of the relative handful of Britons who manage politics, the civil service, the press, the church, and the other governing institutions of the country. As one nonpracticing British barrister—he has turned journalist—said, "We are a country of men, not laws."

American freedom is based on law. We have no old-boy network, no House of Lords, no Pall Mall clubs, no unwritten sense of propriety to protect us. Left to the British reliance on character, we should be at the mercy of the first adventurer from southern California. Lacking a reassuring network of personal relationships, lacking any deep respect for tradition, we must rely on law and institutional arrangements. That is why we are so shocked when institutions fail or are abused, as they were in the Nixon White House.

In one crucial respect Watergate was surely a sign of health in the American body politic: it demonstrated that the public could still rise in outrage at what was seen as an official attempt to twist the processes of law. There was an extraordinary response—3 million telegrams to Congress—when President Nixon forced out the Special Watergate Prosecutor, Archibald Cox, and Attorney General Elliot Richardson and his deputy, William Ruckelshaus, resigned. The President had resisted Mr. Cox's subpoena for White House tapes and documents. The United States Court of Appeals for the District of Columbia, in an historic judgment, rejected his claim of "executive privilege." Mr. Nixon chose not to take that judgment to the Supreme Court—and then announced, unilaterally, that he would supply "summaries" through the chosen medium of Senator John Stennis rather than follow the judicial decision he had allowed to become final. Mr. Cox's resistance to that course, and his consequent dismissal, were rightly seen by the country as an ultimate test of law. In the face of an aroused public, the President backed down on the substance of the issue, supplying the subpoenaed material and agreeing to the appointment of another Special Prosecutor. The struggle to make a lawless President respect the law was hardly over, but the public had understood the issue.

Thus secrecy and lawlessness work together in the United States. The more public opinion can be kept inert, the better chance there is that abuse of official power will go uncorrected.

And that is true not only on the exalted level of the American Presidency. One of the most revealing discussions in this conference concerned secrecy in local government. Professor M. L. Stein of NYU's Journalism Department showed that local governments across America often operate "in an aura of secrecy and distrust of both the press and the public. Clandestine meetings, hidden records and unavailable officials are commonplace even in states with open-record and open-meeting laws." Local secrecy, he suggested, may have "created a public tolerance" for the attitudes displayed in Watergate.

Ira Glasser, executive director of the New York Civil Liberties Union, echoed this thought. Most Americans begin experiencing official secrecy and arrogance, he said, when they are six or seven years old—in public schools. He gave examples of school principals simply refusing to follow the law by saying: "I don't care what the law is, I run my school the way I see fit." Mr. Glasser said he had heard this many times, not only from school principals but from the officials of city housing, welfare, sanitation, and police departments. And so, he said, people learn at an early age and from their closest local institutions that "you say one thing, you subscribe to a set of ideals, but you act in another way."

The concern aroused by such widespread local practice was summed up by Mr. Glasser in these words: "Hannah Arendt wrote a book about the Eichmann trial which was subtitled *The Banality of Evil.* I think we might well begin to look at the banality of secrecy and the banality of official lawlessness. What is terrifying about official lawlessness and official secrecy is not that it is an aberration, but precisely that it is routine."

II

American history is filled with incongruities, with conflicts of principle and practice, with opposing trends that gather momentum together and struggle for dominance. Something like that may have been happening in the field of government secrecy.

Any fair appraisal would have to conclude that the United States is one of the most open societies in the world today. Certainly, foreign journalists are impressed by the freedom of the press to comment on official activity and dig out official secrets. It hardly has to worry about contempt of court, a power used by judges elsewhere to restrain the press. There is no equivalent of Britain's Official Secrets Act, making it a crime in the vaguest terms to publish anything not formally authorized. Almost anything can be said here about an official or any other public personality, true or false, without fear of a libel action. And recent legal developments continue to move in the direction of freedom. It was only in 1964, for example, in the libel case of *New York Times* v. *Sullivan*, that the Supreme Court found false comment on public officials constitutionally protected unless made with malice—a standard unimaginable a few years earlier.

On the other hand, one also sees menacing developments. Locally, there is the atmosphere of secrecy and arrogance—met, according to Messrs. Stein and Glasser, by widespread public indifference. In the federal government, there is the growth of something never known in peacetime before this generation: an enormous national-security apparatus, including vast intelligence operations, all steeped in secrecy. And there is the effort, uncovered by Watergate, to apply secret and illegal methods to domestic affairs under the guise of "national security."

In these conflicting trends there must be at work the familiar process of action and reaction. Government secrecy was not often a great issue in America's past because governments did not have so many secrets. Governments did not matter so much altogether: they operated on the margin of American society, with relatively little power to affect the lives of ordinary people. But in the last forty years, say since the inauguration of Franklin Roosevelt in 1933, all this has changed. Domestically, the economy and therefore the expectations of individuals have become dependent on official decisions; in welfare, police, health, higher education, and many other areas the influence of government has grown enormously. And of course the same is true in foreign and military affairs: the role of the United States has been transformed from a minor to a central one on the world stage.

As government power over our lives has increased, so have the countervailing protections of the Constitution been enlarged by judicial interpretation. Again and again the Supreme Court has reinterpreted the standards of freedom to meet a new problem. *The New York Times* libel case is a local example: the Court took the strong position it did because racist forces in the South had begun to use libel actions to censor criticism. (Alabama courts had returned judgments totaling $3 million against the *Times* for publishing an advertisement which inferentially criticized some local and state officials, without naming them, and made minor errors of fact.)

Similarly, in the federal sphere, new attempts to control or repress speech and association have been met by developing legal doctrine. Until 1965, no federal statute had ever been found in violation of the First Amendment. In that year, the Supreme Court unanimously struck down a law which required the Post Office to detain "Communist political propaganda" mailed from abroad unless the addressee requested its delivery.

If the courts have enlarged freedom of speech and inquiry, and if the press has been somewhat more aggressive in using its rights, then to that extent balance has been maintained in the American system: power has been restrained by other power. But the more important balance of power is between the President and Congress. And there one cannot be so confident.

The main threat lies in the growing power—especially the secret power—of the Presidency. As a matter of history, the growth of government in the United States over these last forty years has largely been the growth of the federal executive.

The divisions of authority designed by the Framers to prevent concentration of power—divisions between the states and the national government and among the federal, executive, legislative, and judicial branches—have gone askew. When we want peace or a better welfare system or an end to rising prices, we look to the President.

It would be a man of unusual modesty and simplicity of character who could resist the human temptations of such power. And the United States has not been blessed lately by a Jefferson or a Linclon. It had in succession two Presidents, who, though very different in their personalities, shared an obsession with secrecy. Lyndon Johnson so detested leaks that he was said to have changed some decisions rather than confirm accurate stories; he led the United States into its most terrible war while denying, even after many thousands of American troops were in Vietnam, that they were there in a combat role. Richard Nixon's paranoia about newspapers so infected his White House that it reacted to leaks with the gross illegalities of wiretapping and burglary.

Even in less morbid circumstances, secrecy is the handmaiden of increasing Presidential power. That is the highly practical, political meaning of the so-called doctrine of executive privilege—the right to keep things secret from Congress and the courts. It should be described as "so-called" because, according to scholars on the subject, it has no basis in history or in judicial decisions. For the first one hundred years of the United States, no President successfully asserted a right to withhold information from Congress. George Washington was troubled when a House committee in 1792 sought documents on a disastrous military expedition; but after expressing his doubts privately in cabinet, he supplied the papers. Lincoln complied with every request for information during the exigencies of the Civil War, including requests for military and diplomatic secrets.

It is in our time, when power has been running to the White House, that the practice of saying no to Congressional questions has become so common. The conference was told that executive privilege had been claimed 49 times since 1952—more than twice the number of prior cases. Shortly after the conference, claim number 50 was made: President Nixon's refusal to let the Senate Watergate Committee see White House documents that might throw light on the crimes under investigation. And then came number 51: Nixon's withholding of the tapes he had made of conversations in his office relevant to the Watergate inquiries. Of these 51 recent assertions of the doctrine, 22—by far the largest number—were made by the Nixon administration.

Professor Norman Dorsen of the NYU Law School and John H. F. Shattuck, staff counsel of the American Civil Liberties Union, made the point in their essay on executive privilege that this claim is the stuff of power. "It is used to cut off Congressional inquiry into the very issues over which Congress and the President are most sharply divided." Thus, in the Kennedy administration, General Maxwell Taylor declined to testify about the Bay of Pigs invasion. In the Nixon administration, Secretary of the Treasury John Connally would not talk about the government's loan to the Lockheed Aircraft Corporation. The most brazen assertion of the doctine came in the early stages of the Watergate inquiry, when Attorney General Richard Kleindienst claimed that the President could order any federal employee, past or present, not to testify on any subject—and that Congress' only recourse was impeachment of the President. That extreme view was abandoned by President Nixon when Watergate developments made it politically untenable: as a matter of public opinion and power, in short, not law.

The assertion of executive privilege is not by any means the only device used by Presidents and their officials in resisting Congressional requests for information. Stonewalling—a word inadvertently made famous by the plotters of the Watergate cover-up—is often simpler: over a period of months the Secretary of State, for example, tells the Senate Foreign Relations Committee that he is too busy to testify on some subject. Or the Defense Department takes months to answer a letter. Members of Congress have other concerns and tend to be short-winded, so the cabinet member can reasonably hope that the request will eventually be forgotten.

In Chapter 1 of this book a good example is given of stonewalling. When a Senate committee sought the facts on the Army's program of surveillance of domestic politics—a program whose disclosure greatly embarrassed the military—the Pentagon said no a dozen different ways. It said that generals wanted for the inquiry were overseas or that they were not able to speak on the "broader issues." It withheld documents and witnesses on the ground that they might prejudice Pentagon investigations. And so on.

Classification of documents, a subject treated in detail at the conference, also plays a part in executive-Congressional relationships. Sometimes, Congress or one of its committees may be denied papers because they are classified. Other times, the papers may be provided with the proviso that they not be released to the public—a condition that effectively removes Congress' most important lever, public debate on an issue.

Then there is what Morton Halperin, a senior fellow of The Brookings Institution and one-time assistant to Henry Kissinger in the White House, called the "you did not ask me the right question, so I did not give you the right answer" game. The best-known player recently was Richard Helms, then director of the Central Intelligence Agency, who said "No" when asked in 1972 whether the agency had been involved in Watergate. He explained later that he had not been asked the right specific questions—for example, whether the CIA had lent anyone equipment to help in a burglary or whether it had been asked to help conceal the laundering of checks related to the crime. He took the question about involvement as relating only to the actual break-in at Democratic headquarters. Oh yes.

There is also plain old lying. Mr. Halperin gave the example of the repeated testimony, by officials of the Johnson and Nixon administrations, that American forces were sent to Vietnam at the request of the South Vietnamese government. "In fact," Mr. Halperin pointed out, "it took a great deal of arm-twisting by the American government to persuade the South Vietnamese to permit our troops to come in. But Congress can ask all the questions it wants about how the troops got there, and the President does not have to invoke executive privilege if he decides just not to tell the truth."

Finally, among the devices by which the executive branch can hope to avoid Congressional questions, there is the new technique of transferring operating responsibility from cabinet members to White House aides, called personal advisers to the President. Congress has understandably been reluctant to intrude into intimate relationships inside the White House itself; perhaps the President should have someone around him—a Harry Hopkins or a McGeorge Bundy—who could give the most uninhibited advice. But it is quite another matter if he takes over the actual power of administering a vital area of government business, as Henry Kissinger did in the first Nixon administration: not only advising the President but negotiating himself in crucial foreign situations, briefing the press, directing the apparatus. When, before he became Secretary of State, Mr. Kissinger refused to testify because he was a "White House adviser," Congress was deprived of a chance to question the man who knew about foreign policy.

What is to be done about this armory of executive weapons for denying Congress the knowledge that is power? The conference canvassed many ideas. The Dorsen-Shattuck paper (Chapter 1) laid out a sophisticated set of standards for what the executive may reasonably claim as privileged—genuinely personal advice to the President, for instance—and what it may not; and the paper urged that disputes about the scope of executive privilege be resolved by the courts. The conferees saw merit in rejecting the claims of successive Presidents to unreviewable discretion in deciding what should be privileged. But some thought that these issues between the legislative and executive branches would have to be resolved in terms of what they represented: power.

When Andrew Jackson refused to give the Senate some documents about his removal of a federal official in 1835, the Senate simply refused to confirm his appointment of a successor. That was answering in terms of power. So it was in our own time when Senator William Proxmire of Wisconsin announced that the Appropriations Committee would not report out the relevant bill unless the executive ended its long practice of concealing the amounts of U.S. military aid going to various countries. Similarly, the way for Congress to deal with its inability to get foreign policy facts from a White House "adviser" who is really acting as Secretary of State is to insist that normal standards of accountability apply to officials with operating functions, no matter what their titles.

Whether or not the courts are brought in to pass on claims of executive privilege, the fundamental way to restore the balance between Congress and President, and thus to reopen the most important channels of information about government policy, is for Congress to cure its own weakness and incompetence. It is as Cassius said in explaining why Caesar did "bestride the narrow world like a Colossus": "The fault, dear Brutus, is not in our stars, but in ourselves, that we are underlings."

III

Some time ago there was an American ambassador in a very small, very remote country. Nobody paid much attention to what he did. For eighteen months that ambassador put the label "Top Secret" on every single cable that he sent to the Secretary of State, whatever the subject. He did it in the hope that someone would look at the cables.

That story was told to the conference by William Phillips, staff director of the House Government Information Subcommittee. It indicates how "national security" has become in part an attention-getting device, how the coinage of genuine security has been debased. It helps to explain why there should be at least 100 million classified documents in the active files of the United States government today, as David Wise, author of *The Politics of Lying*, estimated. The whole apparatus of classification and security clearance is to a large extent a product of the bureaucratic mentality, used to enhance individual prestige and power.

But it would be a great mistake to believe that there are no real secrets in the American government. There are. In fact, as Daniel Ellsberg put it at the conference, the regular classification system could be regarded as a mere cover for a much higher category of secrets, available only to an inner group of officials who amount to a government within a government.

They carry on covert operations that never become known except by some fluke of political history such as Watergate.

Morton Halperin and Jeremy Stone, director of the Federation of American Scientists, echoed this contention in their paper on covert foreign operations (Chapter 4). One example they gave was American operations in China during the 1950s, including large-scale support of a Tibetan independence movement and the dropping of agents from planes over Chinese territory. The Chinese knew of these things, but Americans did not. The result was that when an assessment was being made of the chances of Chinese intervention in the Korean War as U.S. troops moved up toward the Yalu River, members of Congress and scholars did not have the key information that might well have made them understand why the Chinese were nervous about those American troops approaching the Yalu and were quite likely to intervene in Korea.

A number of the operations conducted by the CIA's "department of dirty tricks" have come to light: the coup in Guatemala, for example, and the financing of the Christian Democratic Right in Italian elections. Halperin and Stone were concerned not with the result of particular adventures but with the damaging effect on a democracy when it uses such covert techniques regularly and on a large scale.

The credibility of the United States is naturally damaged abroad: After the past record of CIA tricks, it is hard to deny involvement when there is a coup in Cambodia or Greece or Chile. At home, the whole process of decision-making within the government is distorted. An official reads a national-security estimate marked "Top Secret," for example. He thinks that he now knows the facts of that subject, on which the top officials will base their decision. But they see a different piece of paper, with a far higher classification—a classification that he does not even know exists. Secrecy means lying: government colleagues have to lie to each other about the existence of special clearances and covert plans. And there is a terrible risk of inbreeding, of conformity among the handful of people allowed to know about any one operation—because only those already committed to a certain policy will be allowed to participate. The detached scrutiny essential to making wise government policy is lacking. The result can be such a disaster of false assumptions as the Bay of Pigs.

The larger danger is the one that came to life in Watergate. Professor Harry Ransom of Vanderbilt University put it: "At the highest levels of our government we . . . discovered that there are people who don't know the difference between war and politics." If they commit burglaries and fix elections abroad, it becomes easy to do those things at home, too. The excuse is the same: the President says it is in the interest of national security.

The President says. . . . Justice Robert H. Jackson remarked, "Security is like liberty, in that many are the crimes committed in its name." That may be true in all countries, at all times. What is special about the crimes of security in contemporary America is that they so often invoke the mystique of the Presidency.

Daniel Ellsberg came to the conference after spending a morning at the Senate hearings watching James McCord, the Watergate burglar who decided to speak out. "I recognized myself in him," Ellsberg told the conference. "I, like Mr. McCord, spent a large part—well, really all—of my professional life under the belief that the wishes of the President were the law: the kind of law that really goes beyond the Constitution and the statutes of Congress. At a certain point in my life I discovered that was a mistake, and I acted differently; and at a certain point in his life Mr. McCord realized that was a mistake, and he began acting differently."

Ellsberg spoke of how conspiratorial methods were first used abroad after World War II in response to the perceived threat of Stalinist communism, then moved home. He described how people on the inside of the government become convinced that they are acting for the good of the country, develop a contempt for those who do not have the secrets, and come to consider them really unfit to participate "in determining who shall run the country."

Robert Saloschin, a senior staff attorney in the Justice Department, was a participant in the conference. When Ellsberg had finished, he intervened to say that he found it "incredible that any educated person" could think "the wishes of the President were law over the Constitution and statutes." That any person holding responsibility should have that idea, he said, was "very shocking."

"Sir," Ellsberg replied, "I have been the subject of not only prosecution but bugging, burglary, and attempted assault by your colleagues. . . ."

There were more exchanges. Others joined in. Emotions ran high. But what seems most significant in retrospect is Mr. Saloschin's incredulity at the idea that any responsible person could put the President's wishes above the Constitution and laws. That a senior Justice Department lawyer could hold such a view after the Watergate disclosures began is a monumental testament to something: naïveté, perhaps, or a refusal to face unpleasantness. For a large number of men did precisely that in Watergate: treated the wish or the inferred interest of Richard Nixon as the higher law. Many of them were lawyers, and one of them was a former Attorney General of the United States.

Watergate may have curbed some of the worst excesses of secrecy and lawlessness done in the name of the President. But the systemic problems remain. One is the area of covert operations. An ironic result of Watergate, with the sudden shifts in personnel made by President Nixon, was his naming as director of the CIA its long-time deputy director for plans—the dirty tricks department—William E. Colby. Sooner or later Congress will have to think seriously about regulating the CIA, perhaps by establishing the long-discussed Congressional oversight committee, perhaps by adopting the more fundamental reform urged by Messrs. Halperin and Stone to dismantle the entire CIA covert-operations department, leaving any such future activities to be handled on an *ad hoc* basis by others. In the autumn of 1973 that same view was expressed by Nicholas deB. Katzenbach, former Attorney General and Under Secretary of State. Writing in *Foreign Affairs,* he said there should be no more covert operations abroad, except the gathering of intelligence.

On the domestic side, the outlook for the law itself is a cause for concern. The Nixon administration made a major effort to turn law and the courts in a repressive direction. In the

Pentagon Papers case, it became the first U.S. government to get an injunction against publication of newspaper articles—until the Supreme Court decided otherwise by the not-very-comfortable majority of 6–3. Then, in the Ellsberg-Russo prosecution, it tried to use laws on espionage, theft, and conspiracy that had never been applied to leaks of government information. It was an astonishing attempt to create an American Official Secrets Act by distorted interpretation of old statutes on other subjects. If the attempt had succeeded, it would thereafter have been a crime for any person to give official information to a newspaper without formal authorization—and for the newspaper to receive it.

The danger to the press in the Ellsberg-Russo case was related to another legal phenomenon: the growing practice of bringing reporters before grand juries and demanding that they testify about the sources of any story bearing on a crime. That tactic, upheld by the Supreme Court, means that if leaking became a crime, any reporter who published a story based on a leak could be ordered, by a grand jury investigating the leak, to name his source or face a contempt of court sentence. Those who spoke on the subject at the conference were divided about the wisdom of a national shield law protecting journalists from compelled testimony; the newspaper men present took the view that the press had had plenty of abuse in the past and could take care of itself. But the use of this new tactic, especially by local officials, indicates the fragility of reliance on the law to maintain an open society. The conference also heard about the struggle to make the federal Freedom of Information Act effective, an uphill effort. And there were warnings about the secrecy provisions of an omnibus new Criminal Code proposed by the Nixon administration, S. 1400, 93rd Congress. The bill would for the first time create a statutory classification of "state secrets" through proposed evidentiary rules in a new federal criminal code.

But the reasons for continuing concern about secrecy in the American government are broader than any one President or piece of legislation. Our system of government is dependent on an executive who has the attributes of both prime minister and king and who can tell himself that he alone in this continental country was elected by the whole nation. Unless we find a different breed of person willing to undergo the strains of seeking and holding that office, the danger of concentrated power enhanced by secrecy will remain.

The likely direction of life on earth makes one's concern about secrecy the greater. Competition for natural resources is already sharpening. National governments are going to be more and more involved in a global effort to find food and fuel for their people. The risk of armed struggle will be there, and so will the risk of an Orwellian peace: a state of continuous tension justifying totalitarian order at home. What James Madison wrote Thomas Jefferson in 1798 will be even more to the point: "Perhaps it is a universal truth that the loss of liberty at home is to be charged to provisions against danger, real or pretended, from abroad."

Finally, the temptation to enlarge secrecy—to keep knowledge to oneself—will grow as societies become more complex and more dependent on knowledge. Jerome Wiesner, President of the Massachusetts Institute of Technology, spoke to the conference about the fight that he and a handful of other scientists carried on against ABM deployment. They were up against the enormous resources, financial and technical and human, of the Pentagon and the White House and the Rand Corporation. In the end they made their case, but only because these few men happened to know the ABM technology, because they had enough information. But that was "unique," Mr. Wiesner said: On almost any other military-technical issue those on the inside will have a monopoly on information. Secrecy will be decisive.

Issues of great technical complexity are going to increase in number. For that reason Professor Alan F. Westin of Columbia University, a student of computers' impact on society, urged civil libertarians not to reject computers and modern technology as such but to harness them. "It simply is no longer good enough," he said, "to assemble a small group of lawyers who will take on tilting with the computerized dragon."

Leading American scientists have said again and again that secrecy holds back discovery and development, that our strength lies in open competition. Mr. Wiesner, from his experience as a scientist and an advisor to Presidents, told the conference he was convinced that many of the worst American policy errors of the last twenty years would "not have been made if Congress and the people had been told even a small amount of the quality and character of the information those decisions were based on." But there will always be resistance to disclosure.

In the end, these issues are a matter of faith—of faith in the democratic process. At its birth the United States staked its all on the belief that openness leads to truth, secrecy to superstition. As Justice Brandeis said in arguing for free speech to let in the light: "Men feared witches and burned women."

PART ONE

— SECRET GOVERNMENT

Executive Privilege: The President Won't Tell

—by Norman Dorsen and John H.F. Shattuck

On July 23, 1973, the Senate Watergate Committee took the extraordinary step of directing a subpoena for documents to the President of the United States. At issue were the tapes of certain conversations between the President and his former top aides, purportedly about the Watergate case.

None of Richard Nixon's thirty-six predecessors in office ever faced such a dramatic confrontation with Congress, short of an impeachment proceeding. Furthermore, the President also faced a subpoena from Special Prosecutor Archibald Cox, whose formal request for the tapes "as material and important evidence" in forthcoming criminal proceedings had also been denied.[1] * Since these subpoenas were issued on the heels of an emphatic refusal by the President to surrender the tapes on the ground of executive privilege, a constitutional crisis loomed beyond the court tests ahead.

In the exchange of public statements which preceded the subpoenas, the parties staked out virtually irreconcilable positions. The President in a letter to Senator Sam Ervin claimed that the tapes "contain comments that persons with different perspectives and motivations would inevitably interpret in dif-

* The superior figures refer to the Notes, which begin on page 351.

ferent ways," asserting that "they are the clearest possible example of why Presidential documents must be kept confidential.[2] Senator Ervin, in response, honed in on what he saw as a fatal inconsistency in the President's position: "If you will notice, the President says he has heard the tapes, or some of them, and they sustain his position. But he says he's not going to let anybody else hear them for fear they might draw a different conclusion." [3] The Special Prosecutor, for his part, was silent, although he was soon the first to take the President to court to compel compliance with the subpoena.

It is clear in retrospect that the controversy over the White House tapes raised fundamental constitutional questions which went far beyond the political rhetoric of the parties. Senator Ervin wisely pointed out when the tapes issue was first joined that "the people of the United States are not interested so much in abstruse arguments about the separation of powers or executive privilege as they are in finding the answer" to whether the President was involved in criminal activities.[4] But there could be no answer to that question until the constitutional conflict was resolved.

The confused rhetoric of executive privilege is well illustrated by an incident early in the political career of Richard Nixon. During the course of a debate in the House of Representatives on April 22, 1948, concerning the refusal of President Harry S. Truman to turn over to the House Un-American Activities Committee an FBI report on a prominent government scientist, Nixon, a member of the Committee rose in the chamber and said:

> I am now going to address myself to an issue which is very important. The point has been made that the President of the United States has issued an order that none of this information can be released to the Congress and that therefore the Congress has no right to question the judgment of the President in making that decision.
>
> I say that that proposition cannot stand from a constitutional standpoint or on the basis of the merits for this very good reason: That would mean that the President could have arbitrarily issued an Executive Order in the Meyers case, the Teapot Dome case, or any other case denying the Congress of the United States information it needed to con-

> duct an investigation of the executive department and the Congress would have no right to question his decision.
>
> Any such order of the President can be questioned by the Congress as to whether or not that order is justified on the merits.[5]

It is clear, as this episode demonstrates, that the executive's claimed privilege to withhold information from Congress is often clouded by political controversy. The doctrine of executive privilege has proliferated over the decades very much as executive power itself has grown. The origins of the doctrine were modest, asserted by early Presidents rarely, in narrow circumstances and often under a formulation which implied that the executive could withhold information only with the consent of Congress.

Modern Presidential government, on the other hand, is symbolized by the frequency with which information is withheld from Congress at the sole discretion of the executive. The Library of Congress reported in March 1973 that executive privilege had been asserted 49 times since 1952, including 19 times by the Nixon Administration alone.[6] The Nixon Administration has invoked the privilege at least twice more since March 1973.

Executive privilege is a vital pressure point in the struggle between Congress and the President because it is often used to cut off Congressional inquiry into the very issues over which Congress and the President are most sharply divided. By withholding crucial information or witnesses, modern Presidents have discovered that they can effectively thwart attempts by Congress to investigate in certain areas, particularly foreign affairs and official misconduct. It should come as no surprise, therefore, that General Maxwell Taylor declined to appear before the House Subcommittee on Defense Appropriations in April 1963 to discuss the Bay of Pigs invasion,[7] that the SEC refused to give certain information to the House Interstate and Foreign Commerce Subcommittee in November 1972 concerning its ITT investigation, or that the Defense Department refused in December 1972 to supply documents requested by the House Armed Services Committee during its hearing on the firing of General John D. Lavelle, who reportedly conducted unauthorized raids over North Vietnam.[8]

Incidents like these have helped to create the impression that a President and his subordinates often balk at requests for information simply in order to prevent embarrassing subjects from being explored by a hostile Congress. Nor is this assumption unfounded, since the modern doctrine of executive privilege is in many respects a product of the efforts of the Eisenhower administration in 1954 to block the investigation being conducted by Senator Joseph McCarthy. During the Army-McCarthy hearings, President Eisenhower issued a statement formally rejecting Senator McCarthy's requests for details about the loyalty of Army personnel.

This was a wise and necessary decision. But the Justice Department memorandum that accompanied the Eisenhower statement was written in broad and unqualified terms, often embroidering history. It has spawned a conception of executive privilege that is indefensible in law, mischievous in practice, and indeed at the root of our present constitutional crisis.

I The Claim of a Discretionary Executive Privilege

Former Attorney General Richard Kleindienst, speaking for the Nixon administration, asserted in April 1973 that the Congress had no power to order an employee of the executive branch to appear and testify without the President's express consent.[9] It is important to distinguish the several strands in his testimony. First, its breadth: Mr. Kleindienst did not limit the application of the privilege to Mr. Nixon's personal advisers in the White House or to persons playing a policy-making role in other parts of the executive branch. He claimed that *all* employees of the federal government could be totally insulated from Congress at the order of the President. Second, the Attorney General did not spell out in any detail the constitutional or other legal basis for this sweeping power. Third, and most important, he claimed that the President's judgment on whether to produce documents or witnesses to the Congress was final and that neither the Congress nor the courts had the constitutional authority to interfere.

It was not always so. Even while the executive branch during previous administrations was asserting a broad privilege, there were many attempts to define its limits and a hesitancy to proclaim an unreviewable Presidential discretion. The first major assertion of executive privilege during the modern era came in 1941, when Attorney General Robert Jackson declined to comply with a request by the House Committee on Naval Affairs to inspect FBI reports on the strikes and labor disputes then plaguing defense industries and jeopardizing the war effort. In a letter to the Committee Chairman, Jackson gratuitously observed that the documents in question "can be of little if any value in connection with the framing of legislation or the performance of any other constitutional duty of Congress," [10] but he did not assert an unreviewable executive power to withhold information from Congress. That claim was reserved for a later day.

On May 17, 1954, President Eisenhower sent a letter to Defense Secretary Charles Wilson, with an accompanying memorandum from Attorney General Herbert Brownell, Jr., directing the Secretary to order his subordinates not to testify before Senator Joseph McCarthy's special subcommittee.[11] However laudable its purpose, the Brownell memorandum had a negative impact on the doctrinal development of executive privilege. According to Attorney General William Rogers (who succeeded Brownell), while heads of departments ". . . have frequently obeyed congressional demands . . . and have furnished papers and information to congressional committees, they have done so only in a spirit of comity and good-will, and not because there has been an effective legal means to compel them to do so." [12]

Perhaps because the Presidency and the Congress were controlled by the same political party, the issue lay largely dormant during the Kennedy and Johnson administrations, although President Kennedy in his own name once exercised executive privilege, and executive departments and agencies did so three times during each of the Democratic administrations.

The subject matters that have been included in executive privilege as it has been broadly asserted during the last two decades have not varied much since the Eisenhower administration. In a memorandum frequently cited by succeeding Attorneys General, Attorney General Rogers identified in 1957 at least five categories of executive information privileged from disclosure to Congress:

1. military and diplomatic secrets and foreign affairs;
2. information made confidential by statute;
3. investigations relating to pending litigation, and investigative files and reports;
4. information relating to internal government affairs privileged from disclosure in the public interest; and
5. records incidental to the making of policy, including interdepartmental memoranda, advisory opinions, recommendations of subordinates and informal working papers.[13]

Mr. Kleindienst's claims exceeded even those of the Eisenhower administration because Attorney General Rodgers had sought to insulate not all executive-branch employees but only those who were engaged in the "making of policy."

The Kleindienst position was enunciated just before the main Watergate disclosures began to occur, and it had the effect of temporarily insulating the President's White House advisors from Senator Ervin's Committee. One month later, however, after the resignations of Messrs. Haldeman, Ehrlichman, Dean and Kleindienst, and in the face of growing pressures from Congress and the press for more information from the White House, a more modest position on executive privilege was announced by Leonard Garment, the new Counsel to the President. The new policy permitted testimony by any executive department employee, including past and present members of the President's staff, but it prevented disclosure to Congress or the courts of any conversations with the President, documents received or produced by the President or any member of the White House staff in connection with their duties, and classified information. Any exercise of the privilege would continue to be at the President's unreviewable discretion.

In the remainder of this chapter we shall express our reasons for concluding that the assertion of a discretionary privilege by the President is without basis in historical or judicial precedent or in the constitutional doctrine of separation of powers. We shall also try to show that two of the three basic categories of privilege—national security and investigatory files—while raising issues about the propriety and scope of executive secrecy, can be explained and defined wholly apart from a constitutional privilege. The third category—internal advice within the executive branch—raises more difficult problems. While there may be a necessity for executive secrecy in this area, it is based on the same limited constitutional premise that justifies secrecy among members of Congress and judges: each branch of government has an implied power to protect its legitimate decision-making processes from scrutiny by the other branches. As we shall see, this does not mean that any branch can keep secret its actual decisions or the facts underlying them as distinguished from "advice," nor that it can shield criminal wrongdoing by its officials or employees.

II The Untenability of a Discretionary Executive Privilege

It is vital to be clear about the precise question before us, which is *not* whether there are certain types of information that the executive needs to keep secret in order to function properly. There well may be. Nor is the question whether the Congress generally requires access to information in the hands of the executive in order to legislate properly. Of course it does. The issue is whether the President has the implied authority under the Constitution to withhold data from the Congress or the courts solely in his discretion or whether his decision to do so is subject to constitutional limitation and judicial review.

History lends little support to the claims now being advanced by the executive. Until the turn of the twentieth century, there was but a single instance—during the Presidency of Andrew Jackson—of an arguably successful assertion of executive power to withhold documents requested by the Congress, and the courts did not rule on it. The earlier incidents of executive questioning of Congressional authority, during Washington's administration, were cases in which the President eventually acceded to the requests of Congress and never confronted the legislature with a refusal to disclose.[14]

During this same period, a Congressional practice developed of extending to the President a privilege or discretion to withhold certain investigative reports and state secrets from public disclosure. In the instances where the offer extended by Congress was actually accepted by the President and documents were withheld, the Congressional power to compel their release was explicitly recognized by both parties. When Jefferson declined, for example, to produce certain information on the Burr conspiracy in 1807, he was acting upon a House request that excepted "such [information] as he may deem the public welfare to require not to be disclosed." [15]

The judicial record is equally barren of authority sustaining the broad claims of the executive. Although no Supreme Court case explicitly rejects such a privilege, there are no decisions in this country or in England that uphold it. The Queen's Bench in 1845, for example, established what is still the rule in England today: "the Commons are . . . the general inquisitors of the realm. . . . They may inquire into everything which it concerns the public weal for them to know." [16]

Prior to the White House attorneys' briefing of their position in the Tapes case, the most comprehensive attempt to muster judicial authority on behalf of an executive privilege had been made by Attorney General Robert Jackson when he sought to justify his refusal in 1941 to turn over FBI reports to the House Committee on Naval Affairs. While some of the cases cited by Jackson support a limited power to withhold security data and confidential informers' communications from the courts, none lends credence to a discretionary executive privilege.

In the absence of historical and judicial precedents, we must turn to even more fundamental sources of potential power, in particular, the constitutional doctrine of separation of powers. In our judgment, three distinct facets are involved, none of which supports executive discretion.

1 *Legislative authority.* The first is the power of the Congress under Article I of the Constitution to conduct inves-

tigations. Long before 1789, the English Parliament, in the words of Pitt the elder, was inquiring "into every step of public Management, either Abroad or at Home, in order to see that nothing has been done amiss." [17]

Legislative practice in the American colonies followed the parliamentary model. Examples abound of investigations by colonial assemblies "into the conduct of the other departments of government." So deeply rooted was this legislative right of access to executive documents that the Continental Congress refused to create a Secretary of Foreign Affairs until a resolution was adopted that "any member of Congress shall have access [to] all . . . papers of his office: provided that no copy shall be taken of matters of a secret nature without the special leave of *Congress.*" [18]

There is no express mention in the Constitution of a Congressional power to investigate and gain access to the documents of executive departments, but from the very beginning such a power was assumed to be a fundamental attribute of Congress. In one of its first legislative acts, Congress provided in the Treasury Reporting Act of 1789 that: "[It] shall be the duty of the Secretary of the Treasury . . . to make reports, and give information to either branch of the legislature in person or in writing (as may be required), respecting all matters referred to him by the Senate or House of Representatives, or which shall appertain to his office." [19]

This statute was drafted by Treasury Secretary Alexander Hamilton, hardly an advocate of limited executive powers. It is reasonable to assume that Hamilton would never have imposed a duty on an executive department to report to Congress unless he felt such a duty was constitutionally compelled.

During the first half of the nineteenth century, Congress conducted continuous investigations into the expenditure of public funds in virtually every area of government activity. The authority underlying these investigations was derived both from the Appropriations Clause in Article I of the Constitution and from Hamilton's Treasury Reporting Act. Congressional inquiries into the executive were in fact so common during this period that a nineteenth-century observer commented wryly that "Committees instituted inquiries, ran the eye up and down accounts, pointed out little items, snuffed about dark corners, peeped under curtains and under beds, and exploited every cupboard of the Executive household." [20]

An instructive definition of the scope of the investigating power is found in *Watkins* v. *United States*, where Chief Justice Earl Warren said in 1957: "The power of the Congress to conduct investigations is inherent in the legislative process. That power is broad. It encompasses inquiries concerning the administration of existing laws as well as proposed or possible needed statutes. It includes surveys of defects in our social, economic or political system for the purpose of enabling the Congress to remedy them. It comprehends probes into departments of the Federal Government to expose corruption, inefficiency or waste." [21]

The *Watkins* case is especially suggestive because it is rightly remembered as a decision *restricting* the power of Congress, and in particular the House Committee on Un-American Activities. Chief Justice Warren explicitly stated, "Broad as is the power of [Congressional] inquiry, it is not unlimited. There is no general authority to expose the private affairs of individuals without justification in terms of the functions of the Congress. . . . Nor is the Congress a law-enforcement or trial agency. . . . No inquiry is an end in itself; it must be related to, and in furtherance of, a legitimate task of the Congress."

These limitations, however, are designed to protect the rights of witnesses and do not support a discretionary executive privilege.

The *Watkins* decision dealt with the power of Congress to obtain information from a private individual, and it would be disingenuous to suppose that the Supreme Court was thinking of such recondite matters as executive privilege. But its broad appraisal of congressional power is consistent with history and with earlier judicial pronouncements.

2 *Presidential authority.* The second aspect of separation of powers concerns the implications of the President's power under Article II of the Constitution to "take care that the laws be faithfully executed." It is this constitutional provision on

which Presidents and their Attorneys General have chiefly relied to buttress their claims of unlimited discretionary privilege to withhold executive documents and witnesses from the Congress.

Taken to its essentials it is a claim of inherent or implied power, because the general constitutional language surely does not authorize a broad discretionary withholding of information. The Supreme Court has reviewed and rejected a similarly broad claim of inherent executive power. In the celebrated steel seizure case President Truman was denied the authority to override the will of Congress by seizing steel mills during the Korean War in order to maintain production during a threatened strike. Concluding that "the Founders of this Nation entrusted the lawmaking power to the Congress alone in good and bad times," Justice Hugo Black's majority opinion agreed with the conclusion of Justice Holmes, among others, that "The duty of the President to see that the laws be faithfully executed does not go beyond the laws." [22]

It is unnecessary to accept Justice Black's broad assertions about the lack of inherent Presidential power to reach an identical conclusion. In a separate analysis in the same case, Justice Robert Jackson (the former Attorney General) distinguished three situations: 1) those in which the President acts pursuant to an express or implied authorization of Congress, where his authority is at a maximum; 2) those in which Congress is silent, where the President can rely only on his own powers and frequently the result is uncertain; and 3) those in which the President takes measures "incompatible with the expressed or implied will" of Congress. In the latter situation, according to Justice Jackson and at least two other Justices in the steel case, the President's power "is at its lowest ebb." [23]

The case of executive privilege is plainly of the third type. While Congress has not legislated explicitly on the privilege, it has expressed its intention unmistakably to obtain all necessary information from the executive branch in statutes going back to the Hamilton Treasury Reporting Act. There certainly is no doubt about the desire of the Senate Watergate Committee to obtain pertinent information from the executive branch.

The only reference to secrecy in the text of the Constitution is the requirement that Congress keep and publish a Journal, except "such parts as may in their judgment require secrecy." On the other hand, the only reference in the text to making information available to another branch of government is the duty imposed on the President "from time to time to give to the Congress information on the State of the Union." While nothing definitive can be read into these clauses, their presence in the Constitution cuts in the direction of legislative access to executive documents and away from executive discretionary authority.

Other portions of the Constitution are of little help. Some informed observers have stressed the inherent weakness of the President. For example, Joseph Bishop, a professor at the Yale Law School, has minimized the danger to constitutional government by "an executive which has to go to Congress for every cent it spends, which has no power by itself to raise and maintain armed forces and which cannot jail its citizens except under a law passed by Congress and after proceedings presided over by an independent judiciary." [24] But Bishop wrote in 1957, during the incumbency of a passive President. Today he might stress other constitutional powers which lead in a different direction—for example, the President's role as Commander-in-Chief and his *de facto* status as virtually sole representative of the United States in foreign affairs. Even more important than the powers explicitly found or reasonably implied in the Constitution are the numerous examples, multiplying in recent years, of executive action that seems to go beyond traditional bounds. For instance, Professor Philip Kurland of the University of Chicago Law School has prophesied, without enthusiasm, that "we will continue . . . to see the President wage war without Congressional declaration, to see executive orders substitute for legislation, to see secret executive agreements substitute for treaties, and to see Presidential decisions not to carry out Congressional programs under the label of 'impoundment of funds.' " [25]

Other examples are available: President Nixon has expanded the use of the Pocket Veto, tightened White House budgetary and political controls over what used to be known as the "independent" regulatory agencies, and set up a secret White House investigative unit to look into activities deemed by the President to be a threat to the national security. Taken as a whole, these developments represent a significant change in the balance of power between the executive and legislative branches. An experienced foreign observer, Louis Heren, recently stated; "The main difference between the modern American President and a medieval monarch is that there has been a steady increase rather than diminution of his power. In comparative historical terms the United States has been moving steadily backward." [26]

All this suggests that we should be slow to permit the executive branch to accrete further power by uncontrolled discretion over the information it provides to other branches of government. To acknowledge such power would increase the constitutional imbalance at a time when counter measures seem called for.

Two recently evolved features of the executive bureaucracy further underscore the danger of uncontrolled executive discretion: (1) the vast expansion in the size and function of the White House staff, and (2) the practice of assigning one person the dual role of cabinet officer and Presidential adviser. The former development is partly a matter of numbers. During 1971, for example, Henry Kissinger directed a National Security Council staff of more than 140 persons, of whom 54 were substantive experts—a long way from the small and rather clubby retinue of earlier Presidents.

The second problem—multiple executive responsibilities—is even more serious. A cabinet member who is called to testify on the actions of his department may be asked questions which touch on his activities as adviser to the President. As Dean Cramton has stated, "matters shade into one another and the distinction is difficult to maintain, especially when a cabinet member is housed in the White House and has a separate role as Counselor to the President." [27]

These modern executive practices emphasize the difficulty of accepting the President as final arbiter of the privilege issue. It is the President who decides the size of the White House staff, the allocation of responsibilities between it and the cabinet departments, and whether or not to fuse in one individual both line and staff assignments that formerly were kept distinct. To permit the President also to determine, finally, when an individual may be immunized from legislative or judicial questioning or when a document may be withheld, is to defeat the goal of a balanced federal government.

3 *Judicial authority.* If an issue concerning the privilege cannot be settled by negotiation, it should be for the courts to resolve. Neither the President nor the Congress should be the judge in its own case. Accordingly, just as we deny the right of the President to settle the issue definitively, we also reject the view, taken at an early stage of the Watergate controversy by Senator Ervin, that a Congressional committee should be "the final judge of whether a White House aide could refuse to answer any of the committee's questions." [28]

The courts have a general responsibility to decide cases that involve disputes over the allocation of power as between the political branches of the federal government. The Supreme Court, for example, ruled on the power of the President as Commander-in-Chief to order a blockade in the early nineteenth century without Congress' approval, and, as we have seen, it also determined the scope of Presidential power during the Korean War to seize private property without Congressional authorization.

It is sometimes suggested that executive privilege controversies should be left entirely to what has been called "the accommodations and realities of the political process." Of course, political accommodation permits informal disclosures of information from the executive to the Congress that could not be provided on the record, as well as meetings between Congressmen and Presidential advisers at which, presumably, valuable data may be provided.[29] But we reject this *modus operandi*, and we are pleased that many Congressional leaders likewise reject it. A surreptitious and informal means of communication demeans the Congress and indeed the entire governmental process. We agree with Justice Louis Brandeis, who once said that "sunlight is the best disinfectant." Neither the leak nor the Old School Tie is a satisfactory substitute for open disclosures that the executive branch must be able to defend publicly.

The problem of judicial review, while complicated, is not a sufficient reason to prefer a political rather than a judicial resolution of the issue. The enforcement of a legislative contempt citation against an executive officer for refusing to testify or produce documents would not appear to present the courts with more than an ordinary contempt case, although admittedly in an unusual context. The real problem would lie in compelling the disclosure of a contested document. We dismiss the notion that the President or one of his aides would have to be physically coerced to hand over a document, because we do not believe that matters would ever reach such a pass. The political impact on the President of an adverse judicial decision should not be underestimated. Thus, in the Tapes case Richard Nixon apparently chose to comply with the Special Prosecutor's subpoenas after losing twice in the lower federal courts because the risk of an adverse Supreme Court decision was simply too great.

Since a court would not find it difficult to frame the appropriate relief, speculation about the executive's willingness to comply with a judicial order should not enter into consideration of whether the order should issue in the first instance. As the Supreme Court pointed out in its decision ordering the reinstatement of Congressman Adam Clayton Powell after the House had voted to deprive him of his seat, "it is an 'inadmissible suggestion' that action might be taken in disregard of a judicial determination." [30]

An executive privilege dispute is not a "political question." Its resolution by the courts would not create any of the dangers against which the Supreme Court fashioned the political question doctrine: it would not "risk embarrassment abroad, or grave disturbance at home," nor would it embroil the courts in "overwhelming party or intraparty contests." [31] For these reasons, we do not believe that the executive would refuse to comply with a judicial resolution of the issue. But if a President were to ignore or attempt to evade a judicial order in such a way as to obstruct justice, legal procedures would then give way to political remedies. Impeachment would be the only remaining constitutional means to unravel the impasse, and the country would be in an ominous domestic crisis.

Two Supreme Court decisions in 1972 emphasized that the separation of powers doctrine is a two-way street.[32] The Court ruled that the immunity of Congressmen from criminal process for their legislative activity does not protect them from being required to disclose information "relevant to investigating third-party crime," nor from being the subjects of criminal investigations themselves. There is no basis in the principle of separation of powers for a different result with respect to the President.

We do not maintain that an absolute Congressional power to compel information should be substituted for an absolute executive power to withhold it. All "unlimited power" is inherently dangerous, and it is the function of the courts to circumscribe the executive and legislative powers so that neither branch is exalted at the expense of the other.

III The Proper Scope of Executive Privilege

If our conclusion is correct that a discretionary executive privilege is untenable, this does not foreclose the question whether secrecy can properly be maintained by the President and his assistants in the three types of cases where the privilege has most frequently been asserted.

1 *Foreign or military affairs.* The Congress must have access to foreign and military information if it is to exercise its express constitutional powers under Article I to advise the President in making treaties, to declare war, and to appropriate funds for raising and supporting armies. Congress can, should, and does delegate authority to the President to shield certain foreign and military activities from the public. And it has authorized him to enforce administrative secrecy through the espionage laws and the classification system. But this does not mean that a constitutional power to classify information rests solely with the President. On the contrary, as the Supreme Court pointed out in a 1973 decision, "Congress could certainly have provided that the Executive Branch adopt new

procedures [for classifying documents], or it could have established its own procedures." [33]

Congress, therefore, is theoretically an active partner with the President not only in conducting foreign affairs but in maintaining a system of confidentiality, balanced against the public's right to know what the government is doing in its name.

There is probably a need for secrecy in foreign and military affairs. This means that information properly classified under statutory authority may be withheld in certain circumstances from the general public and provided only to reliable persons within the executive branch on a need-to-know basis. But this does not justify denying Congress the foreign and military information it requires to fulfill its constitutional responsibilities.

2 *Investigatory files and litigation materials.* Attorney General Jackson maintained that disclosure of investigatory files and other litigation materials would prejudice law enforcement, impede the development of confidential sources, and result in injustice to innocent individuals. One does not have to dispute these conclusions to demonstrate that these files need not be protected by anything so grand as an executive privilege. The government's law-enforcement interest, as well as the privacy of individuals under investigation, are amply safeguarded by statutes, by common law evidentiary privileges, and by the constitutional protections against self-incrimination and denials of free speech and due process, which apply with equal force in legislative and judicial settings.

The hallmark of the evidentiary privileges is that the judiciary and not the executive determines when the circumstances are appropriate for a governmental claim of privilege. As the Supreme Court said in 1953, "Judicial control over the evidence in a case cannot be abdicated to the caprice of executive officers." [34] If information is not privileged, the government can be compelled to choose between losing its civil case or dropping its criminal prosecution and producing the documents which it had claimed were privileged.

In addition, the Congress has demonstrated a sensitivity to the executive's need for confidentiality in this area by enacting exemptions to the Freedom of Information Act which protect both "investigatory files compiled for law-enforcement purposes," and "files the disclosure of which would constitute a clearly unwarranted invasion of personal privacy." [35] It is significant again that the application of these exemptions in cases where executive agencies have sought to invoke them has been made by *judicial* intermediaries, not by the executive.

Unlike the blunderbuss of an unreviewable executive privilege, these doctrines assimilate and attempt to balance competing interests in disclosure which are frequently advanced by private litigants, by Congress and by the public. It would be difficult to imagine a greater inconsistency in the law than that a private individual in a lawsuit could compel the disclosure of information from the executive branch not accessible to Congress. But this would be the precise effect of extending a blanket executive privilege into the area of investigatory files and litigation materials.

3 *Advice within the executive branch.* This brings us to the only aspect of the so-called executive privilege that deserves scrutiny as a possible constitutional privilege based on the separation of powers. That is, in the words of President Eisenhower, the power to withhold "conversations or communications, or any documents or reproductions" that relate solely to internal advice within the Executive Branch.[36]

This "advice" privilege, as we think it should be called, has been interpreted very broadly by the executive. But the privilege should not be exclusively "executive." Insofar as it exists, it should apply equally to attempts to extract the advice that judicial law clerks or legislative assistants render to their superiors. The principle involved is the necessity to protect the delicate internal decision-making process of each branch of government.

The chief justification for this principle is that the development of public policy will be inhibited if individuals in government cannot rely on the confidentiality of their communicated opinions. A tragic example of such inhibition was the stagnation of American policy toward China as a result of the public censure of China experts after the Communist regime came to power in 1949.

A second reason for protecting the "advice" that flows from one official to another is based on the realities of power and personal vulnerability. As stated by Professor Bishop, "It is one thing for a cabinet officer to defend a decision which, however just, offends the prejudices of a powerful Congressman and, very probably, a highly vocal section of the public; it is quite another thing for a middle-aged, middle-ranking civil servant, who needs his job, to do so." [37]

In many cases, though not all, it will be sufficient if the middle-aged bureaucrat's superior appears and testifies as to government decisions actually made. The Congress will obtain what it seeks, but it will have to do without the pelt of a worker in the vineyard. Protecting the lower ranking individual is especially needed because Members of Congress, in their desire to score a point for the folks back home, may run roughshod over the reputation and sensibilities, if not the legal rights, of an honest but uninspired bureaucrat. If this can be avoided, it should be. This is why we conclude that if an implied constitutional privilege is admitted on practical grounds to allow executive officers to decline to testify, at the direction of the President, it should apply down the line to the lesser and weaker members of the bureaucracy.

We shall now attempt, not without apprehension, to block out a workable and coherent set of rules applying the "advice privilege."

A No witness summoned by a Congressional committee may refuse to appear on the ground that he intends to invoke the advice privilege as to all or some of the questions that may be asked.

It has been suggested that certain officers in the executive branch—notably those who are White House aides—may decline altogether to appear. The difficulty is that we are no longer in an era when close personal advisers act purely in a counseling capacity. Fully apart from the individuals who occupy dual positions as cabinet members and advisers to the

President, it is plain that the chief White House aides are action officers as well as advisers. This has certainly been true about the principal figures in the Nixon White House, and it was undoubtedly also true about Messrs. Bundy, Califano, Moyers, Rostow, and others under Presidents Kennedy and Johnson. Accordingly, if an employee of the executive branch is directed by a superior not to testify, he should make himself available to explain the reasons for the refusal. Any other practice would open the door to unjustified and arbitrary assertions of privilege.

B (i) The advice privilege may be claimed on behalf of a witness summoned by a Congressional committee only at the direction of the President personally.

(ii) This privilege may be asserted only with respect to questions about recommendations, advice and suggestions passed on to members of the executive branch acting under lawful authority for consideration in the formulation of policy.

(iii) A witness may not decline to answer questions concerning what has been *done,* as distinct from what has been advised. Whatever the title of an individual, and whether or not he is called an "adviser," he should be accountable for actions he took in the name of the government and decisions that he made leading to action by others.

(iv) A witness may not decline to answer questions about *facts* that he acquired while acting in an official capacity.

The separation of "fact" from "advice," while sometimes difficult, is not impossible, and is often performed by courts in order to comply with requests under the Freedom of Information Act. Without the separation an advice privilege invites abuse. As one witness pointed out in the 1971 Senate hearings on executive privilege, the protection of "advice" is potentially "a most mischievous privilege": "Virtually every scrap written in the executive branch can, if desired, be labeled facts, opinions or advice. It can be used as readily to shield opinion corrupted by graft and disloyalty as to protect candor and honest judgment." [38]

(v) Executive privilege may not be claimed as to material relating to a President's role as leader of his political party as distinguished from his position as head of the government.

(vi) If the President or some other official has already made statements about the matter under inquiry by the Congress, the privilege is waived as to that subject. The net effect of selectively withholding information could be to mislead the public as well as the legislative branch.

C (i) Documents or other recorded information may be withheld from Congress or a Committee of Congress only at the discretion of the President personally.

(ii) As in the case of oral testimony, the privilege should extend not to entire documents but only to those portions of documents which meet the criteria justifying an exercise of the "advice privilege."

4 *Crime.* Whatever the effect of these rules in other circumstances, there should be no executive privilege when the Congress or a prosecutor has already acquired substantial evidence that the information requested concerns criminal wrongdoing by executive officials or Presidential aides.* There is obviously an overriding policy justification for the position, since an opposing view would permit criminal conspiracy at the seat of power to be shrouded by the veil of advice privilege.

As we have seen, the Supreme Court in two 1972 cases underscored its impatience with claims of constitutional privilege that shield investigations concerning "possible third-party crime." [39] In the first case, the Court ruled that Senator Mike Gravel's assistant could be compelled to testify about publication of the Pentagon Papers, which Senator Gravel had read on the Senate floor. Justice Byron White, speaking for himself and the four Nixon appointees to the Supreme Court, stated that the Senator himself could be interrogated by a grand jury if his sources of information related to crime. The Constitution "provides no protection for criminal conduct threatening the security of the person or property of others."

* In such situations, of course, individuals summoned to testify are entitled to exercise their constitutional rights such as the Fifth Amendment privilege against self-incrimination. They might also, for example, seek to suppress wiretap evidence seized in violation of their Fourth Amendment rights.

The second Supreme Court case involved former Senator Daniel Brewster of Maryland, who was prosecuted for having received a bribe to influence his action on postal legislation. A lower court had held that his indictment was invalid because it put into question Mr. Brewster's motives for legislative action—a subject that is constitutionally protected. Chief Justice Warren Burger, however, ruled that "taking a bribe is, obviously, no part of the legislative process or function."

Nathan Lewin, a former Justice Department official, has perceptively written that the Gravel and Brewster cases are powerful precedents against discretionary privilege, because in those cases the Supreme Court was dealing with an *explicit* constitutional immunity.[40] In setting forth the privileges of Senators and Representatives, Article I, Section 6 of the Constitution provides that "for any speech or debate in either House, they shall not be questioned in any other place."

There is no such specific immunity based on executive privilege. It is therefore all the more plain that the privilege, whatever its reach, does not permit the President to withhold information concerning criminal conduct. President Nixon, before the existence of the White House tapes became known, said on May 22, 1973, "Executive privilege will not be invoked as to any testimony concerning possible criminal conduct or discussions of possible criminal conduct, in the matters under investigation." In the gathering storm over the tapes, the President retreated from this statement. The ensuing litigation resulted in a rejection of the most extreme presidential claim of inherent executive power.[41] It would be surprising if subsequent judicial decisions did not continue to limit the president's power to withhold information from the Congress and the people.

IV Discussion

MR. KAHN: We all know that news is not what happens, but what happens to get reported. When the executive branch of the government furnishes information to Congress, it is not news. But when executive privilege is invoked, which is in a tiny fraction of one percent of the number of requests the executive branch receives from Congress, then it is news, and because that fraction has become slightly larger in the last few years, there is a tendency on the part of the general public, to believe that the executive branch is in the habit of refusing information to Congress.

The fact is that in the last generation, because of the expansion of the executive branch, because it has moved into many new fields and because it now employs many more people than ever before, Congress needs more information from the executive branch, and it gets it. Furnishing information to Congress has become a major industry in the executive branch. It has become a commonplace among newspaper reporters and political scientists that heads of government departments now spend as much as half of their time testifying before committees of Congress. The average governmental department has an entire division whose sole function it is to answer requests for information from Congress. If you ask a Congressional aide about this, you will find that he or she is astonished at the extent to which executive agencies will go in complying with requests for information.

This, of course, is not news, and there is no reason why it should be news. I mention it only because we ought to remind ourselves, when we see occasionally that executive privilege has been invoked, that this is a comparatively rare occurrence.

I think that the paper we have just heard has overlooked one important distinction in its discussion of the right to invoke executive privilege. I am not a lawyer, but this is a question which my work has involved me in for a great many years, and I know what lawyers have said about it. It seems to me that we must consider that certain offices were created by act of Congress but that the Presidency was created by the Constitution, not by act of Congress. Shattuck and Dorsen point out that in the act establishing the Treasury Department, the Secretary is required to report to and furnish information to the Congress. That is not unique. All of the acts that have created agencies in the executive branch contain a similar provision. Whereas, as we all know, since the beginning of our history, Presidents have loved to point out that the Presidential office was not created by Congress, but by the Constitution, that the President of the United States holds office by virtue of the vote of the people, not by virtue of the creation of his office by

Congress, and, that, therefore, he does not have the responsibility of reporting to Congress except in his annual State of the Union message.

Several years ago I had occasion to investigate this point and found that the White House office is not an agency in the executive branch of the government. In the laws that require government agencies to perform certain acts or to follow certain procedures, the White House office is not interpreted as falling within the meaning of "government agencies." If the White House does comply with requests, it does so as a matter of comity rather than because it is required to do so.

The real question here is, now that the White House has become so large, to what extent does executive privilege extend to and embrace the men who work for the President? How far does this Presidential prerogative of not having to respond to inquiries from Congress extend? Does it extend to his immediate aides? Does it extend to White House file clerks? Does it extend outside the immediate White House office into the whole Executive office of the President, including such agencies as the Council of Economic Advisers and the National Security Council? This is the major issue.

The writers of this paper seem to feel that in order to defend the right of Congress to request information from the White House, they had to adopt what may be called the Taftian view of the Presidency, that the President has no residual powers, no inherent powers not specifically given to him by the Constitution. I hope that is not so. This is a view of the Presidency shared by James Buchanan and Calvin Coolidge and, to a certain extent, by Dwight Eisenhower, but it is not the view of the Presidency that has been adopted by the men who historians and political scientists consider our great Presidents. Nor was it even the view of Thomas Jefferson. As every schoolboy knows, he negotiated the Louisiana Purchase without any specific constitutional power to do so, and he chose to tell the Congress about it afterward.

I think we ought to remember that secrecy in government is as American as apple pie. It is certainly not necessary to remind this group that when the men who wrote our Constitution gathered, the first thing they decided to do was to hold their conversations and negotiations and discussions in secret. Not only was the public not to be admitted but no record was to be kept of their debates or their proceedings, and none was ever to be published.

We know of what took place at the Constitutional Convention only because of Madison's decision to keep some notes of his own as a private person, from the diaries of a few men who were there, and from some of the letters they wrote. The reasons advanced at that time for keeping the discussions at the Constitutional Convention secret are precisely the reasons advanced today in defense of the doctrine of executive privilege. So executive privilege is not something new, nor unprecedented in our history.

MR. MARSHALL: The basic thrust of the paper seems to be a rejection of *unreviewable* discretion to invoke executive privilege, not of executive privilege in all its forms. That conclusion seems to me to be indisputable and, in fact, inevitable. I suppose if Congress and the executive branch come into an unresolved contest, that conflict will go into court as other conflicts do.

It seems to me, though, that for two reasons this is not necessarily a desirable way of resolving these conflicts. First, as Dr. Kahn has stated, executive privilege is somewhat overblown as a constitutional issue. Congress is not really denied information it needs to perform its function. Executive privilege is less an issue of information than of the distribution of power. The distribution of political power is not the kind of issue it is desirable for the courts to resolve. They are likely to do so in the context of another kind of issue they are used to dealing with, that is, evidentiary privilege. The question is not really evidentiary privilege but, as I say, a matter of power, and that is better resolved in a political context and by political forces than by judicial process, which will be focusing its attention mainly on an issue which is peripheral to the real issue.

I question the wisdom of the position taken in the last part of the essay, that Presidential aides should invoke executive privilege on a question-by-question basis, not by immunity against compulsory testimony before Congressional committees. I think this rule would affect the kind of advice and the freedom with which advice is given the President by his aides if they believe that they can be called down to appear before a political or public constituency to whom they are not really responsible.

The problem, of course, lies in the expansion of the White House. Immunity from testifying may have been true when the White House was peopled by Presidential aides, but now it is peopled by a whole organization. But this issue should not be dealt with on an executive-privilege basis: it is a distribution-of-power issue. If the National Security Council should be responsible to Congress as well as to the President, then that is a matter which Congress has clear power to resolve. It is Congress that appropriates money for the National Security Agency. I would agree that Dr. Kissinger and his staff, and their predecessors, have functioned as an agency of government rather than as an adviser to the President, and they should be treated that way. But it seems to me that if you respond to the increase and other changes in the White House staff by saying that all Presidential aides should be called before Congress, you are answering the wrong question.

MR. DORSEN: Dr. Kahn is plainly right that a great deal of information goes to Congress from the executive branch. I spent a couple of years in the Pentagon, at a very low level, and a great deal of my own time was spent giving information to Congress.

The reason Mr. Shattuck and I spent so much time dealing with the executive's claim of an unreviewable discretion to withhold information from Congress is that that is the position taken by Mr. Kleindienst, the former Attorney General, apparently with the approval of the President. We hope our paper has put it to rest.

We think that having the court resolve the tension between the Congress and the President is a bad solution to the problem. Unfortunately, it is also the best solution. Ideally, the tensions should be worked out between the President and his aides on one hand, and the Congressional committees on the other. But if they cannot be worked out, we see no better solution than having the courts act. The alternatives are for the

President and his aides to make the final decision or for Congressional committees to make it. We don't see either one as the right answer.

There are problems of justiciability, and problems of enforceability in going to the courts. We have not spelled those out in this essay, but we think those problems can be dealt with.

Two final points. Mr. Marshall's comment about the impediment to free and open advice within the executive branch is correct, and I think the solution might be one he suggests—a reorientation of the power structure within the executive branch to separate the advisers from those who perform governing functions. Maybe Congress should not appropriate money for Dr. Kissinger's staff of over one hundred and forty people, a sort of mini-State Department. Should we permit whole operating agencies within the White House to be insulated from questioning by Congress? I don't think so. Presidential aides like Kissinger and Ehrlichman should be subject to Senate confirmation, and they should be absorbed within the normal agencies of the executive branch, responsible to Congress. But until that day comes, I don't see how we can live with a situation where entire areas are closed off to Congressional inquiry.

Lastly, regarding Dr. Kahn's point about our passive view of the Presidency. My rejoinder is that our passive view is really premised less on political-science considerations than on what the Supreme Court has said in its principal confrontation with this issue, in the steel seizure case, where it directly faced up to the question of inherent Presidential power. The majority opinion, by Justice Black, and what I thought was the more discriminating and interesting concurring opinion, by Justice Jackson, both rejected the idea of inherent Presidential power.

We think this idea, even apart from what the Supreme Court has said, is a dangerous one, but we are content to rely on what the Supreme Court said in the steel seizure case.

MR. SALOSCHIN: I am struck by what Mr. Marshall says about the need for uninhibited discussion within the executive branch. At the time when Mr. Marshall and I were both in the Justice Department, when Bobby Kennedy was Attorney General, there were situations which had to be dealt with with great speed. One example that comes to my mind was, what do you do about the freedom-rider crisis, the bus burnings that were going on in Alabama? These were not problems that could be dealt with effectively by the same type of deliberation—on the record and with full discourse—that is used in processing legislative proposals.

There is a tendency which should be watched in the development of American constitutional law—the tendency to buck a lot of tough questions to the Supreme Court, which other branches of government should decide. If an umpire is needed, if another tribunal is needed, and if these matters cannot be reconciled between the legislative and executive branches through the exercise of comity and statesmanship, then there is another forum besides the courts. This, after all, is still supposed to be a democracy: these questions are known to the public, and they can be resolved through the political process, as Mr. Marshall suggested. There is no need to fall back upon a doctrine of judicial supremacy *sub silentio,* when we still have, I hope, the people, who act through the political process.

The statement was made that executive privilege is an effective veto on Congressional debate. Some of us would feel from our experience and observation that an exercise of executive privilege is more likely to stimulate Congressional debate and public debate than it is to silence it.

The Army-McCarthy hearings, in which another implied constitutional power, the power of Congress to investigate, came in conflict with executive privilege, is another good reason why the doctrine should not be confined to giving advice to the President. As I recall that incident in history, what Senator McCarthy wanted from Army Secretary Stevens was not just advice that had been given to executive officials. He wanted the files, the personnel security files on Major Peress, and he had been demanding FBI files and other types of information—not advice. These types of government files, as I think you know, contain a great deal of raw unevaluated information, which may be sincere or may be misinformation or malicious. This is the sort of stuff that Senator McCarthy was seeking when executive privilege was exercised.

With regard to the conclusions at the end of the paper, I think it would be helpful to keep in mind the distinction between executive privilege as a legal, constitutional doctrine which seeks to define a power necessary to enable the President to discharge his constitutional duties, and proposed guidelines for the exercise of that power. Lawyers are familiar with the distinction between a legal power and what would be a discrete and proper exercise of that power as a matter of policy in particular circumstances. I think it might be more helpful to debate these suggested guidelines *as guidelines* than to define the legal powers.

MR. SCHWARTZ: I should like to discuss both the law and the history of executive privilege, particularly the history. I wonder how many of us realize that, from legal and historical points of view, most of the support for the doctrine of executive privilege is built upon fantasy. The claims made for it have little justification. Historically speaking, and I refer to Professor Kahn's statement, it has made little difference whether the President is a weak or a strong one. For more than a hundred years, no claim of executive privilege was successfully asserted against Congress. The first attempt to assert the privilege, by Washington in 1792, gave way in the face of a Congressional claim. In 1835 Andrew Jackson removed a minor federal official named Wurtz and nominated a successor. The nomination went before the Senate for confirmation. The Senate, before voting approval, asked for the documents relative to Wurtz's removal. The President refused, largely, I think, as a personal matter. He felt Congress had asked for too much. So the Senate simply refused to confirm the successor and the matter was dropped—hardly a successful assertion of the claim.

After Jackson, until almost our day, the President has given in to every request for information, documents, etc., made by Congress. Think of the periods in our history. We tend to think that we alone are living through crisis times. Think of the Civil War. During the War, Lincoln gave in to every demand for information made by Congress, particularly by the famous (or infamous, depending on your viewpoint) Committee on the Conduct of the War. Military secrets, conduct of operations, and diplomatic matters were all provided by the President.

In 1886 Senator George Edmonds, one of the outstanding Senators in our history, gave a long historical survey of the practice. He said that in the previous forty years, not one demand by Congress for information had been refused.

In 1860 Congress conducted a very broad investigation into whether the President himself had improperly influenced action by Congress or any state legislature. The President made a protest, but then he yielded. More than sixty witnesses were questioned, and they went into intimate details of what the President himself had done.

A better illustration occurred in 1846. The State Department had a discretionary fund at its disposal, to be used at the direction of the President. The Senate investigated the manner in which this fund had been misused by Secretary of State Daniel Webster. John Tyler, who had been President at the time, was asked to and voluntarily did testify at some length on how the fund had been used. We would think of this as almost heresy today, but they had no doubt at the time that they could question the President, and they did. Legally, the claim for executive privilege is even less founded.

MR. PHILLIPS: I would like to add one recent example of the use of executive privilege. During the last twelve years, the use of executive privilege has been governed by an informal agreement reached in 1961 with the Chairman of the Government Operations Subcommittee on Government Information, then headed by Congressman John Moss of California. By letter with President Kennedy, and subsequently by letters with President Johnson and President Nixon, the use of executive privilege was limited strictly to a Presidential decision. It would not be invoked by any subordinate in the executive branch, but only by the President. The most elaborate system of guidelines for use of executive privilege was spelled out, during these twelve years, by President Nixon. In a memorandum dated March 24, 1969, his guidelines required the Office of Legal Counsel of the Justice Department to advise the President where there was a dispute whether an executive department or agency should request him to claim "executive privilege." The counsel to the President was to make the final decision on the recommendation to the President. Despite this elaborate series of guidelines, "executive privilege," as the writers indicate, was asserted during the first four and a half years of the Nixon administration nineteen times, and on only four of those nineteen occasions did the President himself assert the claim as required.

This is, of course, an informal agreement. It has no force of law. Senator Fulbright has on several occasions introduced legislation to make law the type of guideline contained in this informal series of letters with the Presidents. Also, our subcommittee has just held hearings on "executive privilege" bills. I think it is clear that we have a situation where executive agencies are not following the precise guideline requirements laid down by the President in 1969 and adhered to by his two predecessors.

MR. HALPERIN: The comment has been made that executive privilege has to be put in perspective, that it is used rarely, and most of the time Congress gets the information it asks for. I think this may give the misleading impression that executive privilege is the only technique the executive branch uses to keep Congress from getting information. I wanted to mention three others, because they don't seem to fit anywhere else on the program, although they go a little beyond executive privilege.

One method is classifying material which, even if it is then given to the Congress, is of little use because Congress depends on public debate. If the information must be kept secret, it is hard for the Congress to use it. For example, for many years Congress tried to get the executive to make publicly available the amount of money going to various countries for military-assistance programs. This information was regularly supplied to Congress, but the executive branch insisted that it be classified, and therefore Congress could not use it. Senator Proxmire discovered the way to get the executive branch to drop these claims. He said the Appropriations Committee would not report out the military-assistance bill until the figures were publicly provided. He discovered that if you are tough enough, you can sometimes get what you want.

Second, the executive controls information through a game called "you did not ask me the right question so I did not give you the right answer." Mr. Helms, you may recall, was asked by the Foreign Relations Committee whether the CIA was involved in Watergate, and he said no. He was not asked, Did you ever give Mr. Hunt and Mr. Liddy equipment with which to burglarize? And he was not asked, Was the CIA ever involved in the cover-up of Watergate? And so, when later confronted with his prior testimony, he explained, "You asked me the wrong question so I did not give you the right information."

The third technique for denying information is lying. Congress was often told, for example, that American forces were sent to Vietnam at the request of the South Vietnamese government. We now know, through the Pentagon Papers, that in fact it took a great deal of arm-twisting by the American government to pursuade the South Vietnamese to permit our troops to come in. But Congress can ask all the questions it wants about how the troops got there and the President does not have to invoke executive privilege if he decides just not to tell the truth.

MR. GOODELL: I have had the experience where the executive has denied the existence of information in its possession.

MR. KRONFELD: I agree with Mr. Halperin on the various techniques used to deny information. One of the most useful techniques I found is for an agency to say Yes, we will supply the information, and then just not to supply it. This has happened on numerous occasions. You must go back to them repeatedly. The agencies know full well that a small Congressional subcommittee cannot spend a lot of time on one item, so they just delay.

I have never heard of a government official who was reticent about giving his views. They will give advice whether they are operating in a fish bowl or not, and in many cases the official gives the advice and releases it himself, often before his superior even gets it.

I think as much as possible, government should operate in a fish bowl. When it does not, we have problems such as Watergate. If there were independent people in the White House, I don't think we would be in this crisis. I agree that although executive privilege is invoked infrequently as a formal doctrine, information is frequently denied. Congress gets an awful lot of information, more than it wants, but much less than it needs. It is often useless information, akin to the press releases that flood the Washington bureaus of newspapers.

MR. LEWIS: I have a question and a comment. A question for Messrs. Shattuck and Dorsen. I am not absolutely clear how procedurally your litigated cases on executive privilege would get into court. Do you suggest that the offending official of the executive branch would be called to the bar of the House or the Senate, or would he be criminally prosecuted under the regular contempt statute? Would there be some declaratory proceeding? I would be interested, and perhaps my question indicates that, like Mr. Marshall, I have some questions about the practicality of frequent litigations.

MR. DORSEN: Any of those techniques could be used to raise the issues in court. There are ways of doing it procedurally. There are problems with this, and we recognize them, but I don't think the justiciability issues are insuperable.

MR. LEWIS: That confirms my partial agreement with Mr. Marshall. You would not want to have too frequent an occurrence of that kind. I think it would obviously be awkward if once a week, once a month, or even once a year you had a lawsuit or criminal prosecution about exactly who had to testify to what extent about what. On the other hand, I am not quite so hopeful as Mr. Marshall about the political process solving all these questions. I think the executive branch does have a very great advantage over Congress under ordinary circumstances. It is not an equal contest, partly for the reasons Mr. Halperin has expressed so well. Executive privilege is not the only weapon in the government armory. It can bury you under the trivial and not give you the answers to important questions. Also Congress can be short-winded. The President is in office for four years. A Secretary of State can just sit there and not answer a letter for two months, as he often does. Meanwhile Congress' attention or a committee's attention turns to something else, an election comes up in another year. So I don't think it is an equal contest. I think in large measure it is luck—luck and, indeed, an indication that we have come very far, a dangerous distance, in giving the executive too much power and too much power to keep things secret.

MR. PLESSER: You don't really say how deep the advice privilege goes. I think that is a problem. What level of government employee can claim the advice privilege?

MR. DORSEN: I would say all levels.

The Government's Classification System

—by William G. Phillips

Any discussion of the government's classification system, the subject of heated controversy during recent years, must be framed in the larger context of its relationship to our over-all national defense and foreign policy and its application to existing criminal statutes.

From the earliest years of our Republic, the President and other executive officials have limited the dissemination of information affecting defense and foreign-policy interests. Few argue that government should not have such power to safeguard vital military and foreign-policy secrets. It is likewise obvious that, in a representative system, the citizenry must be informed to the maximum extent possible of defense and foreign commitments made by their government so as to make sound electoral judgments in the selection of public officials. Further, if the public has a "right to know," Congress has a constitutional "need to know" as the people's representatives so that it can act intelligently and responsibly as a coordinate branch of government in investigating, legislating, and appropriating public funds for weapons systems, defense installations, and foreign-policy programs. The classic dilemma is thus posed between the need for governmental secrecy, as weighed against the public's and Congress' "right to know."

The classification system is an administrative mechanism, applying to federal employees and military personnel, that assigns certain levels of security protection over various types of sensitive military and foreign-policy information, equipment, devices, or other material, the disclosure of which—in the judgment of the classifier—would in various degrees be harmful to the national security. It is presently embodied in Executive Order 11652, issued by President Nixon in March 1972. [1]

The general public is denied access to information classified under the executive order, but Members of Congress and certain Congressional staff members who work for committees involved in defense or foreign policy jurisdictions have limited access to classified documents on a "need-to-know" basis. Traditionally, Members of Congress are not subjected to the in-depth security-clearance procedures that apply to both executive branch personnel and Congressional staff personnel who have access to such classified information.

Since the executive order governing classification procedures does not have the force of law, except for internal administrative purposes, it provides no criminal sanctions for the unauthorized disclosure of classified information. The major deterrent to such unauthorized disclosure is the criminal penalties attached to the Espionage Act of 1917 and a provision of the Internal Security Act of 1950.[2] However, except for classified information dealing with cryptologic systems or communications intelligence, the Espionage Act contains additional legal requirements to sustain an action for unauthorized disclosure of classified data. Legislation is pending in Congress that would make it a federal crime to disclose "classified information to an unauthorized person and to bar as a defense the question as to whether the particular document may have been improperly classified." [3] Many experts feel that the enactment of this bill, as drafted by the Justice Department, would result in an American equivalent of the British Official Secrets Act.

I Evolution of the Modern Classification System

The systematic use of classification markings having precise definitions was first established during World War I, patterned after British and French procedures.[4] Several modifications were incorporated in 1917, 1921, 1935, and 1936. This system applied to military information only and was contained in Army and Navy regulations. Other executive agencies, including the State Department, relied on a 1789 "housekeeping" statute to withhold information from the public.[5] Diplomatic correspondence, cables, and other sensitive types of foreign-policy information were not covered by the classification markings or procedures used by the armed forces.

President Roosevelt's Executive Order 8381, issued in 1940, was the first use of this instrument in the classification field.[6] It applied classification markings and procedures to military and naval installations, equipment, maps, photographs, documents, military designs, and similar items.

Shortly after the outbreak of World War II, the Office of War Information created a governmentwide classification system by regulation issued under authority of Executive Orders 9103 and 9182.[7] The military services, however, utilized their own classification system based on the 1940 executive order and regulations implementing and preceding it.

Over-all security and classification responsibilities were subsequently vested in the National Security Council, created by the National Security Act of 1947,[8] although the military services continued to operate under their established classification system.

In 1950 President Truman issued Executive Order 10104, which revised and updated the 1940 order as applied to military and naval installations and equipment.[9] The following year he issued Executive Order 10290, which was the first one that formalized a security classification system applying to nonmilitary agencies.[10] It authorized any executive department or agency to classify information on a uniform basis and defined "classified security information" to mean "official information the safeguarding of which is necessary in the interest of national security, and which is classified for such purposes by appropriate classifying authority." It was strongly criticized by the press and by some Members of Congress for its vagueness.

Soon after he took office, President Eisenhower replaced the Truman order by a new Executive Order 10501.[11] It was amended several times, but for almost twenty years it was the basis for the nation's classification system. A provision of the Atomic Energy Act of 1954 established a separate statutory classification system governing the AEC's classification and declassification procedures.[12] It operates within the over-all framework of the executive order. The Eisenhower order reduced the number of federal agencies authorized to classify, redefined the "Tot Secret," "Secret," and "Confidential" categories of classification markings, and provided for declassification procedures. This latter provision was substantially improved by "automatic" downgrading and declassification procedures amendments provided by President Kennedy's Executive Order 10964 in 1961.[13]

Executive Order 11652, which replaced the 1953 Eisenhower order on June 1, 1972, was the result of more than a year of effort by a special interdepartmental committee headed by former Assistant Attorney General Rehnquist. It was aimed at remedying major defects in the operation of the twenty-year-old order under which hundreds of millions of classified documents had accumulated, declassification had lagged, and administrative procedures had become a bureaucratic nightmare. Perhaps the best indictment of the classification system that has evolved under executive orders was leveled by President Nixon. In his March 8, 1972, statement accompanying the new order he said:

> Unfortunately, the system of classification which has evolved in the United States has failed to meet the standards of an open and democratic society, allowing too many papers to be classified for too long a time. The controls which have been imposed on classification authority have proved unworkable, and classification has frequently served to conceal bureaucratic mistakes or to prevent embarrassment to officials and administrations. . . .
>
> The many abuses of the security system can no longer be tolerated. Fundamental to our way of life is the belief that when information which properly belongs to the public is systematically withheld by those in power, the people soon become ignorant of their own affairs, distrustful of those who manage them, and—eventually—incapable of determining their own destinies.[14]

These ringing words of Presidential commitment to the public's "right to know," promulgated some three months before the Watergate break-in, somehow seem hollow in the light of the shocking series of revelations of the past year. But they do accurately describe the basic weaknesses of the executive order system of classification and the consequences of continued abuses of classification authority by the military and civilian bureaucracy of the federal government.

II Earlier Studies of the Security Classification System

During the mid-1950s, increasing attention was directed to the government security measures, the classification system, public access to government information, and the right of Congress to information from the executive. The new awareness to such problem areas was sparked by the nation's preoccupation with alleged domestic subversion, "spy trials," the widespread "loyalty-security" investigations associated with the late Senator Joseph McCarthy, and an outbreak of "leaks" of Pentagon documents—part of an interservice rivalry over military missions in the atomic age. It was perhaps also related to the uneasinesss over the global leadership of the United States in the "cold war" period of conflict with the Soviets, the outbreak of the Korean War, and the growth of defense alliances such as NATO.

At the same time, there was renewed effort on the part of scholars, news organizations, and legal authorities to challenge the government's virtually unlimited power to withhold from the public even the most trivial types of information. "The people's right to know" became a rallying cry for those who strongly advocated more open access to government records and the cudgels were soon taken up in the Congress, led by Congressman John Moss of California, Senator Thomas Hennings of Missouri, and, later, Senator Edward Long of Missouri. The Moss Subcommittee on Government Information was created in 1955 and the following year began extensive hearings into all aspects of government information policies and practices, including the classification system.[15]

Over the next year, two other groups were also established to examine government information access, classification procedures, and security procedures. They were the Defense Department's Coolidge Committee and the Commission on Government Security (Wright Commission), which was created by Congress.[16]

In November 1956, after a three-month study, the Coolidge Committee reported to Secretary of Defense Wilson that:

> The two major shortcomings in the operation of the classification system are overclassification and deliberate unauthorized disclosures. . . . Little, if any, progress can be made without a successful attack on these major shortcomings. . . .
>
> The Committee has found a tendency on the part of Pentagon officials to "play it safe" and overclassify; an abuse of security to classify administrative matters; attempts to classify the unclassifiable; confusion from basing security on shifting foreign policy; and a failure to declassify material which no longer requires a secrecy label. . . .
>
> For all these reasons overclassification has reached serious proportions. The result is not only that the system fails to supply to the public information which its proper operation would supply, but the system has become so overloaded that proper protection of information which should be protected has suffered. The press regards the stamp of classification with feelings which vary from indifference to active contempt. Within the Department of Defense itself the mass of classified papers has inevitably resulted in a casual attitude toward classified information, at least on the part of many.[17]

In its recommendations, the Coolidge Committee made a number of suggestions for plugging "leaks" of classified information, although some were characterized by the Government Information Subcommittee as being "repressive and restrictive." In addition, the Coolidge group made some constructive recommendations for eliminating unnecessary secrecy. Among these were recommendations for a "declassification director," a halt to secrecy changes based on temporary shifts in foreign policy, an explanation to the press when information is refused because it is classified, a determined attack on overclassification, a halt to attempts to classify the unclassifiable, a prohibition on the use of secrecy classification for administrative matters, and improved procedures for releasing information about differences of opinion between the services.

Secretary Wilson issued a new DOD directive covering the procedures for classification of security information under Executive Order 10501. His July 8, 1957, action replaced a dozen previous directives and memorandums and consolidated classification instructions into a single new document—DOD Directive 5200.1—entitled "Safeguarding Official Information in the Interests of the Defense of the United States." It incorporated a number of the specific recommendations made by the Coolidge Committee.[18]

Despite concern over the problem of overclassification, the Coolidge Committee made no recommendation for penalties or disciplinary action in cases of misuse or abuse of classification. The new DOD directive did mention disciplinary action for overclassification, but there is no evidence of its ever having been used.

The Wright Commission on Government Security, established in 1955, studied the broader aspects of the Government Security Program, such as the federal civilian loyalty program, industrial security, atomic-energy program, port security, passport-security program, criminal statutes, as well as the document-classification system.

The Commission report issued in June 1957, found that some 1.5 million employees of federal departments and agencies had the authority to classify documents as of January 1, 1957. It recommended that the "Confidential" category of information under Executive Order 10501 be eliminated, criticizing the overuse of this label and its restriction upon the free exchange of scientific and technological information which retards progress necessary to national security. It estimated that 59 per cent of all Defense Department classified information and 76 per cent of classified information in the State and Commerce Departments was "Confidential." It also recommended that the number of persons in each agency authorized to classify documents under Executive Order 10501 be reduced. Another recommendation urged the creation of a statutory Central Security Office having "review and advisory functions with respect to the Federal document classification program and [able] to make recommendations for its improvement as needed." [19]

The most controversial portion of the Wright Commission recommendations was its proposal urging Congress to "enact legislation making it a crime for any person willfully to disclose without proper authorization, for any purpose whatever, information classified 'secret' or 'top secret,' knowing, or having reasonable grounds to believe, such information to have been so classified." The recommended bill would impose a $10,000 fine and jail term of up to five years for those convicted of violating its provisions. The Commission made it clear that its proposal was aimed at persons outside of government, such as newsmen. The recommendation was soundly criticized in articles and editorials in the daily press. One article by James Reston of *The New York Times* pointed out that it would have even resulted in the prosecution of the reporter Paul Anderson, of the *St. Louis Post-Dispatch*, who uncovered and published "secret" documents in the "Teapot Dome" scandal during the 1920s.[20]

In its two-year study of security-classification policies that spanned the Coolidge and Wright groups, the House Government Information Subcommittee concentrated heavily on the Defense Department. The conclusions and recommendations made through reports of the full Government Operations Committee are particularly important to recall. Had the recommendations of these reports been properly implemented by Pentagon officials, it is possible that the security-classification "mess" referred to by President Nixon almost fourteen years after the issuance of the first of the reports could have long since been corrected. Many of the Committee's conclusions might have been written today instead of in 1958. For example, in discussing the handling of information by the Military Establishment, the committee concluded:

> Never before in our democratic form of government has the need for candor been so great. The nation can no longer afford the danger of withholding information merely because the facts fail to fit a predetermined "policy." Withholding

> for any reason other than true military security inevitably results in the loss of public confidence—or a greater tragedy. Unfortunately, in no other part of our government has it been so easy to substitute secrecy for candor and to equate suppression with security.
>
> . . . In a conflict between the right to know and the need to protect true military secrets from a potential enemy, there can be no valid argument against secrecy. The right to know has suffered, however, in the confusion over the demarcation between secrecy for true security reasons and secrecy for "policy" reasons. The proper imposition of secrecy in some situations is a matter of judgment. Although an official faces disciplinary action for the failure to classify information which should be secret, no instance has been found of an official being disciplined for classifying material which should have been made public. The tendency to "play it safe" and use the secrecy stamp, has, therefore, been virtually inevitable.[21]

When the Kennedy administration took office in January 1961, the House Government Information Subcommittee urged the President to take action to implement previous Committee recommendations to tighten up the administration of the classification system.

Subcommittee Chairman Moss also advised incoming Defense Secretary Robert McNamara of previous recommendations concerning security classification and public information, including one urging that "The Secretary of Defense should direct that disciplinary action be taken in cases of overclassification," which had been made in H. Rept. 1884 in 1958. On May 31, 1961, Secretary McNamara issued DOD Directive 5230–13, setting forth four basic principles of public-information policy at the Defense Department, among which was the following: "Secondly it is essential to avoid disclosure of information that can be of material assistance to our potential enemies, and thereby weaken our defense position. It is equally important to avoid overclassification, and therefore, I suggest that we follow this principle: when in doubt, underclassify. In no event should overclassification be used to avoid public discussion of controversial matters."[22] Unfortunately, this "underclassification" principle and the warning against overclassification was not implemented by the imposition of penalties against overclassification, as recommended by the Subcommittee.

Today, more than a decade after the urgent and repeated recommendations of three separate and independent groups for specific action to correct administrative abuses inherent in the operation of the executive-order classification system, such abuses still exist in abundance and, in some cases, have actually multiplied. The classification bureaucracy continues to flourish and still maintains firm control over the system. Mired in the excesses of its own operation, wallowing amid mountains of documents often bearing meaningless and long-since outdated classification markings, the bureaucracy continues on its blind, "stamp-happy" course. Many close observers of the classification machinery fear that the over-all integrity of the system has reached the point where the protection of the relatively few truly vital defense and foreign-policy secrets may no longer be possible.

III Dimensions of the Classification Problem

The publication in the press of the Pentagon Papers in 1971, and the attempts by the administration to restrain their publication, made millions of Americans more aware of the classification system. The 6–3 Supreme Court decision against the government in *The New York Times* and *The Washington Post* cases, and the depositions presented in those cases by both government and outside classification experts revealed operational details of the system. Witnesses who testified at hearings of the House Foreign Operations and Government Information Subcommittee during the controversy uncovered other salient facts.[23]

Leaks of government documents during the India-Pakistan conflict in December 1971, the leak early in 1972 of a National Security Council memorandum revealing administration policy conflicts on Vietnam war strategy, and the Ellsberg-Russo trial in connection with the Pentagon Papers, have all contributed to a broader interest in the security-classification problem.

The House Foreign Operations and Government Information Subcommittee held hearings in May 1972 on security classification problems involving Section 552 (b)(1) of the Freedom of Information Act.[24] They supplemented the Subcommittee's June 1971 hearings on the "Pentagon Papers" and their relationship to the security-classification system.

Chairman William Moorhead described the dimension of the problem in his opening statement:

> There are 55,000 arms pumping up and down in Government offices stamping "confidential" on stacks of Government documents; more than 18,000 Government employees are wielding "secret" stamps, and a censorship elite of nearly 3,000 bureaucrats have authority to stamp "top secret" on public records.
>
> These are not wild estimates. These numbers were provided by the Government agencies, themselves. But even this huge number of Government censors is just the top of the secrecy iceberg.
>
> These Government officials are the ones who have been granted authority, under a Presidential order, to put "top secret," "secret," and "confidential" on Government records which are to be hidden from the public in the interests of national defense. It seems to me that this sort of national defense effort creates little more than a Maginot Line made of paper—and it is even more dangerous than France's concrete and steel Maginot line which gave that country false confidence in its safety just before it was overrun by the German Army in World War II.[25]

Witnesses who testified before the Subcommittee during the 1971 and 1972 classification hearings—from executive agencies as well as outside experts—presented examples of specific abuses of the classification system as well as broad criticism of its over-all operational efficiency.

1 *Massive volumes of classified material.* Dr. James Rhoads, Archivist of the United States, testified that the Archives contain some 470 million pages of classified documents that cover the period 1939–1954. Mr. William Florence, a retired Air Force classification expert, testified that the Defense

Department alone has at least 20 million classified documents (not pages but documents). One State Department witness testified that his department had some 35 million classified documents in its possession, but another State Department representative who testified estimated the total to be only 2 million.[26] The fact is clear that no one really knows just how many classified documents there are in any Federal agency.

2 *Authority to classify.* A 1971 survey by the Subcommittee of twelve federal agencies having primary classification authority indicated that some 55,000 persons were authorized to originally classify "Top Secret," "Secret," or "Confidential" information or material under the provisions of Executive Order 10501. Of this number, 2849 could classify "Top Secret," as well as the two lower categories; another 18,029 had authority to classify "Secret" and "Confidential," while the remaining 34,122 had "Confidential" classification authority.[27]

These statistics, however, apply only to original classifications and do not take into account the extent of "derivative" classification—the clerical reassignment or transfer of an existing marking on information contained in a classified document when it is used in another memorandum, letter, cable, report, or other communication. One witness estimated that "hundreds of thousands" of low-level military and civilian employees thus wield classification stamps under this "derivative" marking system for millions of additional papers that circulate within the federal bureaucracy.[28]

There has been a gradual reduction in the number of federal agencies that are authorized to exercise classification authority under the various executive orders. President Truman's Executive Order 10290 gave such authority to all agencies. This was reduced drastically to forty-seven under Executive Order 10501 and still further reduced to thirty-five, including various White House and executive office agencies, in the new Executive Order 11652. Only thirteen of these agencies now have "Top Secret" classification authority.[29]

A recent report of the Interagency Classification Review Committee, created by the new order to oversee its operations, indicates that there has been a 63-per-cent reduction in the number of persons authorized to classify. The number is now said to be in the 17,000 range from the previously reported total of more than 50,000.[30] These figures, however, have not yet been verified by the Subcommittee.

3 *Overclassification.* There has been virtually unanimous agreement that serious abuses of overclassification continue. Former Defense Secretary Melvin Laird told an Associated Press group in April 1970, "Let me emphasize my conviction that the American people have a right to know even more than has been available in the past about matters which affect their safety and security. There has been too much clasification in this country." [31] And Mr. Florence testified; "I sincerely believe that less than one-half of one per cent of the different documents which bear currently assigned classification markings actually contain information qualifying even for the lowest (Confidential) defense classification under Executive Order 10501. In other words, the disclosure of information in at least 99.5 per cent of those classified documents could not be prejudicial to the defense interests of the nation." [32]

Other witnesses provided examples of the overclassification of information. For instance, Gene LaRocque, Rear Admiral (retired), U.S. Navy, a much-decorated veteran of thirty-one years of naval service, testified:

> In the military the best way to prevent disclosure of information is to classify it. Classification is made for a variety of reasons. First, to prevent it from falling into the hands of a potential enemy; this is legitimate but accounts for only a small portion of the material classified. Other reasons for classifying material are: to keep it from the other military services; from civilians in their own service; from civilians in the Defense Department; from the State Department; and, of course, from the Congress. Sometimes, information is classified to withhold it for later release to maximize the effect on the public or the Congress.
>
> Frequently, information is classified so that only portions of it can be released selectively to the press to influence the public or the Congress. These time-released capsules have a lasting effect.[33]

Repeated urgings by the Government Information Subcommittee and the House Government Operations Committee to the executive departments to impose severe administrative penalties on those who repeatedly overclassify have fallen on deaf ears. A survey of administrative penalities imposed by federal agencies for violations of security-classification regulations, conducted last year by the Subcommittee, showed that of the 2505 reported administrative penalties against civilian and military personnel—*not one was for overclassification.*

4 *Classification costs.* In June 1971 the Subcommittee asked the General Accounting Office to investigate all aspects of security-classification costs—including storage, protection, classification and declassification, transmission, and other related expenditures. Four agencies were chosen by the GAO for the pilot study—Defense, State, Atomic Energy Commission, and National Aeronautics and Space Administration. Direct costs for these four agencies totaled some $60 million for the most recent fiscal year.[34]

This does not take into consideration the more than $60 million spent annually on security-clearance investigations of military and civilian employees of the government, nor does it include an estimated $49 million in annual security-classification costs related to government contracts and included in the "overhead" of major defense-industry contracts for weapons systems, ammunition, and other military equipment.

5 *Lack of historical perspective.* Less subject to precise measurement is the crippling of historical perspective that results from the decades of hiding information about major events. This point was well expressed during the Subcommittee's hearings by history professor Lloyd Gardner of Rutgers University:

> Nations, like individuals, depend in part upon memory in order to be able to function rationally in the present. Historians are to a degree responsible for what stands out in a nation's memory; they supply experience longer than one generation's life-span, and broader than that of any group of individuals.

As one approaches the present, the historian's most valuable asset, perspective, is diminished chronologically, and in a secrecy-conscious nation, by the lack of available evidence as well.

The nation's memory is thus weakest for the years of the recent past, a serious defect, unless one is prepared to concede that the public should reach its conclusions on the basis of little or no information, or that the policy-maker is the only one who needs the memory.[35]

IV Executive Order 11652

As noted earlier, President Nixon's Executive Order 11652 was issued in March, and took effect on June 1, 1972. House Foreign Operations and Government Information Subcommittee Chairman Moorhead requested National Security Council personnel working on the draft order in February for an opportunity to comment on the draft. He believed that the Subcommittee's long study of the classification system could provide some useful material for the NSC's deliberative process. Mr. Moorhead's request was refused by David Young, NSC's chief staff official, who replaced William Rehnquist as head of the drafting committee when Mr. Rehnquist was appointed to the Supreme Court.

The new Executive Order 11652 is entitled "Classification and Declassification of National Security Information and Material." President Nixon has outlined its "most significant features" as follows:

> The rules for classifying documents are more restrictive.
>
> The number of departments and people who can originally classify information has been substantially reduced.
>
> Timetables ranging from six to ten years have been set for the automatic declassification of documents. Exceptions will be allowed only for such information as falls within four specifically defined categories.
>
> Any document exempted from automatic declassification will be subject to mandatory review after a ten-year period. Thus, for the first time, a private citizen is given a clear right to have national security information reviewed on the basis of specified criteria to determine if continued

classification is warranted so long as the document can be adequately identified and obtained by the government with a reasonable amount of effort.

If information is still classified thirty years after origination, it will then be automatically declassified unless the head of the originating department determines in writing that its continued protection is still necessary and he sets a time for declassification.

Sanctions may be imposed upon those who abuse the system.

And a continuing monitoring process will be set up under the National Security Council and an interagency classification review committee, whose chairman is to be appointed by the President.[36]

A White House "Fact Sheet on Executive Order 11652," issued on August 3, 1972, listed "the three basic objectives of the new executive order as: 1) to reduce the amount of material classified by the government; 2) to provide for speedier declassification under automatic schedules; and 3) to insure implementation of the order through the establishment of an Interagency Classification Review Committee." [37]

The preamble of the executive order directly links the authority for its issuance to the Freedom of Information Act:

> The interests of the United States and its citizens are best served by making information regarding the affairs of government readily available to the public. This concept of an informed citizenry is reflected in the Freedom of Information Act and in the current public information policies of the executive branch. . . .
>
> This official information or material, referred to as classified information or material in this order, is expressly exempted from public disclosure by Section 552 (b)(1) of Title 5, United States Code. Wrongful disclosure of such information or material is recognized in the Federal Criminal Code as providing a basis for prosecution.[38]

Exemption (b)(1) of the Freedom of Information Act contains one of the very few statutory references to the executive order classification system. It reads as follows:

> (b) This section does not apply to matters that are—
>
> (1) specifically required by Executive order to be kept

secret in the interest of national defense or foreign policy. . . .

The government used this exemption to withhold information relating to the Amchitka nuclear test in Alaska two years ago. Representative Patsy Mink and thirty-two other Members of Congress sued as individuals under the Freedom of Information Act when they were denied such information. The Supreme Court, overturning the Court of Appeals, ruled in January 1973 that a claim of exemption under (b)(1) of the Act was satisfied by an affidavit of the government that the documents sought were properly classified under the applicable executive order and involved "highly sensitive matter . . . vital to our national defense and foreign policy." The District Court refused to order an *in camera* judicial examination of the contents of the disputed documents to determine whether or not they were properly classified.[39]

The Subcommittee has concluded hearings on legislation to reverse the Court's decision in the *Mink* case and to make other strengthening amendments to the Freedom of Information Act.[40]

Members argue that the Congress never intended to give blanket authority to the executive to determine whether information sought under the Act by the public is "properly classified," without requiring judicial review of all cases brought under the Act.

The Subcommittee's staff identified the following defects in Executive Order 11652:

— It totally misconstrues the basic meaning of the Freedom of Information Act.

— It confuses the sanctions of the Criminal Code that apply to the wrongful disclosure of classified information.

— It confuses the legal meaning of the terms "national defense" and "national security" and the terms "foreign policy" and "foreign relations" while failing to provide an adequate definition of these terms.

— It provides no specific penalties for overclassification or misclassification.

— It permits executive departments to hide the identity of classifiers of specific documents.

— It permits full details of major defense or foreign-policy errors of an administration to be cloaked for a minimum of three four-year Presidential terms, but loopholes could extend this secrecy for thirty years or more.

— It provides no public accountability to Congress for the newly created Interagency Classification Review Committee.

— It legitimizes and broadens authority for the use of special categories of "classification" governing access and distribution of classified information and material beyond the three specified categories.

— And it creates a "special privilege" for former Presidential appointees for access to certain papers that could serve as the basis for their private profit through the sale of articles, books, and memoirs to publishing houses.[41]

While a number of these points were subsequently clarified, either during the cross-examination of executive branch witnesses or in the National Security Council guideline directive interpreting the new order, the majority of them remain unchallenged.

Several other major problems affecting the classification system under the new order also surfaced during the hearings:

— There was an administrative lag between the effective date of the new order and its implementation by affected executive departments and agencies. Only six agencies had issued regulations some sixty-four days after the effective date of the new order. Another three agencies published such regulations in October 1972, while an additional four came out in November, eight more in December, and the final four agencies finally published their implementing regulations in January 1973.[42]

— The new order omitted a "savings clause" that would have protected against legal questions concerning the status of information classified after the effective date of the new order, but *before* agency regulations could be written, promulgated, and implemented.

— Conflicting interpretations were given by executive-branch witnesses over the extent to which "domestic surveillance" activities by federal agencies involving American citizens are subject to classification under the new executive order.[43]

— Provisions of the new order affecting the access of historian, researchers, and scholars to classified data of the post-World War II period fall far short of the policies necessary to permit the Congress and the public to benefit from insights into defense and foreign policy during this crucial period.

Only time will determine the extent to which apparent loopholes and administrative deficiencies will hinder the operation of the classification system under the new order.

V Conclusions and Recommended Reform

For well over a decade a subcommittee of the House Government Operations Committee has conducted studies and investigations and has held months of hearings covering many thousands of printed pages of testimony. It has issued more than a dozen reports and other publications dealing with the nation's security-classification system as it has operated during the past five administrations.[44]

Over the years, the Committee's findings and conclusions have documented widespread overclassification, abuses in the use of the classification stamps, and other serious defects. These Committee documents have revealed dangerous shortcomings of a system that has been administratively loose and uncoordinated, unenforced and perhaps unenforceable. It has functioned in a way to deny public access to essential information. It has spawned a strangling mass of classified documents that finally weakened and threatened a breakdown of the entire system.

These same reports have repeatedly made constructive recommendations to help correct the deficiencies of the security-classification system. Unfortunately for the integrity of the system and for the taxpayers who must pay millions of dollars annually to keep the classification machine running, many of these recommendations have gone unheeded.

There is an unquestioned need for federal agencies to avoid the release or dissemination to the public of certain sensitive information, the safeguarding of which is vital to national defense and to the necessary confidentiality of dealings between our country and foreign nations.

But the nation is strengthened when the American public

is informed of our international commitments and our defense posture, insofar as this can be done consistent with security requirements. Fundamental liberties are endangered whenever abuses in the security system occur. Within these constraints, when information that should be made available to the people is unnecessarily withheld by government—for whatever reason—our representative system is undermined and our people become less able to judge for themselves the stewardship of government officials. Information is essential to knowledge—and knowledge is the basis for political power. Under our governmental system, maximum access to information must, therefore, always reside firmly in the hands of the American people.

The efficiency and integrity of a security-classification system rests in large part on proper use of clearly defined gradations of secrecy. Unnecessary classification of marginal information and overclassification must be strictly avoided. When the mass of currently used classified information aggregates many millions of pages—much of which is overclassified—there no longer can be the degree of respect or selectivity upon which classification markings depend for their integrity. To the extent that a classification system does not punish participating officials who abuse the system, who classify unnecessarily, or who "play it safe" by overclassifying, it adds immeasurably to the proliferation of classified documents, gradually weakening and eventually destroying its own integrity and effectiveness.

The inescapable conclusion drawn from any serious study of the classification system is that the executive-order approach must be replaced by a workable, realistic, and enforceable statutory system. The power of Congress to legislate is clear. In the *Mink* decision, Justice White said that "Congress could certainly have provided that the Executive Branch adopt new procedures [for classifying documents], or it could have established its own procedures. . . ."

A statutory system should be established, perhaps as an amendment to the Freedom of Information Act, to make it clear that Congress intends a proper balancing between the safeguarding of information classified under strict guidelines to protect defense and foreign-policy secrets and the right of the American public to know how the affairs of their government are being conducted. Congress should also take this necessary action to assure maximum credibility of all citizens in our governmental institutions and in our elected and appointed officials. Classification legislation should include the following:

1. It should provide for precise definitions of the categories of information subject to classification.

2. It should be strictly limited to the relatively few executive departments and agencies directly involved in national-defense and foreign-policy matters, intelligence-gathering, and related areas.

3. Only key policy-making officials in these departments and agencies should be entrusted with original classification authority; they should be clearly identified on each document they classify; they should be held fully accountable for their classification judgments; and they should be subject to severe and enforceable disciplinary action for misuse of their authority.

4. It should provide that the vast amounts of more "routine" classified information remain frozen in each category for only a relatively short time, establish a workable administrative mechanism for regular periodic review, downgrading, and ultimate declassification—based on a determination of the need for continued protection at the various classification levels. (Such determinations are not always measurable in absolute time periods as they are dependent on the rapidly moving sequence of events involving scientific development, defense technology, changing diplomatic and military situations, and the like.)

5. Certain highly sensitive types of information—cryptologic systems, intelligence reports, identification of intelligence sources, information provided by foreign governments in confidence, contingency military plans, details of weapons systems or military installations requiring the highest degree of security protection—should be governed by procedures that permit maximum discretion by responsible high-ranking government officials. In most instances, such informa-

tion should be exempt from automatic downgrading and de-classification procedures that apply to more "routine" categories of classified information, but their classification status should be periodically reviewed by higher authority.

6. It should provide a vigorously enforced mechanism for reviewing and policing all aspects of the classification program, perhaps by an independent regulatory body within the executive branch that would be assigned administrative, enforcement, and adjudicatory functions. It must assure that Congressional committees have full access to classified information held by the executive branch when such information is relevant to their investigative or legislative jurisdiction.

7. It should assure proper administrative efficiency of the classification system to safeguard against the compromise of vital defense or foreign-policy secrets, while at the same time upholding to the maximum extent possible the right of the American public to know about national-security commitments being made in their name.

8. Finally, it should provide for full judicial review of classification decisions by requiring *in camera* examination of classified information by federal courts in cases involving disputes over the use of proper classification markings authorized by the legislation.

Congress has an overriding responsibility to act promptly by enacting a sound and workable classification law. Several proposals have already been advanced in both the House and Senate. Senator Edmund Muskie introduced such a bill in December 1971, and Chairman William Moorhead offered another version in May 1972. These measures have been the subject of considerable study and discussion and will soon be reintroduced in revised form. Another comprehensive classification bill has recently been introduced in the Senate by Senator Mike Gravel.[45] This is the time for action.

VI Discussion

MR. TAYLOR: There is a close relation between government classification and executive privilege. Mr. Halperin's comments on Messrs. Dorsen's and Shattuck's paper brought that out. With regard to the privilege, the key is the relationship between the person who is providing the information and the person to whom he is providing it. For example, if judges are sitting in conference over a case, what they say to each other may not be interesting or damaging if it were disclosed, but their relationship is such that we discourage inquiry. With classification, we deal with information. The content of a document is protected, perhaps irrespective of its source or recipient. This does not give us a perfect delineation, and Mr. Halperin quite rightly pointed to the overlap, but there is that conceptual difference which is helpful to make at the start.

Classification reminds me a little bit of the way in which Professor Thomas Powell of the Harvard Law School used to close his lecture on the extent, if any, to which the states could regulate interstate commerce. He used to say, "Can the states regulate interstate commerce? Yes.

"How much can the states regulate interstate commerce? Some, but not too much.

"How much is too much? That is outside the scope of this lecture."

That is the nature of the problem here. Everybody seems to agree there must be some classification, but not too much; and most everybody agrees there is too much.

MR. FUTTERMAN: The problem is simply that the public does not always get the information it needs to play its proper role in a democracy. This issue goes beyond the classification problem. Even if there were no classification system, there would be no assurance that the public would get the facts it needs. A document can be hidden in a file drawer whether or not it has a "top secret" stamp on it. The next logical question is, can we identify in fairly precise terms the kinds of information that the people have a need and right to know? If we can do that, I think we can look to Congress to identify not only information which should not be classified but information which the government should affirmatively disclose.

What information might this be? It is sometimes said that the people have a right to know what the government is doing, as distinguished from what it is thinking or planning. I think this may be a bit broad. For example, it is not clear to me that the people had a right to know, in the spring of 1971, that Washington was talking to Peking about a summit meeting. But there are categories of information of such importance that the public has a clear need and right to know about them. Various people would differ on how long the list should be, but I think any list would have to include the right to information about military action the government is taking and where U.S. military forces are stationed around the world. For a long time it was unknown, for example, that there were large contingents of the U.S. Army in Thailand. People should also be told what assistance the United States is providing foreign countries.

At least with respect to these three areas, and there may be others, secrecy is not necessary—unlike intelligence-gathering or the conduct of negotiations. Yet it is interesting that the government seems to get most exercised about leaks in these very areas. It was the revelation, in 1969, of the Cambodia bombing that led the White House to take the I hope, unusual step of tapping the private phones of White House aides.

Trying to identify categories of information that must be made public has one major advantage over using standards like "grave danger to national security" to classify information. In the present situation, I think the courts are not likely to enter this area with the judicial review Mr. Phillips refers to. We must decide that certain categories of information bear such a vital relationship to the ability of the public to fulfill its role in a democracy that they must be made public, and whatever convenience there is in keeping them secret must simply be foregone.

MR. PHILLIPS: This problem of definition is certainly most difficult. Executive Order 11652 did something quite unique. For the first time, it gave examples. Thus, information is "top secret" if its release may lead to armed hostilities against the United States or its allies, disrupt foreign relations vitally affecting the national security, compromise vital national-defense plans, cryptologic codes or communications intelligence systems, reveal sensitive intelligence operations, or disclose scientific or technological developments vital to the national security.

MR. TAYLOR: Is release of classified information, without more, a basis for penal sanctions? Or do you believe that the information must also damage the national defense before a person could be prosecuted for releasing it?

MR. PHILLIPS: None of the classification bills introduced thus far—and I don't believe any of the drafts that have circulated in this area—provide for criminal sanctions. I think most of the sponsors feel that they would prefer to rely on the existing espionage statutes and court decisions.

MR. WISE: I think this a problem without a solution. That is a terrible thing to say, because we live in a country where we think everything can be solved and all differences accommodated; but I don't think there is a solution to this problem. For example, we talk about trying to set standards. I really don't think you can set standards. The Nixon administration has apparently attempted to classify a burglary. It was an indecent act, a burglary of a psychiatrist's office, and I can't think of anything comparable except perhaps putting a bug in a confessional. So, whatever the standards, any group of people exercising power will interpret the standards their own way. That is what is wrong with standards.

I am skittish about the statutory approach Mr. Phillips has proposed because first I think it is impossible to provide the definitions, and secondly I have come around to the feeling that the correct solution is to junk the present classification system entirely. If the government feels there are certain things that must be kept secret, it can put them in the file and lock them up. It does not matter whether the file has a fancy label on it.

I think there is a great danger that any regulatory body set up by legislation would end up as a board of censors rather than an agency that increases the flow of information. I can foresee a situation where Neil Sheehan has the Pentagon Papers and, before he could publish a story, he would have to run it through a committee on secrecy. Legislation of this sort could also bring with it sanctions for violation of the standards that Congress sets up.

I agree with what Professor Emerson said in another context, that if the cat is out of the bag, it is out. I think government has a right to keep secrets, or to try to keep secrets, in areas it thinks are important. The press has the right to inform the public under the First Amendment, and if it gets secrets, whether they are stamped or not stamped, it has the right to print them. I think that there is always going to be that tension. It is not reconcilable, either by executive order or by legislation.

MR. BLACK: I do not think it has been made clear enough that the real purpose of the federal government's classification systems is to limit the flow of information, whether between agencies, branches, or individuals. The only way the information can be protected is physically. The classification systems themselves are only bureaucratic devices to provide guidelines and rules for control.

I was the Classified Material Control Officer in one military command and responsible for Restricted Data security in another, including nuclear weapons themselves. In each instance, there were numbers of diverse instructions and regulations to read and implement. They were awfully ambiguous, but were clear enough on one point: I was to permit no one to get or see the items under my control unless they were officially given "access" to them—a *Catch-22* type of status which most often amounted to the commander's saying that a particular person had a "need to know." This is where the real protection or seclusion came. If the commander said that someone was to see or get a particular item, it happened; if he said "no," it did not happen. The classification system itself played a minimal role in this game, and was basically not needed.

This is generally true of the rest of the federal government. If someone wants you to know the information, you get it. If you ask the right questions in the right way and the government officials are relatively neutral, you get the information. Otherwise, you never will, regardless of any laws dealing with classification, freedom of information, access, executive privilege, or secrecy in general.

The classification systems are only bureaucratic devices, are costly in terms of time and dollars to operate, and are just not necessary. The only proper system for protecting valid government secrets is a *physical* one. In my experience, that is the only real system that existed in the first place. I would suggest getting rid of the formal classification systems altogether.

MR. CALLEN: Mr. Phillips commented on the need to keep certain scientific things classified. Scientists don't always feel that way. Edward Teller, the "father of the hydrogen bomb," recently commented that he thinks everything should be declassified after one year—scientific things and technological things—and the burden of proof should be on anyone who wants to have something remain classified to show that it is in the interest of the government that it be done. Mr. Teller and many other scientists feel that in fact security classification holds back scientific progress. Much of what a researcher does is done by serendipity. He does not know what he has a need to know until he knows it. Something is classified and he does not know that he needs to know it. He just has no access to it. The result is that the unclassified fields move ahead fastest—for example, in electronic computers, the United States leads the world. This field has never been classified. On the other hand, fusion and laser-inducted fusion, where we are not doing well, is a highly classified field.

MR. PHILLIPS: I would like to quote from the Wright Commission Report of 1957. The Wright Commission was not known as a liberal group. In fact it was very conservative, and some of the recommendations it made were repressive. But one of the major recommendations was that the "confidential" category of information under Executive Order 10501 be eliminated; the main reason was that it was overused. It definitely restricted the free exchange of information in the scientific and technological areas, and this retarded progress necessary to national security. Remember, this was when Sputnik went up; there was concern that the scientific community in the United States was lagging behind the rest of the world. Unfortunately, the Wright Commission recommendation was never adopted.

MR. CALLEN: Professor Teller said the Russians know not only what we know now but everything we will discover and classify in the next two years.

MR. HALPERIN: I agree that this is not a problem that can be solved. I am skeptical that a rewritten executive order or new legislation can deal with the overclassification problem. I think it reeks of the bureaucratic. We have to identify specific problems which arise out of the classification system, and then ask ourselves how they can be dealt with. I would like to mention three of these.

First, there are activities which the government keeps secret and which it should not even be engaging in without public debate—such as bombing Cambodia or Laos or carrying on covert intelligence operations against North Vietnam. The way to deal with this is by positive legislation that requires Congressional consent for the activity and reporting to Congress on it.

Second is the declassification issue. Here it seems to me one does need some kind of body, separate and independent from the executive branch. Anybody who has tried to get a document from an executive agency, no matter how old, knows it is hopeless. It should be made clear that this body may not deal with information in the hands of a person not in the government, however it got to that person. That is, this commission should not have a right to deal with material that has reached *The New York Times* or anybody else. It should be a body that takes away from the executive branch the power to keep things classified beyond a certain number of years, if at all, depending on the information.

Third is the issue of criminal penalties. I disagree with the suggestion that criminal penalties should be left to current legislation and cases. Senator Goodell and I sat through a good deal of the Pentagon Papers trial, and I think it was absolutely clear that the legislation is totally unintelligible. The notion that one should rely on the plain meaning of the words in the case of the espionage legislation is absurd, because the words have no plain meaning. But the government is asserting that the legislation as it now exists can send a person to jail for a great many years if he gives any classified document to someone without a clearance. Given that assertion, I believe there is a definite need for new legislation. It should not be a crime to reveal information unless one's intent is to harm the national defense. Nobody has ever gone to jail up until now without having that intent, but, as I say, it has now become ambiguous whether that is the law.

MR. KRONFELD: Government agencies say that the release of classified information might allow a foreign power or potential enemy to learn something it did not know. But in many cases, the foreign power already knows the information. In the U-2 incident, the Russians knew full well we were flying U-2s over their country. That information was classified. And all parties involved in the India-Pakistan dispute knew that the United States was leaning toward Pakistan. But that was classified.

This information is classified so as not to force the other party involved in the dispute to take an action which it does not want or have to take so long as the general public does not know what was going on. In the case of the U-2, for a long time the Russians could not act against the U-2s because they did not have the technology. But if the U-2 flights had been generally known to the public, the Russians might have been forced to take some action they did not want to take against the United States. The same is true in the Pakistan-India dispute. The parties knew about the American position, but until it was released, they did not have to act on it. It is just a question of allowing the foreign ministries to play their own game and not having to react to public pressure.

MR. SALOSCHIN: It should be clear that the classification of information is a phenomenon of government which arises out of the constitutional responsibility of the President as Commander-in-Chief. Anyone who has ever had any administrative or executive or management responsibility in any public or private organization which has to function in a milieu of constant rivalries and constant changes, knows that information with regard to one's own capabilities and intentions, and those of others, obviously requires executive concern.

I was very struck by your comment at the beginning, Professor Taylor, and I think there is a lot of truth in it, when you said that it is easy to classify and hard to declassify. I would like to pick that up and ask why is that true? In a nutshell, I think it is because, from the viewpoint of the individual who ultimately has the function of classifying or declassifying in a real life situation in an agency, classification is based upon a determination of risk, whereas declassification is based upon the harder determination of no risk.

I agree that this is not a completely soluble problem. You have to ask yourself, Who is going to do the work and what is it going to cost? If any of you were offered a full-time job declassifying the tremendous accumulation of documents, it would be a tossup whether you would quit your job first, out of sheer boredom and a feeling of uselessness, or whether the taxpayers would tire of keeping you on the payroll when they measured the cost of this activity against the many other demands on the federal budget.

MR. EMERSON: The suggestion has been made by several members of the panel that the problem can be solved by delineating those things which should be made public, rather than to try to describe those things which may be classified. But it is difficult to define the items that should be made public. Although there may be some use in that approach, it is not enough. I would approach it from the other point. I would say that nothing can be classified except in certain very limited categories. Everything else should be open to the public. I would define the exceptions pretty much along the line that the Nixon executive order defines items that will not automatically be declassified. Those would include military operations, intelligence operations, confidential dealings with foreign powers, and a few other limited areas. Otherwise, there is no purpose for classification.

I would also propose, as Mr. Wise did, that once the material gets out, there be no controls, either by way of prior restraint or by way of criminal punishment or anything else. Once information gets into the public domain, it is futile to try to stop it. It can only result in the worst aspects of an official secrets act to try to do so.

MR. STONE: We ought to ask why the rhetoric about the need for national security has stepped up. I think there are two reasons. One is the increasing bureaucratization of society. The most sensitive matters, held in highest classification, have internal political consequences for the bureaucracy. One example of bureaucratization occurred when I first applied for a security clearance; I was given a fairly good going-over and decided to hire a lawyer. People who interceded for me were told, "There is no problem about clearing Stone, but we do not like the politics of his lawyer. If he wants to shake up the system, that is another matter." I also got advice at one point from a friendly security official, that if you want to write a letter of complaint about inordinate delays, make it very calm and cool and show no signs of being about to cause the bureaucrats a lot of trouble. I realized then that the security system was in part if inadvertently, a method of bureaucratic control. The concern of the system, and the bureaucrats, was whether the applicant would "go along." The security system could be used to make sure they would.

The other reason for the enhanced rhetoric about security is habit and the indoctrination of a generation to think in these terms.

MR. GOODELL: I agree with the difficulty of setting standards, but I don't think we should abandon that effort. In most complex things you are going to get an imperfect result. The standards should say that under no circumstances will anything be classified only to deprive American citizens of information. I don't think there should be criminal sanctions connected to the classification law. Congress has not written criminal sanctions. They were not necessary. I think the classification system will work, probably overwork, through administrative sanctions without criminal sanctions.

Congress should always have full access to classified information upon request. It would be helpful if members of the executive branch knew they were not committing an administrative or criminal violation in giving classified information to members of the Congress. It is up to the Member of Congress to decide what he does with the information.

Quite frequently, the best way to keep a secret is not to classify it, because the bureaucrats at the higher levels are so overburdened they frequently say, "Don't show me anything that is not 'top secret.' "

So if you don't classify it, they are not going to have the

time to look at it, or if you only classify it confidential, they say it is not worth looking at anyway.

MR. PHILLIPS: In our Subcommittee's recent study of 2505 administrative penalties assessed for violation of classification rules—about ninety-five per cent of them were in the Department of Defense—we showed that not one of those penalties was for overclassification. I have never known, nor have any of the witnesses who testified before our Subcommittee ever given, one example of an administrative penalty against someone for repeatedly overclassifying. This is one weakness of the executive order.

Conversely, there is also a great deal of overclassification that occurs simply to get attention. The Subcommittee is aware of a situation involving an ambassador to a small, remote country. Nobody in the State Department paid much attention to what he was doing. So every cable he sent to the Secretary of State for eighteen months he classified "top secret," without regard to what was in it. He wanted to get attention. He wanted to make sure that when he sent a cable to Washington someone at State would at least look at it.

What Is the Real Problem with the Classification System?

—by Stanley Futterman

I The Political Issues

Criticisms of the government's classification system have tended to focus on the quantifiable. As with members of a weight-watchers group, measurement of the leviathan has served as the indictment.

An efficiency-oriented, number-obsessed society cannot fail to be impressed with figures indicating that there are hundreds of millions of pages of classified documents, that tens of thousands of government employees exercise classifying authority, and that the total secrecy system costs hundreds of millions of dollars each year. Accordingly, the standard solutions proposed year after year involve cutting down on the number of documents classified, and the people classifying.

Implicit in this approach is the notion that classification is a problem in management, with success something that can be represented on a graph composed of descending lines. There is a management problem here, of course, but it is not the critical issue. There is no threat to the Republic in the overclassification of trivia or in providing a junior with a classification stamp along with his pass to the executive cafeteria. (Indeed, requiring him to seek out his senior whenever he writes a memo referring to sensitive information could make the classification system even more of an obstruction to efficient government than it is now.)

More serious than the manager's concern is that of the historian. We depend on historians to supply society with a usable memory, one that permits us to forge cognitive links between the daily rush of events and the successes, failures, sense, and nonsense of the past. An accelerating pace of change pushes the present ever more quickly into the past. Our need for historians to be able to explicate the recent past, to give us the power to relate it to present problems, increases apace.

Happily, the historian's problem may be susceptible to managerial amelioration. A limit of ten years, say, on the length of time that government records may remain closed—with an exception for records specifically determined by responsible officials at the expiration of that period to require further withholding for a limited period—could go far to insure accurate knowledge of the past.

But we are still not at the critical issue. If the political need for information about the past is to equip us to deal with the present, an even more insistent imperative is that we know the present. For this we must look to reporters, not historians. The press is the fourth branch of government because without it the process of governing would be unrelievedly oligarchic. There is no democracy without a concerned public, and there can be no concern about that which is not known. If a system of secrecy is working at high efficiency, the public will not even know that it does not know.

The critical issue is no less than this: how can a government of and by the people be achieved when the government can keep—and to some extent must keep—information from the people?

Putting the issue this way suggests that the problem transcends the classification system. The problem is not simply to assure that information which should not be kept secret is not classified. Rather, it is to assure, to the extent that it can be assured, that information which should not be kept secret is actually and contemporaneously disclosed.

Classification does, of course, bear on disclosure. A classification stamp on a document alerts insiders that they are expected not to disclose its contents to outsiders, and that they will be subject to administrative, perhaps even criminal, penalties if they do so and are discovered. The classification stamp also serves as a justification for turning aside specific requests for information from the press and public. This procedure has been given statutory blessing by the self-styled Freedom of Information Act. The Act requires that agencies make "identifiable records" available to any person requesting them, but exempts nine categories of information, including matters "specifically required by executive order to be kept secret in the interest of national defense or foreign policy." [1]

An unclassified document can be hidden just as deeply in a file drawer, however, as a classified document can. The Freedom of Information Act never even becomes relevant until someone knows enough to ask for an "identifiable" document.

It is instructive that the government doesn't rely on the normal working of the classification system to protect information it is most concerned not get out. Rather, the technique is to restrict the information to a tight circle of trusted officials. Filling the classified stamp pads of these officials with disappearing ink would have little effect on what information comes to the public's attention.

If the critical problem is disclosure, then, we are not likely to go very far toward solving it without imposing a positive disclosure requirement—one which does not wait upon an informed request, as does the Freedom of Information Act, but imposes a positive duty on the government to keep the public informed.

In a general sense, this duty seems implicit in the organizing principles of our polity. Hannah Arendt has applied to America Montesquieu's conception of a spirit of the laws "which varies from country to country and is different in the various forms of government," and concluded that "consent, not in the very old sense of mere acquiescence with its distinction between rule over willing subjects and rule over unwilling ones, but in the sense of active support and continuing participation in all matters of public interest, is the spirit of American law." [2]

This is the philosophic starting point. But it proves too

much to be transposed directly into law. Everything that concerns the government, after all, is a matter of public interest. The people have a right to know—but what? Perhaps to know what the government is doing as distinguished from what it is considering; but perhaps not all the government is doing lest, for reasons having nothing to do with consent, it not be able to do it. The secret negotiations with China in the spring of 1971, leading to President Nixon's visit to Peking, is a ready example of an important undertaking by the government to which secrecy was important and about which there was no pressing need for the public to be contemporaneously informed.

A practical starting point in giving content to a duty of contemporaneous disclosure is the recognition that it is more important for the people to know about some things the government is doing than others. At the top of the list must be the involvement of U.S. forces in combat, the ultimate act of sovereignty.

Recent history indicates that this view is not universally shared. In the spring of 1969 the Nixon administration was apparently so disturbed by the "leak" about U.S. warplanes bombing Cambodia that it instituted taps on the home telephones of White House staff aides to discover the traitor.[3] To take an example that spans two administrations, American warplanes had been bombing and strafing in behalf of the Royal Laotian government in its contest against the Pathet Lao for seven years before it was officially admitted in 1971.[4]

In both cases it may seem that the only audience being kept in the dark was the American public—hardly a sufficient justification for secrecy. In fairness, it should be noted that in both situations there was a plausible rationale for concealment in national-security terms. The heads of government of Cambodia and Laos—Prince Sihanouk and Souvanna Phouma respectively—were avowed neutralists, and official admission that American warplanes were bombing their countries with their consent or at their request might have imperiled their political position. Since it was and is one of the tenets of our Indochina policy that our national security is promoted by having stable non-Communist governments in Laos and

Cambodia, the basis for classifying information on U.S. combat activities in those countries was clear, if a bit involuted. A "doveish" rationale for classification also existed: military activity in behalf of or merely of assistance to another government could be more readily terminated, if that should seem advantageous at some point in the future, if the activity remained covert.

Thus, these are not cases that can simply be dismissed as obvious abuses of the prerogative of secrecy on the ground that since the enemy knew it was being bombed and almost surely by whom, only the American people were being denied the relevant information. But the point of a positive disclosure requirement is not to deny that there may be real tactical advantages at times in keeping the fact of American combat activities secret. Rather it is to insist that there are decisive countervailing values. Yet no law of Congress insists on the supremacy of these values over the advantages of secrecy in any situation involving foreign affairs. Everything is left to the judgment of the executive.*

The commitment of forces to combat is the most obvious candidate for a disclosure requirement. It is surely not the only one. Closely allied is U.S. support for military actions of other government and insurgent groups. Beginning in February 1964, seven months before the Tonkin Gulf incident, the United States planned and financed a series of covert military operations by South Vietnamese forces against North Vietnam that were not disclosed until the publication of the Pentagon Papers in 1971.[5] Contemporaneous disclosure of these activities might well have produced an early public and Congressional concern over the course of events in Vietnam, if it did not rule them out altogether. At the least there might have been a somewhat different reaction in Congress in August 1964, when President Johnson reported that American naval ships had finally come under fire—immediately following, it

* One may go further and insist that the commitment of American forces to combat not only must not be secret but must receive the positive authorization of the Congress. That, however, is another subject. The point being argued is simply that no matter how expansive a view one takes of the President's inherent power to commit forces to combat it is intolerable that this power be exercised in secret.

later came out, South Vietnamese naval harassment operations under U.S. command—and that he had ordered retaliatory strikes.

U.S. involvement in the overthrow of governments by insurgent forces, most familiarly the Arbenz government in Guatemala in 1954,[6] is never officially acknowledged, with the single exception of the failed Bay of Pigs expedition. This practice has served not only the executive but Congress as well, for it has facilitated Congress' preference to avoid having to deal by law with the question of whether or in what circumstances we should be engaging in those activities.

Other candidates for disclosure as one proceeds down the list from the most obvious possibilities are the presence of U.S. forces in foreign countries, all manner of assistance being provided foreign countries, and, depending on one's view of the significance to be attached to secret commitments, commitments to send military forces or provide assistance.[7]

Some would no doubt wish to extend this list; others to shorten it. I offer one caution—that disclosure requirements not be made to do the work of prohibitions. All or most of the instances cited above are cases where secrecy is no necessary part of the enterprise. To require disclosure of military action the United States is taking or supporting or of assistance provided to foreign countries, or even of certain commitments, may be inconvenient, but there is no inherent reason the United States could not do these things in open view and, indeed, most of the time it does. If the duty of disclosure will act as a deterrent to undertaking these activities at times, it will be because the government fears the force of public response. This can never be an acceptable argument for secrecy. A disclosure requirement should exist precisely to provide an opportunity for public response.

Other activities cannot tolerate disclosure for quite different reasons. The provision of U.S. assistance to insurgent groups, for example, is a matter of keen public interest. But such groups could not exist if there were a duty to disclose assistance to them even before they began to engage in overt activity. Thus we may be content to require that U.S. involvement in an action such as the Bay of Pigs be fully disclosed once the landing has been made, without requiring that the American role in forming and training the invading force be disclosed beforehand. Disclosure of preparations would do more than disclose; it would necessarily abort.

On the other hand, the Congress may decide that the United States should never under any circumstances provide assistance to covert groups or, more likely, that this should be done only in certain situations or under certain procedures. In that event, an explicit and carefully drawn prohibition would be more appropriate than a disclosure requirement.

Can a positive disclosure requirement work? If the information is secret to begin with, how is one to know whether the government is failing in its duty of contemporaneous disclosure? There are several answers to this. First, a clear legal duty to disclose certain matters will make it far harder for the government to keep these matters secret. It is not so easy to eliminate all honest men from the circle of the knowledgeable. Once it is clearly understood that concealing certain information is illegal, and that no administrative penalties, much less criminal penalties, may be imposed on officials who reveal the information, it would be a foolhardy administration that would assume secrecy could be maintained.

Second, much information that would seem appropriate for a disclosure requirement—particularly concerning military and paramilitary activities—does tend to surface sooner or later. When it does, the administration responsible, if it is still in office, usually suffers only a temporary embarrassment. The political cost would be far higher, however, if what was being disclosed were matters that the government had violated its legal duty to disclose. This should be a powerful deterrent to concealment for even the most cynical of administrations.

Finally, specific disclosure requirements would make possible effective judicial intervention. Procedures could be established whereby, on a showing of reasonable grounds for suspicion that disclosure requirements were violated, a court could order responsible officials to produce all information covered by the relevant disclosure category. A response that was later shown to be false would be punishable by the power of contempt

II The Legal Limits

The prospect of judicial enforcement of disclosure requirements contrasts sharply with the judiciary's relation to the present classification system. In *Environmental Protection Agency* v. *Mink*,[8] decided in January 1973, the Supreme Court considered for the first time how much change had been wrought by the Freedom of Information Act of 1966. The plaintiffs were an unusual group, comprising thirty-three Members of Congress who had prevailed in the lower court. They asked the Supreme Court to approve a modest procedure ordered by the District of Columbia Circuit to enable a District Court to separate the unclassified portions of certain documents submitted to the President regarding a proposed nuclear test from the classified portions, and to make the former available. Under the Circuit Court's procedure, the District Court would have examined the classified documents *in camera* to determine if there were any nonsecret components. If there were any—and here the District Court would apparently be merely asking the government to decide whether each portion of a document required secrecy—the Court would then determine if the nonsecret components could be read separatly from the secret remainder without distortion of meaning. If there was something left at that point that might be ordered disclosed the District Court would then have to consider the applicability of another exemption to the Act protecting "inter-agency or intra-agency memorandums or letters which would not be available by law to a party other than an agency in litigation with the agency." [9] Only so much of the unclassified portions as consisted of factual data that, as the Circuit Court termed it, were not "inextricably intertwined with policy-making processes" and that could be disclosed "without impinging on the policy-making decisional processes intended to be protected by this exemption," would have to be disclosed. The Supreme Court by a vote of 5–3 (Justice William Rehnquist not participating) agreed with the government that this procedure did not accord classified materials a wide enough berth. Once the District Court is told by the government that a document is classified and that it contains sensitive matters relating to national defense or foreign policy, it may go no further.

The decision can be criticized as affording more deference to a classification stamp than the language, not to mention the general spirit, of the Freedom of Information Act compels. But the more striking feature of the case is how little real difference a contrary decision would have made. A District Court judge would have gotten to see the material. The judge could have asked the government attorneys if every paragraph really had to be classified. He could have frowned skeptically when they solemnly responded in the affirmative. And that is apparently all. Justice William Douglas, perhaps the member of the Court least respectful of security classifications, emphasized in his dissent that "the Court of Appeals never dreamed that the trial judge would reclassify documents." In another section of his opinion, Justice Douglas suggests that the Act empowers the District Court "in its discretion [to] collaborate with the agency to make certain that the congressional policy of disclosure is effectuated." But the terms of this collaboration are not articulated. If it is to stop short of the judge himself reclassifying, it must apparently be limited to moral suasion—the skeptical frown, perhaps a raised voice.

If in the end the District Court could not reclassify documents, how much would be gained by having it inspect them? The majority did not advert to this consideration but it may be a more compelling justification than the Court's exegesis of the Act's inconclusive legislative history.

The Supreme Court, to be sure, is not always so deferential to classification decisions of the executive. In *New York Times Co.* v. *United States*, the Pentagon Papers case, the Court refused to lend its aid to the government to keep highly classified information secret.[10]

At one level the results in *Mink* and *Times* could not seem more contrary. And indeed, only two Justices who voted against the government in *Times* voted for it in *Mink*—Justices Byron White and Potter Stewart.[11] But a unifying theme can be found precisely in the opinions of the two Justices who held the balance of power here as in many other cases. What Justice Stewart, joined by Justice White, said in his *Times* concurrence reveals the perspective the two brought to Mink: "It is clear to me that it is the constitutional duty of the executive—as a matter of sovereign prerogative and not as a matter of law as the courts know law—through the promulgation and enforcement of executive regulations, to protect the confidentiality necessary to carry out its responsibilities in the fields of international relations and national defense."

"As a matter of sovereign prerogative and not as a matter of law as the courts know law"—that view of the classification function supports reluctance both to provide judicial aid to the executive in maintaining secrecy and to the public in probing that secrecy.

The result is to make "possession" even more critical an element in this exotic area of the law than it is proverbially in more traditional areas. How much further the rule of possession could be pushed is not clear. The dismissal of the Ellsberg-Russo prosecution postpones any authoritative consideration of the relevance of classification to a criminal prosecution.[12] And the Supreme Court in 1973 itself postponed clarification of the significance of classification in yet another context. The case was *United States* v. *Marchetti*,[13] and it is well worth notice.

Victor Marchetti is a former CIA employee who has published fiction and nonfiction dealing with the intelligence trade, much to the discomfiture of the CIA. The Fourth Circuit, in an opinion by Judge Clement Haynsworth, approved an injunction requiring Marchetti to submit to the Agency for its approval, thirty days in advance of release, all writings relating to the Agency or intelligence. Marchetti may not release this material if the Agency disapproves. The Agency may only disapprove undisclosed classified information, but such disapproval is final. Judge Haynsworth took pains to point out that the court would not review classified information. He rejected the suggestion of a concurring judge that Marchetti should have the chance to demonstrate "by clear and convincing evidence that a classification is arbitrary and capricious."

The regime of censorship imposed on Marchetti makes the prior restraint at stake in *Times* seem modest by comparison. There, at least, the government's effort was restricted to the protection of specific documents that its employees had brought into being. The *Marchetti* injunction is closer to the classic situation of requiring official examination before publication of materials as yet unwritten. It closely resembles in this respect the injuction disapproved in the Supreme Court's landmark prior restraint case, *Near* v. *Minnesota,*[14] which enjoined individuals from publishing a "malicious, scandalous or defamatory newspaper."

The *Marchetti* decision is thus highly vulnerable on the issue of prior restraint. The only question is whether the fact that Marchetti agreed when he joined the Agency never to disclose classified information, an agreement the court said it probably would find implied in the relationship if it had not been expressed, somehow excuses the procedure.

The Fourth Circuit was on much more solid ground in what it said about the reviewability of classification decisions as such, especially in view of what the Supreme Court had indicated previously in *Times* and would indicate subsequently in *Mink.*

Once the court decided that Marchetti's agreement not to disclose classified information was enforceable by prior restraint, it was up against the fact that under the present classification system what is classified is determined by the executive. This obtains not just because the Supreme Court has said so but because the nature of the classification decision as it has so far existed largely commands it.

The problem is that the classification system rests entirely on subjective decisions about contingent political effect. The present standard is whether it is reasonable to expect that disclosure would cause damage to the national security.[15] One may tinker with this standard, but so long as the critical element remains exclusively a political judgment, the courts will not interfere. They may disregard the classification entirely as in *Times,* or give it total deference as in *Mink* and *Marchetti.* There is no model for something in between.

This absurd rigidity is nowhere better revealed than by *Marchetti.* The enforcement of a system of censorship over whatever a writer may wish to publish in his chosen subject area for the rest of his life is breath-taking in itself. To carry it out without any inquiry into the importance to the public of the censored information is staggering.

III Secrecy v. Democracy

The answer does not lie in a statutory direction to the courts simply to examine classified documents in order to separate classified portions from the unclassified, that is, a reversal of the precise point decided in *Mink*. Nor does it lie in legislating an "arbitrary and capricious" standard for classification decisions. Enough has been said to indicate that the government will be able to duck under that standard, even in respect to information that the people have the most vital need to know if they are to control their country's course. Nor, to repeat an earlier refrain, does a full answer lie in legislation that treats of what may be classified but does not positively compel disclosure.

No satisfactory answer will emerge unless Congress is willing to come to grips with specific conflicts between secrecy and democracy and to designate by law categories of information with respect to which the values of democracy must prevail. These determinations could be enforced by the courts without feeling that it was their political judgment that was being substituted for that of the executive.

Congressional determinations of this sort would no doubt encounter assertions of executive prerogatives founded on the Constitution. Indeed, these assertions may be presaged by Justice Stewart's language in the Pentagon Papers case referring to the "constitutional duty of the executive . . . to protect . . . confidentiality," and by Justice White's statement in *Mink* that Congress could have legislated differently than it did in the Freedom of Information Act "subject only to whatever limitations the executive privilege may be held to impose upon such Congressional ordering." Yet there is every reason to hope that the Congress, the Court, perhaps the executive too, will be able to distinguish what is constitutionally required from what is familiar.

Secrecy and Covert Intelligence Collection and Operations

—by Morton H. Halperin and Jeremy J. Stone

We aim in this paper to assess the effects of secrecy on the conduct of American covert intelligence collection and covert operations, and the effects of those programs on American society and foreign policy. We begin with a description of the structure by which the executive branch plans and carries out covert intelligence collection and operations and then briefly discuss covert activities in which the United States has engaged since World War II. This is followed by an analysis of the costs of such operations, with particular emphasis on the decision-making within the executive branch, the effect on American society, and the effects on American foreign policy. We conclude with an analysis of the covert operations and intelligence programs and some specific recommendations.

I The Structure of Covert Intelligence and Operations

The only Congressional authorization for covert intelligence operations is contained in the Congressional Act of 1947, which created the entire national security system as well as the Central Intelligence Agency. The Act listed the primary functions of the CIA as advising the National Security Council on intelligence matters and correlating and evaluating intelligence related to national security. The fifth item listed under the functions of the CIA, under the direction of the National Security Council, was: "to perform such other functions and duties related to intelligence affecting the national security as the National Security Council may from time to time direct."

Based upon this very general Congressional authority, Presidents have authorized the CIA to engage in covert intelligence collection and covert operations. Over the years, a structure has grown up within the American government for devising such programs and for implementing them.

At the heart of the covert operations is the CIA. Within the CIA such operations are centered in the "Plans Directorate," under the Deputy Director of the CIA for Plans (known as the DDP). Under the DDP there is an assistant in charge of each region of the world and operators dealing with particular countries or areas. These officials are drawn largely from a career service of covert operators within the CIA. This group is distinct from the career intelligence analysts, who serve only in Washington and only in the evaluation of intelligence material. The covert operators (who have a "cover" identification indicating that they work for the Department of Defense, the State Department, or some other agency or private organization) alternate between assignments in the CIA headquarters in Langley, Virginia, and assignments overseas.

American embassies have a separate section staffed by career covert intelligence operators from the CIA. The head of this unit, who is one of the senior officials of the embassy below the ambassador, is known as the CAS (apparently standing for Chief at Station). This unit maintains its own communications systems with Washington. In friendly countries, its members often operate as liaison with the local intelligence services, but in all cases they are available for the planning of covert intelligence collection and operations.

The only other resources known to be in the field to conduct covert intelligence operations are the military attachés attached to most American embassies. In addition, the service intelligence divisions operate intelligence-collection stations on land, and aboard ships and airplanes. Many of these operations are under the auspices of the National Security Agency, the group charged with the collecting of communications signals and their evaluation.

The National Security Council Act provided that other activities should be conducted only when the National Security Council shall direct them from time to time. In fact, procedures have grown up which provide for continuing authorization to the CIA to conduct covert operations and which put the initiative in the hands of the CIA to come forward with proposals. Beginning in the late 1950s, covert intelligence collection and operations have been approved by a committee chaired by the Special Assistant to the President for National Security Affairs. The existence of the committee and its membership have never been publicly announced, and its name (or rather the number by which it is designated) has changed from time to time. It is now apparently known as the Forty Committee, because its duties were redefined in National Security Decision Memorandum number 40.

In addition to the Assistant to the President for National Security Affairs, the members of the Forty Committee are the Deputy Secretary of Defense, the Chairman of the Joint Chiefs of Staff, the Under Secretary of State for Political Affairs, and the Director of Central Intelligence. Each member is staffed by his own department or agency. For the Director of Central Intelligence, the staffing is done by his Deputy Director of Operations and staff; for the Under Secretary of State, by a small group under an Assistant Director of the Bureau of Intelligence and Research in the Department of State; for the Chairman of the Joint Chiefs, by the Special Assistant to the Chairman for Counter Insurgency and Special Activities (SACSA). Until very recently, the Deputy Secretary of Defense was staffed simply by one of his military assistants, who relied primarily on the evaluations from the Joint Chiefs of Staff. It is possible that this function has more recently been taken over by the new Assistant Secretary of Defense for Intelligence. The Chairman of the Forty Committee, the President's Assistant for National Security Affairs, has in the past been staffed simply by a liaison officer assigned by the CIA.

Proposals for covert intelligence collection or operations

normally come from the section of the DDP charged with the relevant geographic area, and, after informal discussion among the staffs of the members of the Forty Committee, they are approved by the Committee itself. In some cases, the proposals come from other members of the committee.

Evaluation of the proposals is limited to the members of this Committee and the staffs designated for this purpose. Under normal procedures, a proposal for a covert operation in Latin America, for example, would not be cleared by the State Department desk officer dealing with that Latin American country or by the Deputy Assistant Secretary, or even, in some cases, the Assistant Secretary for Latin American Affairs. Likewise, it would not be cleared by the Regional Deputy Assistant Secretary in the Office of International Security Affairs in the Pentagon, or even by the Assistant Secretary or the military officers in the Joint Staff charged with planning and policy toward the particular Latin American country. Within the CIA itself, proposals for covert operations are normally not staffed by the Intelligence Branch of the CIA charged with collating and evaluating intelligence materials from all sources. In exceptional cases, particular people from these various organizations may be brought in to consult on a particular problem, but only at the sufferance of the officials formally involved.

Covert operations and intelligence-gathering is conducted, then, under a cloak of what we will call Super Secrecy. Executive Order 10501 specifically prohibited any classification other than the three categories it set out ("top secret," "secret," "confidential") and others authorized by law (such as those involving cryptology and atomic energy). Nevertheless, covert operations carry additional classification markings, and access to them depends on an additional set of clearances whose very existence is classified. Thus, information about them is limited very severely, even within the executive branch. Most of this paper is devoted to an analysis of the consequences of this Super Secrecy for executive-branch decision-making, for the American constitutional system, and for the conduct of American foreign policy.

II The Range of Covert Intelligence Collection and Operations

Covert intelligence operations are of many different kinds and raise quite different issues. The best known concern covert intelligence-gathering. At the beginning of the cold war, the United States had planes engaged in short dashes into Soviet territory. Later, the U-2 flights overflew the territory and a special technology was developed for just this purpose. Stationed around the "Communist bloc," there are planes and ships gathering electronic intelligence—information on the planes flying through Soviet airspace, transcripts of the conversations of the pilots in them, characteristics of Soviet radars, information on Soviet space and missile firings, and so on. The *Pueblo*, captured off North Korean shores, was such a ship. More information comes from satellites encircling the globe and transmitting or dropping information to earth. From satellites, very good pictures of the ground can now be developed.

Covert intelligence gathering also involves the more traditional spy, although the relative effectiveness of spying has greatly decreased. Spies run the gamut from agents injected into a foreign territory, to foreigners recruited for this purpose, to paid informers in friendly or neutral governments, to sympathizers of many kinds and degrees. The Soviet colonel Oleg Penkovsky is probably the best-known example of a spy.

Beyond covert intelligence-gathering lie the activities in support of political groups in a foreign country. Here a line is crossed between efforts to get information and efforts to manipulate. Political parties, labor unions, student groups, and military officers, etc., may be given funds, information, or other help in an effort to win influence over them and to advance shared aims. The first such operation was apparently the massive American intervention in the 1948 Italian election. Later, the United States apparently sought to buy votes in the French National Assembly to secure ratification of the European Defense Community Treaty.

Still greater involvement occurs when insurgent movements get covert support. Here, the United States takes a hand in active struggle. Examples include Indonesia in 1948, Tibet after 1949, Cuba under Batista, China immediately after the Communist revolution, and Katanga. In Iran, the United States sponsored a countercoup to restore the Shah.

Still greater support is involved when the United States seeks to give covert aid to foreign military forces. Here we have assistance to the South Vietnamese against the North, to the secret army in Laos, and to the King of Jordan.

At the end of this spectrum lie major covert military operations. In 1949 the United States air-dropped hundreds of agents into Albania in an effort, much like that of the Bay of Pigs (another example), to overthrow the Albanian government. Tipped off by the Soviet spy Harold Philby, the Albanians had no trouble putting down the revolution.

Sometimes, covert operations involve domestic manipulations, and foreign operations abroad require domestic covers. Travel organizations, student organizations, businesses, foundations, and American labor unions may all be asked to help in providing a base for covert CIA operations. Alternately, they may be infiltrated—with few, if any, of their own higher-ups being aware of it.

Lastly, the United States government cannot credibly deny involvement in dramatic attacks or incidents abroad. A coup in Cambodia or an Israeli attack on Lebanon promptly brings charges of CIA involvement.

III Distortions in Decision-Making

The Super Secrecy system under which decisions about covert operations are made increases the chances that such operations will be chosen over more desirable alternatives, reduces the effectiveness with which they are designed and carried out, distorts decision-making within the executive branch, and reduces the effectiveness of intelligence evaluation.

The Super Secrecy of covert operations increases the chances that the President will choose covert action rather than other, desirable options, which might be adopted given a free and open debate within the executive branch—and even more clearly if the Congress and the public were involved.

American Presidents face multiple audiences. Whatever the President does is seen not only by the foreign group against which he may be directing his action but also by leaders and active groups in other countries, by the Congress, and by the American public. One of the major attractions of covert operations is that with them one avoids the multiple-audience problem. If something is conducted in secret, then one can avoid the fight over means (as well as ends) which erupts when other audiences perceive an ongoing operation. For example, when President Nixon was asked in the summer of 1970 why the United States had been willing to send military forces to Vietnam to prevent the Communist take-over but was not willing to send American military forces to Chile to prevent a Marxist government from coming into power, he replied that the United States could not send military forces to Chile without provoking an adverse political reaction in the rest of Latin America. Though he did not make it clear at the time, it was later revealed that the United States government had engaged in *covert* operations in Chile. These operations avoided the political outcry which would come from an overt step, such as the introduction of American forces.

As compared to alternatives, the necessary approval for covert operations is easier to obtain. The President himself can often usually authorize them without having to go to Congress for funds or to make a public justification. They also seem cheap and easy because they can usually be disavowed, if necessary. Indeed, the working definition of a covert operation appears to be that it is one which can be disavowed with impunity. As with many other aspects of covert operations of this extreme optimism seems to accompany the evaluation of this factor. Thus, in the cases of both the U-2 and the Bay of Pigs, an explicit element of the calculation leading to the authorization of the plan was the belief that it could be disavowed with a cover story if it was discovered.

The mechanism of decision-making also tends to bias the system toward the choosing of covert options. When the United States government is faced with a problem, meetings are held to discuss the range of overt possibilities; they are weighed against each other in an adversary procedure that will permit critics of one proposal to be heard while the proponents of that proposal are present. Covert operations are not discussed at such meetings, but are considered separately at meetings from which advocates of other proposals, and critics of covert operations, are excluded. Indeed, participants in meetings considering overt options are often not aware that covert alternatives are being considered at other meetings. Those advocating covert operations can bring them up through the mechanism of the Forty Committee, and thus do not have to compete for the time and attention of top-level decision-makers.

These same factors serve to reduce efficiency in the design and execution of covert operations. The Super Secrecy increases the probability that covert operations will be designed and implemented poorly and with little regard for the realities of the external world or for appropriate principles of American behavior. Many problems arise precisely because the circle of people involved in covert operations is kept so very small and is limited to people who tend to be sympathetic to such operations.

Other aspects of covert operations add to the general difficulties of getting any operation evaluated by the people responsible for devising it and later responsible for its execution. For example, the "play god" aspect of covert work—involving as it often does intervention in the internal affairs of other nations—tends to attract people who are likely to be insensitive to the difficulties of the work and to its implications for American constitutional procedures. Moreover, the cabalism—the close working relationship between the small number of people involved—substantially reduces the chance that any insider will object to somebody else's favorite scheme. Officials involved from other agencies are often simply on loan from the CIA or intimately connected with CIA operations.

As in all policy areas, the responsible officials have an interest in keeping the number of participants down and to exclude those who are likely to be critics. In covert intelligence operations, a special tool facilitates such exclusion: the special clearances required for such operations. A "top secret" clearance is not sufficient; one must get special clearances the existence of which are not even known to officials who do not have such clearances. Moreover, authority to grant them is in the hands of the officials who manage the programs, who can use this tool to exclude anyone they fear might be skeptical or critical.

Normally, an official observing an ongoing policy which he sees as a threat to his organization's interests, or to the national-security interest as he defines it, would attempt to fight his way into the process. He would argue that he has a special expertise to contribute or that the interests of his organization are involved. In covert operations, Super Secrecy makes it extremely difficult for this to occur.

First of all, the official usually does not know that the activities are under consideration or being implemented. The existence of the special clearances makes it difficult to assert a right to be involved, since one is asserting the need for a clearance whose existence one is not supposed to know and which is supposedly kept to a small number of people. Thus, someone attempting to fight his way into the evaluation of a covert operation faces not only the normal difficulties of getting into a new policy arena but special problems of appearing to be jeopardizing security requirements.

As a result, a person who finally does get cleared for a particular operation is likely to feel that he has been admitted on the sufferance of the planners. He knows he will continue to be involved only if he accepts the basic principles involved and presents his criticism on the edges of the operation. Someone who is skeptical about covert operations in general, or covert operations in a particular area, is likely not to get the necessary clearances. If he does, he may feel that he must mute his views or find himself isolated and, ultimately, have his clearance withdrawn.

With the circle of those "in the know" kept so small, those in it tend to discount the views of other government officials who are not aware of the details of covert operations. For example, expert estimates of the unlikelihood of a successful anti-Castro operation in Cuba in 1961 were discounted by the officials who knew about the Bay of Pigs operation. These officials knew they were the only ones receiving all the reports from our covert operations in Cuba; intelligence analysts in the CIA and State Department were discounted because they had not received some of the reports from covert agents operating within Cuba.

The process by which proposals for covert operations move up through the narrow group of those with necessary clearances reduces the likelihood that the senior officials on the Forty Committee will examine them critically. Proposals that come before the Committee are usually unanimous because of the close working relationships of the staffs involved, and they tend to be rubber-stamped by the committee. Presumably, they are also rubber-stamped by the President when they are brought to his attention. The lack of vigorous dissent, so common with other proposals of a controversial nature, leads to routine approval.

The inability of top officials to maintain control is particularly acute when an operation is very large. For then the danger of adverse political consequences exists if the operation is halted after it is well on its way. In the case of the Bay of Pigs, President Kennedy was confronted with statements from Allen Dulles that if the operation were to be canceled, Cuban refugees who had been recruited would talk about it and cause political problems because of the intense anti-Castro feeling then rampant in the United States.

One form of monitoring is often entirely absent in the case of covert activities. The press provides one critical aspect of the monitoring system over the President and other top officials. This does not occur with a covert operation unless it reaches such proportions that the press in the field begins to learn of it. (Paradoxically, in such cases the press may serve to alert other parts of the United States government to what is going on. This appears to have been the case in Laos through the 1960s, where covert activities came to the attention of many government officials through press reports from Laos.)

Super Secrecy also reduces the possibility of effective monitoring within the American government. The acknowledged need for flexibility in covert operations often makes it easy to justify discretionary authority for officials in the field to implement an approved plan. Ambassadors who sometimes provide effective monitoring or control often do not know, and do not want to know, about CIA operations in their countries. Moreover, the CIA controls its own money, people, and communications channels to Washington, often enabling it to move without normal internal executive-branch monitoring, bypassing skeptics who might otherwise try to persuade the President that it was an error and should be abandoned.

Super Secrecy of decision-making and execution of covert operations also casts a shadow over executive-branch decision-making in general on national security matters. Creating a special class of those with a "need to know" for covert operations tends to give those people a sense that on all matters they are better informed than others.

Moreover, within the government, lying becomes an accepted habit. In order to protect the existence of additional clearances and of covert operations, officials with access to information about these things must routinely deceive other officials. This lying breeds cynicism and contempt for those who are lied to, and this must influence the entire pattern of decision-making.

The most obvious demonstration of how Super Secrecy distorts executive-branch decision-making is in the CIA itself. The CIA was envisioned by President Truman, who called for its creation, and by the Congress that authorized it, primarily if not exclusively as an intelligence-evaluation organization. Prior to its creation, President Truman received intelligence reports from each of the armed services and from the State Department. He felt the need for a single agency which would collate and evaluate these reports and which would do so without the bias that an operating agency had in favor of its own programs. Thus, Truman wanted a professional and independent intelligence capability.

This conception of the CIA's role differs markedly from reality because of covert intelligence operations. The CIA has always been dominated by officials whose primary concern has been covert operations rather than intelligence or evaluation. The only career officials to be named heads of the CIA—Allen Dulles, Richard Helms, and William Colby—rose through the covert side of the agency, and Helms and Colby were former DDP's before becoming Directors. The dominance of covert operations within the CIA has diminished the quality of personnel on the intelligence side. The officials who work on intelligence evaluation recognize that they are not operating in a totally hospitable environment and are unlikely to rise to the top.

Moreover, because of its involvement in operations, the CIA is not the neutral intelligence-evaluation organ that President Truman and others envisioned. It has a policy ax to grind concerning its covert operations. The Director of Central Intelligence is reluctant to put out intelligence reports that contradict a view that the CIA is pressing in the Forty Committee or in other covert intelligence channels. Super Secrecy of covert operations also reduces the quality of its intelligence over-all in that the evaluators are often uninformed of covert operations and of matters that would enhance their ability to make sensible intelligence inputs.

Thus, the covert operations staff dominating the CIA weakens it in its primary function of providing objective intelligence evaluation of ongoing problems. The Vietnam war illustrates this well. The Pentagon Papers reveal that intelligence analysts in the CIA frequently produced much more sensible estimates of the situation in Vietnam than other parts of the intelligence community did. What the Pentagon Papers do not indicate, because they did not draw on the files of American covert operations, is that the DDP was as wrong on Vietnam as any other part of the government. The CIA was heavily involved in covert operations in Vietnam, including the training and arming of ethnic minorities. The CIA operators were optimistic about the success of their programs, and the great weight of the CIA effort within the government was to defend these programs rather than to push the consequences of the pessimistic intelligence evaluations.

IV How Covert Operations Distort the American Constitutional System

The American constitutional system is fundamentally distorted by secrecy—although the different branches of government are affected in different ways.

The executive branch thrives on secrecy because secrecy frees it from Congressional, judicial, and public oversight. But the Congress suffers from secrecy because its power is based on the ability to expose, to rally public opinion, to maintain a dialogue between constituents and elected officials and with the press. When a Congressman is told that CIA operations are Super Secret, self-interest makes him prefer not to know anything about it. These secret operations are dangerous to him—he may be accused of having breached secrecy if the matter gets out, yet the information is of no political use to him unless it can be made public. Only a sense of duty can sustain his willingness to participate in hearings on such matters. Indeed, in the House of Representatives, the CIA subcommittee of the Appropriations Subcommittee has a membership that is secret. The Congressmen do not want it known who they are!

The Congressmen risk being asked whether they knew of covert operations. In 1971 Senators John Stennis and Allen Ellender—the Chairmen of the Armed Services and Appropriations committees, as well as of their CIA oversight subcommittees—said that they knew nothing about the CIA-financed war in Laos, surely the CIA's biggest operation. It is hard to know whether to believe these denials, which would suggest enormous laxity in oversight.

Covert operations are especially difficult for Congressmen to come to grips with because they involve, or seem to involve, men in the field—"our boys." Every effort has to be made to protect these men and to bring tham back if caught. Thus the flag is wrapped around the personnel, if not the funds, that go into covert operations.

So Super Secrecy is at the heart of Congress's problem in fulfilling its function of oversight of CIA operations. Even the authorization for CIA activities was promptly distorted in secrecy. The National Security Act authorized the CIA to: "perform *for the benefit of the existing intelligence agencies* such additional services of common concern as the National Security Council determines can be more effectively accomplished centrally; perform such other functions and duties *related to intelligence* affecting the national security as the National Security Council may from time to time direct" (italics added).

But secret directives promptly expanded these functions. Overthrowing governments, secret wars, assassinations, and fixing elections are not done "for the benefit of the existing intelligence agencies," nor are they duties "related to intelligence." It is entirely possible that a court might rule such actions unauthorized by statute. Yet within the executive branch, secret directives authorize special operations of all kinds provided they are small enough to be plausibly deniable. Unfortunately, these directives do not cover the impossible-to-deny operations: U-2 flights, Bay of Pigs, the Iranian coup, the Laotian war, etc.

A traditional method of Congressional control is through the power of the purse—the control of funding. The Constitution explicitly supports this power of Congress when it asserts in Article I, Section 9, Clause 7, that: "No Money shall be drawn from the Treasury, but in Consequence of Appropriations made by Law; *and a regular Statement and Account of the Receipts and Expenditures of all public Money shall be published from time to time*" (italics added.). CIA expenditures are in violation of this constitutional clause, since no accounting whatsoever is made public. Indeed, the burial of CIA expenditures in the accounts of other departments puts the latter accounts in violation of law. They cease to be accurate.

Complete control of funding for covert operations is evidently delegated only to subcommittees of the Armed Services and Appropriations committees. Thus, Senator Stuart Symington would not be permitted to discuss CIA appropriations, although he is on the Appropriations Committee and the CIA oversight subcommittee of Armed Services, because he is not one of the five senior members who make up the CIA oversight subcommittee of appropriations. The full committees do not vote on these matters, nor are they discussed on the floor of the Senate sessions on the CIA.

The failure of Congress to approve covert operations hampers its activities in other ways as well. Congressmen cannot properly assess the implications of many foreign events unless they understand the extent to which these events were shaped by covert American operations. The Gulf of Tonkin affair may have been encouraged by ongoing covert operations in the Gulf, but ignorant of these activities, Congressmen considered any attack on U.S. ships to be "unprovoked."

Similarly, interpretations of the true desires of Chileans may have been based on election results in Chile which in fact were manipulated by covert American campaign contributions. The Laotians may desire to avoid fighting, but a secret war financed by a covert operation may persuade Congressmen that Laotians want to continue the struggle.

Today covert operations are what most require the Super Secrecy of the CIA. Electronic intelligence-gathering does not require it, nor does intelligence assessment. It is the potentially explosive disclosure of interference in the internal affairs of other countries that does.

CIA employees must take a special oath to maintain CIA secrets. By restricting them from discussing these matters with their Congressman or Senators, the oaths interfere with our political system. Moreover, they constitute a special security system, unauthorized—on top of a variety of other unauthorized systems ("sensitive," etc.).

Super Secrecy has led to the widespread use, inside the CIA, of lie detectors. This may be a handy method for detecting double agents and for other use in covert operations. But their use spreads to all CIA employees, to other branches of government, and into the society at large. The funds available to the CIA make it possible for it to pioneer in a technology that undermines traditional judicial and ethical processes.

Super Secrecy as required by covert operations threatens the freedom of the press. For fifteen days, in the first prior restraint order in the history of the country against a daily newspaper, *The Washington Post* and *The New York Times* and other papers were restrained from publication of the Pentagon Papers. Part of the government's objection to publication was its fear of revealing covert operations and intelligence collection. And the only permanent injunction against free speech in the history of the United States has been issued against Victor Marchetti, a former CIA official—based partly upon his secrecy oath and partly on the need to keep secret the covert operations of which he might have knowledge.

Covert operations have led to Presidential requests to the press not to publish articles. In the case of the Bay of Pigs, President Kennedy urged *The New York Times* to do just that. When the covert operations are based in the United States, they can also interfere with individual rights. An effort to hide the fact that Tibetans were being trained in Colorado mountains led armed men to surround, and hold at gunpoint, a number of civilians who happened to witness their departure. And then the government apparently asked *The New York Times* not to publish the story.

Covert operations tend to distort the perceptions of foreign policy held not only by Congressmen but also by scholars and, in turn, the public. The entire image of U.S.-Soviet relations during the cold war would have been significantly different if U.S. penetrations of Soviet airspace had been made known. It would have shown that not all the Russians' fear of encirclement was "paranoia."

It is possible, with covert operations, to induce reactions from other nations which are self-fulfilling. Castro's anti-American attitude can be shaped by American sabotage of which he is cognizant but the American public is not. The Chinese knew that Downey and Fecteau were CIA agents; the American public did not. The North Vietnamese gauge our willingness to stay in Indochina by assessing, in part, the commitment shown through covert operations; the American public can not. In these matters, Super Secrecy is effectively directed only at the American public. The "enemy" may understand only too well what is happening, and sophisticated observers in third countries may also. But the American public is the last to know.

Government credibility suffers not only from acts of omission but also from the necessity to lie, to cover up. It was a sensation when President Eisenhower lied to cover up the U-2 incident. The extensive lies covering up the Bay of Pigs included Ambassador Adlai Stevenson's unwittingly untrue assertions in the U.N. Security Council. (Such acts are less sensational now because government credibility has sunk so much lower.) Even Presidential candidates are forced to lie. During the Kennedy-Nixon debates in 1960, both candidates were forced to wrestle with their secret knowledge of plans for the invasion of Cuba. What to say about Cuban policy in the face of this knowledge?

The Watergate affair amply documents the corruption of the political process by graduates of the CIA covert operations branch. Some of the CIA operatives hired at the lower level of the caper thought they were still working for the Agency. A more sophisticated operative is said to have gotten help in locating a suitable locksmith from a CIA roster. Throughout, the skills and techniques of CIA operators were ready and waiting. And those at higher levels directing the operatives had seen *Mission Impossible* and knew, or thought they knew, how the game was played.

The public's response to Watergate was to question why anyone should take such risks for so little. The answer probably lies in the fact that the administration had "institutionalized" dirty tricks. The same people had performed other "mission impossible" assignments, including breaking into a safe in Las Vegas, into Daniel Ellsberg's psychiatrist's office in Los Angeles. The resistance to covert operations was lowered; those who otherwise might have warned of the danger were, to that extent, silenced.

Watergate also reveals the dangers of permitting "hardened" operatives to work freely in American society. Ordinarily, only a criminal would be available to do these break-ins. The criminal element would have few contacts with a normal administration and would lack sophistication and reliability. But a gang of Cubans led by a covert master spy like Howard Hunt is another matter. They can inspire confidence and encourage assignments from an administration.

The use of private institutions for covert operations tends to bring them all under suspicion. This is what happened when it became known that the CIA had financed the National Student Association and about 250 front organizations and conduits. President Johnson appointed a panel headed by Under Secretary of State Nicholas Katzenbach to review the ground rules for such operations. It concluded:

> 1. It should be the policy of the United States Government that no Federal agency shall provide any covert financial assistance or support, direct or indirect, to any of the nation's educational or private voluntary organizations.
>
> 2. The Government should promptly develop and establish a public-private mechanism to provide public funds openly for overseas activities or organizations which are adjudged deserving, in the national interest, of public support.

The first resolution was adopted. But it left a number of loopholes. In the first place, organizations that seemed to be "private voluntary" might not be. They could be quietly organized as "for profit" and few would know. Alternatively, philanthropists might be enriched, perhaps through stock-market operations, and they would then endow organizations with covert uses. Meanwhile, private businesses could continue to be funded by CIA.

The second recommendation does not seem to have been adopted. The infiltration of private organizations forces people to defend their "cover stories" and lose their integrity. Friends become unsure whether they can believe each other. Persons wonder whether they should accept funds from this foundation or that. To this day, legitimate "Stern Foundations" are confused with the conduit "Stern Foundation," which the CIA used in 1966. The Asia Society and the Asia Foundation have both suffered from the decision of the latter to accept CIA funds. Suspicion spreads.

V Distortions of American Foreign Policy

When foreign countries are aware of U.S. covert operations and the American public is not, the possibility arises of having our government blackmailed by foreign governments. For example, they may insist on foreign aid they might not otherwise receive in return for participating in our covert activities. They may seek ransom for captured pilots—as Indonesia did in a case much like that of Gary Powers. They may hold prisoners until the United States admits they were CIA agents—apparently China's approach. And since covert operations, unlike electronic intelligence, require assets in place, the sensitive problems of purchasing and maintaining such assets can increase the risk of blackmail.

But even when pressure is not applied, CIA covert operations can lead to greater recognition of or commitment to a government. A U-2 base at Peshawar can buttress a particular regime in Pakistan. A country that gives us a base for invading Cuba, as Guatemala did, can discover that we are committed to maintaining stability there, if only to protect the base.

Because these commitments are undertaken indirectly and without full debate, it is difficult for anyone to be sure where they will lead. Laos is a good example. The commitment and involvement may outrun the conflict in Vietnam which reinforced them. Meanwhile, the secret war may decimate the population and otherwise dramatically change the original conditions of conflict.

For businesses abroad, the charge of their possible involvement with CIA cannot be answered. The Johnson administration took the view that one could not legislate "private morality" and that, in any case, it was not improper for businesses to cooperate with a government agency in securing information. But here, as elsewhere, the securing of information is something of a "cover concept" for covert operations. While it might not be immoral, it is poor policy to permit a government agency like the CIA to get involved with businesses around the world. In the long run, American business relations will suffer and the inevitable charges of government interference wherever American business rears its head do our foreign policy no good.

The ITT case shows how successive levels of degeneration in function are revealed when dirty tricks are institutionalized. First, the NSC is requested to order covert operations on an occasional basis. In time, the CIA is proposing these operations to a passive NSC. Then, in turn, the businesses through which the CIA operates, as in the ITT case, make proposals to the CIA and try to use the Agency for its own ends. Thus work expands to fill the covert possibilities available. Secrecy debases control.

The credibility, efficiency, and authority of State Department officials are undermined by the presence of covert CIA operatives. The CIA has better communications, better logistics, larger and more available sources of secret money, and greater security of communications. Under these circumstances, its authority in the field can hardly be matched. If there are CIA operatives around, why should sources of information talk to diplomats? The reported closeness of the late President Nasser to American CIA representatives rather than to Foreign Service representatives is a case in point. Nasser may have thought that the real power lay with the CIA.

CIA operatives undermine the effectiveness of the Foreign Service not only by competing with it but by implicitly smearing it. The legitimate diplomatic operations abroad cannot prove that they are legitimate. While some sources are attracted to the CIA, others are repelled. Members of diplomatic missions are suspected of being CIA agents much as American civilians might wonder if a Soviet diplomat is really a KGB agent.

The internal power balance in a foreign country can be distorted by the alliance of the CIA with certain elements in it rather than with others. Ramon Magsaysay in the Philippines may have risen to power on the basis of help or information provided him by the CIA. Others who do not cooperate find themselves disadvantaged, relatively, even if no action is taken against them. From the CIA's point of view, small services can be of great significance—a few weapons, money, some investment advice, dirt on other members of the government, and so on.

Part of the purpose of CIA political operations is to gain just such influence as these operations make possible. But even when these "benefits" are not intended, CIA covert operations can still pervert a foreign government's structure. It is hard for a CIA operative to be passive. Some sources will be cooperating with him; others will not. Gradually, even without direct effort, the CIA—and the United States—may become aligned with and encouraging X rather than Y.

Covert operations seem to encourage rebellions or revolutions without hope. In Laos, teen-agers were encouraged to fight against the North Vietnamese troops until they were destroyed. In Tibet, guerrillas fought against the Chinese in hopeless uprisings. In the Bay of Pigs, miscalculations only somewhat less obvious were made. The dynamic of covert activities seems to have a logic that can produce violence which, on later reflection, is not worth it.

VI Conclusions and Recommendations

The very existence, much less the mode of operation, of the CIA's Directorate of Plans is a legacy of the World War II Office of Strategic Services (OSS). In the hot war of the OSS, any and all tricks were considered consonant with the world-wide struggle against the Axis. Many imaginative and creative persons were drawn into its operations. After World War II, the OSS was institutionalized in the CIA. Many of the OSS operatives left, but some stayed. The pattern of imaginative involvement in covert operations remained. The cold war was seen, as late as the early 1960s, as a "long twilight struggle"; CIA covert operations fell neatly into that twilight—a gray area, whose propriety was buried in secrecy.

Today, with the cold war waning, the CIA is bidding for permanent institutionalization of its structure and role. Richard Helms argued that America's role as a "great power" demands a CIA even if the cold war does not. Thus what began in a hot war and grew in a cold war may come to base its right to exist simply on the permanent fact of American power.

Meanwhile, the effectiveness of the CIA's covert operations in the industrialized world has vastly diminished. In Europe, the instability of the post-World War II period is over. We no longer need to bribe Italian dockworkers to unload our goods. In the Communist industrialized world (and in China), CIA covert operations are of little effect, even if desirable. And electronic intelligence is providing more than we want to know about most subjects of interest.

As a result, the institutionalization of covert operations is certain to lead to its influence being applied to the Third World—an area with which we are not at war, and from which we are not in danger. The governments are penetrable. The agents have room for maneuver. But there is little work that needs to be done.

In the Third World, nationalism is a proven force against the rapid Communist expansion once feared. Soviet, Chinese, and American interference in Third World states tends only to produce resistance to a large power's further involvement. The problem ceases to be one of fighting fire with fire. It becomes one of giving competitors enough rope to hang themselves. No situation better illustrates these principles than Egypt. Unusual needs in Egypt, and unusual Soviet willingness to help, has nevertheless produced a history of strained relations between the Egyptians and the Soviets and a drain on Soviet resources.

The time has come for America to change its strategy from covert intervention to nonintervention. When there is no emergency, it should be an easy choice to stand for principle. In the long battle for respect and support in the Third World, principles and integrity will be the most important force. The short-run opportunist approach embodied in the CIA's Directorate of Plans sells the long run short.

Furthermore, it will be increasingly difficult to keep covert operations secret. As each operation is "blown," our reputation will suffer; we live in an era that is increasingly impatient with such manipulations. Each covert operation is a time bomb waiting to go off.

Covert operations diminish the flexibility of American foreign policy when it is most required, in a stage of disengagement. They tend to link us to established forces and to encourage the existing tendency of American policy to resist the popular aspirations in underdeveloped countries.

Especially important, covert operations pose a serious threat to democracy at home. James Madison wrote to Thomas Jefferson on May 13, 1798: "Perhaps it is a universal truth that the loss of liberty at home is to be charged to provisions against danger, real or pretended, from abroad." The effort to suppress information about covert operations abroad has already damaged freedom of the press and freedom of speech in America. The Pentagon Papers case and the Marchetti case may be precedents for still more ominous incursions on the

First Amendment. Covert interference abroad is interference with freedom at home.

Finally, the greatest Presidential scandal of modern times has arisen from the injection of covert CIA methods, used by CIA graduates, into American society. No greater signal can be given of the danger of these methods to the highest interests of Americans.

We believe, therefore, that it is time for a drastic overhauling of the Super Secrecy system surrounding the planning and conduct of covert intelligence collection and covert operations. We recommend that certain operations and structures be abolished and that the secrecy surrounding others be eliminated.

The United States should continue to conduct operations involving the collection of intelligence materials by technical means, but not in any greater secrecy than other government activities. Implementation of this purpose would mean the elimination of the special classifications surrounding these programs and a public acknowledgment of their existence.

In this category we would put the various satellite collection programs for the gathering of data by photographic and other means, as well as ships and planes carrying electronic equipment. The government should carefully review all such programs to determine which ones in fact produce information of significant importance to the United States. An assessment should be also made of which programs are provocative—running high risks of penetrating the air spaces or territorial waters of other countries. The United States should make a public statement in general terms about the activities to be continued. The budgets for such programs should be publicly identified and be a regular part of the budget of the Defense Department. Officials of the Defense Department should be required to justify them as they justify all other programs. The organizations that operate and conduct them and the responsible officials for them should be publicly identified and be made a matter of public record.

There is, of course, a case for keeping some aspects of a program secret. For example, the technology of the most advanced cameras in satellites might justify continued secrecy.

However, such secrecy should be within the context of an ongoing classification system and should be treated within the government like other classified material.

We do not believe that electronic intelligence-collection programs, if any, which penetrate the air spaces or territorial waters of other countries (or run a high risk of such penetration) should be continued.

Our proposals regarding covert operations are more drastic. We believe that the United States no longer needs a large establishment whose function is to conduct covert operations and gather intelligence covertly. Accordingly, the entire covert-operations section of the CIA should be dismantled. The CIA should become what it was originally meant to be—an intelligence evaluation and coordinating organization with no operational responsibilities. This would mean eliminating the entire Plans division of the CIA and the career service of covert operators. It would mean also that the CIA would no longer have clandestine agents in overseas embassies. Their clandestine contacts with government officials and opposition groups abroad should be taken over, to the extent necessary, by State Department officials and military attachés.

Adoption of this proposal would permit the CIA to emerge from the shadows. Its functions would be discussed publicly. Its budget could be publicly identified and its functions largely explained in a public defense of its budget and operations. The intelligence-analysis branch of the CIA would become the dominant career service, with intelligence analysts rising to top positions, including that of Director.

The gains from these proposals would include the elimination of the costs to executive-branch decision-making, American society, and to American foreign policy discussed above. The adverse consequences would be minimal. If the United States government decided to conduct a limited covert operation—for example, obtaining information from a spy within a potentially hostile government—it could be carried out either by the military attachés or by State Department officials. But there would no longer be a group whose *raison d'être* was such operations, a group constantly looking for ways to employ covert means as an instrument of American foreign policy.

VII Disscussion

MR. LOWENFELD: I am not quite sure why I was asked to be a commentator here. I was told by the organizers that they wanted somebody who had government experience in foreign affairs. As I read the paper and listened to Mr. Halperin and Mr. Stone, I realized what they meant. I was one of those guys who had all the appropriate clearances and worked on some things that I thought were critical and important, and for the most part I did not know about all those other meetings, the Super Secret meetings.

It did come across to me once. I remember in August 1964 I was Acting Deputy Legal Adviser of the State Department. Bill Bundy called up and said, "I want a resolution authorizing the President to act in Southeast Asia." It turned out that my boss, the Acting Legal Adviser, was on leave—it was the middle of August—and I was the one who picked up the phone. I said, "What happened?" He said, "Never mind; just write a resolution."

It was fairly easy to write the resolution. As any good lawyer, I had a form book. We had the Cuba resolution, the Formosa resolution, the Lebanon resolution, all contained in a nice little book called *Legislation on Foreign Affairs*. It was not too hard to dictate a Vietnam resolution. But I said, "Tell me what happened, so I can put in the appropriate 'whereas' clauses." The answer was, "You are not authorized," and I never did find out.

A few days later my boss came back. He had not yet been confirmed. There was some doubt whether he could see the reports from Tonkin Gulf. I think ultimately he did briefly, but only looking over somebody's shoulder. So I knew there was something going on in Tonkin Gulf, and also that there was an attempt to limit access to the information. Whether the news was actually managed, I don't know.

I am sort of depressed by Mr. Halperin's and Mr. Stone's essay. I thought one of the excitements of my job as a government official was that I was really in on a lot of important decisions. Since then, as a teacher and scholar, I have tried to write about them. Now I have to consider that maybe I was just misinformed.

I think it may well be true that espionage is a good thing, a stabilizing influence, a force for peace. Take, for example, Soviet maneuvers in East Germany and Czechoslovakia in 1968. If you had no idea what they were doing, you thought maybe they were going to march to the Rhine or the English Channel, and maybe you got your contingency plan for the Strategic Air Command out of Omaha ready. If, on the other hand, you knew what they were doing, that they were only worried about Dubček, and you had already decided you could not really protect Dubček, you calm down. I think there is a lot of that in both directions. So it may well be that a certain level of espionage is a stabilizing rather than a destabilizing force.

Where does espionage tilt over into operations? That is very hard to say. Take, for example, the U-2—was that an operation or was it information-gathering? It is a bit of both. I am not sure that you can really make the separation that Messrs. Stone and Halperin suggest.

MR. RANSOM: I am an academic observer of this subject. The only time I ever worked with the government was quite a while back, when I joined the U.S. forces to stamp out fascism—which I see returning, I am afraid, in a different uniform. I find the Halperin-Stone essay is a very original analysis, and I think I have read everything else on the subject in English dealing with how Super Secrecy and Super Secret agencies can subvert our policy-making system.

I want to say a word about definitions, because while this may seem elementary and pedantic, I think we have all discovered recently that definitions are important. At the highest levels of our government we have discovered with Watergate that there are people who don't know the difference between war and politics.

Intelligence means evaluated information. Espionage is one of the several techniques for gathering information and is by definition illegal. Counterintelligence is a police and security function. Covert or clandestine political operations are activities having no direct relation to intelligence or espionage functions, although they produce some and use some intelligence. That is all very simple, and I restate it because I feel that at the highest levels of government these distinctions are thoroughly confused.

What did Congress intend when it set up the Central Intelligence Agency? My reading of the legislative history is that Congress did not intend to create a clandestine or covert political action organization. We need further research into the legislative history—and scholarly research on this subject encounters many obstacles—but I am convinced from my research to date that Congress did not intend to authorize anything but a Central Intelligence Agency whose functions were to be related to intelligence, that is, *information.*

If Congress did not intend covert political action, how did it come about? I think it was an American reaction to Stalin and communism. The covert political activities of the last twenty-five years have been justified in the same way that we justify activities in time of war generally. We have been in a gray zone between a war declared by Congress and what has in fact been a wartime condition—a cold war since 1947.

The first big covert operation was the Italian election of 1948. Our government felt that we had to make that election come out right. Ever since then, at least until 1967, we have secretly intervened in a major way in elections all over the world. I was startled to see in *The New York Times* a few days ago that we subsidized one wing of the Italian Christian Democratic party to the tune of three million dollars a year between the early 1950s and 1967. I had no idea that as an American taxpayer I was contributing to a particular wing of an Italian political party. I think most of you here didn't know that.

Since 1948, I estimate that the CIA has conducted hundreds of "Watergates" around the globe. That is, it has waged secret political warfare, has attempted to give history a push here and there and make things happen in what our government considers its favor. As the cold war intensified after Korea, covert operations were stepped up, and came to include the secret subsidy of U.S. domestic organizations. You might say, as the cold war stepped up, covert operations came to be used internally and included, as Messrs. Halperin and

Stone have indicated, the secret CIA subsidy of an estimated two hundred and twenty-five domestic organizations between the early 1950s and 1967. The most famous, of course, was the National Students Association, whose budget at one time was supported ninety per cent by a secret subsidy from the CIA.

These widespread domestic subsidies were perhaps the second greatest mistake in the history of the CIA. I would say the program of subsidizing domestic organizations was clearly against the law. What, then, was the greatest mistake? The greatest mistake was to allow CIA personnel and equipment to be used for doubly illegal acts at home—illegal because burglary is illegal, and illegal because Congress had very explicitly prohibited the use of the Central Intelligence Agency for internal purposes.

In 1971, the then Director of the Central Intelligence, Richard Helms, gave a rare public speech defending the CIA. He raised the problem of the compatibility of its activity with American democracy. He said explicitly and clearly, "We do not target on American citizens." Was he telling the turth? Because I thought he *was* telling the truth, I found something else he said even more shocking. "The nation must to a degree take it on faith that we who lead the CIA are honorable men, devoted to the nation's services." I don't think that any government officials at any level should ask the American people to take it on faith that they are honorable men, because we, I hope, are a government of laws and not of men.

I recommend a thorough audit of all CIA activities, foreign and domestic, by a Hoover Commission-type study, independent of the government. It is an ordinary suggestion, but I remind you that not since 1955 has such a study been made. There have been dozens of studies of the CIA's problems by secret government committees; the government was investigating itself. In 1955, the Hoover Commission task force on intelligence activities, a very Establishment-oriented group, called public attention to the dangers that we now see have become real. We need another such study. I believe such a study should go forward separate and apart from the CIA involvement in the Watergate scandal. Watergate is going to be thoroughly investigated, but there is a much, much larger question: the policy, organization and controls of the intelligence system.

I predict such a study will recommend what Messrs. Stone and Halperin have recommended: that the CIA become again an intelligence agency, as Congress intended, and that covert operations be abolished. If we need a reserve force for covert operations, then we will create and use it. I don't rule out all overseas use of covert operations. But such covert activity is an act of war, so let's call it war and get the CIA out of it.

I predict that such a study will also call, as the Hoover Commission did in 1955, for a joint Congressional committee on intelligence activities. I realize that this is a close question. The Congressional Joint Atomic Energy Committee has not worked the way we wanted it to work. But Congress needs a sustained surveillance group for the intelligence community. Congress gave far too much away in 1947 and 1949. Congress did give the CIA the right to spend funds secretly. Congress did give the director of intelligence the right to tell Senator Fulbright and others, "Sorry, Senator, I cannot tell you that, because Congress has given me the discretion to decide whether I should tell you this or that." Now that the CIA has been disgraced—disgraced to some extent by Watergate in the public eye—I think we have an opportunity to organize for a new Hoover Commission-type study. In 1945 Harry Truman, as President, told his Budget Director, and these are Truman's words, "I am very much against building up an American Gestapo." Tragically, Watergate demonstrated that Truman's fears were not unfounded.

MR. KRONFELD: I think we have to take a rather jaundiced view of Congressional oversight in this area. When something comes up before the Congress, the Congressmen often don't know what they are voting on. They go by what the committee leadership says; it gets down to a very few people. The Armed Services Committee does have an oversight role now, but the oversight is done by the staff. A good example of the quality of the oversight is suggested by the fact that the just-retired chief counsel of the House Armed Services Committee was also a major general in the Marine Reserves. Most of the senior staff on the Armed Services Committee treat the junior dissident

Senators with a certain disdain. They don't talk to them. They don't give them information. These junior members and some middle-rank members don't have a chance. They can't get through to the chairman, they can't get through to the staff, they have to rely on outside people.

MR. LEWIS: I am skeptical of the suggestion that covert operations could continue safely if they were scrutinized by an effective Congressional committee. I don't believe that a joint Congressional committee is ever going to deal effectively with these matters. It won't be in on the operation early enough. It won't have the expertise. Even supposing a Senator thought landing people in Cuba was a bad idea, by the time he found out about it everybody would be all cranked up on the operation and would say, Senator, it is too late to change. It is just not a realistic notion that you can control such operations. Their whole nature is that you cannot control them, and that is the danger.

MR. LOWENFELD: It may be possible to build in some notion of regular accountability. I am skeptical too, but it may be worth the effort.

One footnote to what Professor Ransom said about the historical record. I am more and more skeptical of the historical record. I am skeptical of the notion that in 1947 Congress did not intend the Central Intelligence Agency to do anything but evaluate. I realize that is what the statute says and that is what the formal record says, but that's just the point.

MR. DORSEN: Are you suggesting there were separate meetings in the Congress, with a record that might not have been made public?

MR. LOWENFELD: Sure.

MR. CALLEN: I wish to comment on intelligence-gathering, as distinct from covert operations. I worked at the National Security Agency for eight years, sometimes helping among other things to develop analytical interception and surveillance apparatus. I agree with Professor Lowenfeld that a great deal of what goes on, in NSA at least, is very much in the interests of peace, because you don't really trust what any other government says. You really have much more confidence in what you intercept, in what they are saying among themselves.

Much of what used to be done by people is now done by satellites. You can ring the Soviet Union with interception apparatus, but that only gets at long-range communications. Microwave communications, which are short range, can be intercepted by satellites. You send the satellites high up and they swoop down low over the Soviet Union and gather stuff. So satellites play a major role in the interception of foreign communication.

The thing that interested me for all those years was how little of the surveillance technology actually diffused into our own economy, though some of it was developed right here in this country. This was, I think, because there was no force for such diffusion. Now, there is such a force—the fight against crime. The Law Enforcement Assistance Administration [LEAA] poses a very definite threat to the right of privacy and to civil liberties by funding the use of this technology in domestic affairs. For example, in Washington, we fought very hard and successfully against a group which was going to receive money from LEAA. It was going to have some $150,000 worth of equipment for an electronic surveillance van to use, they said, for fighting organized crime and heavy drug traffic. We are going to see more and more of this across the United States, funded by LEAA.

MR. SCHWARTZ: I want to make two brief points. The first point is with regard to Congressional oversight. I think few people really feel Congressional oversight is adequate. All too often it turns into the primary dictionary meaning of the term. Yet we must use the tools we have. This is, in our constitutional governmental structure, the only real instrument we have for controlling executive action.

Secondly, as one who is not involved in this area at all, my sympathies are with the suggestions made in the paper and discussion. This bloated, elephantine apparatus that has grown up completely distorts the constitutional center of gravity. Of course, it ought to be pruned, refined, improved, and maybe abolished, and yet one has a lingering doubt. You all remember Secretary Stimson's famous remark when he dismantled this kind of operation, at what now seems a very elementary if not infantile level: "Gentlemen don't open other people's mail," he said. But what happens if, in the world, you are not dealing with gentlemen, and all other governments have this kind of thing?

MR. HALPERIN: I want to distinguish between two things. Mr. Stone and I were not proposing the abolition of reading other people's mail. That is precisely one of the things we are proposing to continue. It is very hard to make estimates; but I don't know anybody who has been in the government who would challenge the notion that something over ninety per cent, I would say ninety-eight per cent, of the useful information the United States government has comes either from overt sources: newspapers, public radio broadcasts, or things of that kind—or from technical and intelligence-gathering: satellites, reading other people's mail, the kinds of things the National Security Agency supposedly does.

We are not proposing to abolish that range of activity. What we are proposing is to move it out of its Super Secrecy. For example, it is now clear to anybody who reads anything that the United States has a very large satellite program. It is still the case that anybody with a security clearance is violating the law if he says so publicly. The budget for spy satellites and the office that runs them are buried. If you go as a Congressman or a citizen and say, "Who runs the satellite program which we read about in the newspapers all the time?" you can't find out. If you say, "How much does it cost?" you can't find out.

There is absolutely no reason in the world for either of those two facts to be secret, and no reason in the world for Congress not to be able to get into that program in executive session on a classified basis, the way it gets into the Minuteman missile program or any other military program.

Legislative Secrecy

— by Albert Gore

Secrecy in the legislative branch of the government is neither newer nor more to be condemned than in the judicial and executive branches. Though maximum public procedure must be our goal, I am convinced from experience that some privacy in the discussion and procedure that leads to legislative decision and action is not only consistent with our traditions but useful to the public interest, especially where public discussion would jeopardize national security, impair court procedure, or inhibit exploratory and informative sessions.

The Senate Watergate Committee held nationally televised hearings, and many people applauded and some deplored the public disclosures. Yet these highly public hearings were preceded by closed Committee sessions in which decisions were made as to what witnesses to call and as to the principal thrust of the questions. Without such exploration, a hit-or-miss procedure would be unavoidable. So the most educational, prudent, and effective public procedure is frequently preceded by closed-door sessions, each adding zest and quality to the other.

But to acknowledge that there is a justification for secrecy in some instances only underlines the general virtue of public procedure. As I contemplate the many secret sessions of the U.S. Senate Foreign Relations Committee, on which I served during the tragic years of the Vietnam war, I now believe the national interest would have been vastly better served if all these sessions had been public. The bombing of Cambodia was surely no secret to the Cambodians. The "security" involved was domestic politics. The release of the Pentagon Papers by Daniel Ellsberg would not then have been a very dramatic event; indeed, the Vietnam war might never have occurred; it surely would not have been so prolonged had the public not been so deceived.

The peculiar circumstances that characterize our times lend point and drama to the issue of secrecy. The President of the United States is now at all times our chief legislator. This position and power stems not only from his veto, which can be overturned only by a two-thirds majority of both House and Senate, but from the office itself—its dramatic character, its newsworthiness, its prestige, which has been greatly magnified by the many events and trends of our day. Not the least among these is the President's management and command of the news media, especially of television and radio. A vast portion of news about government comes from the President and is about the President, but an even vaster majority is subject to his suppression or release in whole or in part, both as to time and as to emphasis. In very important respects, government is now by White House public relations. Public opinion is thus molded, sometimes manufactured.

Now and then, public curiosity and the diligence of the press will overcome the secrecy of even the Presidential office. But so pervasive an operation as Watergate, we must recall, was successfully covered up for a long while, during which it was widely and lightly, if not humorously, dismissed as an irresponsible "caper." It appeared we had achieved "burglary with honor."

In the day-to-day legislative process, the President exercises a truly vast influence not only by bringing pressures and influences to bear on a specific pending issue but also by creating and fashioning the political atmosphere in which legislative proposals are considered. The President speaks with a concentrated, authoritative, magnified voice while the Congress is a babble of many and mostly controverting tongues.

A new development—the refusal of administration witnesses to testify before Congressional committees—must now be considered. Not only have officials of the present administration repeatedly declined polite invitations to testify, but President Nixon's Attorney General Kleindienst asserted an unprecedented extension of the President's executive privilege to include the right to prevent testimony before the Congress by any employee of the entire executive branch of government. Though this is executive secrecy per se, it is in fact legislative secrecy when its use so deeply affects the legislative process.

As I see it, the present obsession with secrecy by the executive branch is an intolerable perversion of the American democratic process and a threat to the American principle of tripartite coequality, which the Congress must be quick to challenge. A chief executive determined to conduct war and foreign affairs without restraints or even without consultation with Congress, determined to shield policy-makers from cross-examination by the elected representatives of the people, and determined to cover up the crimes of his most intimate, and thus his most powerful aides, is a President whose acts must be diligently illuminated.

Still another new factor that further intrudes upon the legislative process is the denigration of the cabinet. Current cabinet members are no longer the principal policy-makers or spokesmen for governmental departments. Who would expect Secretary of State William Rogers to define U.S. foreign policy? I observed his attempt to respond to questions about a foreign policy when it was obvious he did not know what the policy was. Henry Kissinger was all along *de facto* Secretary of State! Or who expected Mr. Kleindienst either to uncover or to prosecute the commission of burglary or the cover-up of same by his *de facto* superiors on the White House staff?

These unprecedented conditions hinder public legislative sessions. Indeed, the whole atmosphere of deception and secrecy that accompanied our embroilment in the Vietnam war has survived it and smites mightily at the very base of our representative democracy.

There are, as I have said, instances where secrecy in the legislative process is advisable—examination of individual tax returns in the course of study for tax legislation, for example. I recall being astounded to see from its tax return that a large U.S. corporation with far-flung world operations had actually not been required by law to pay any income tax on its vast overseas profits. I could and did make speeches about it, although I did not consider it proper to identify the taxpayer. Nevertheless, the legislative purpose was served by a mixture sometimes called—not entirely inappropriately—a "public secret."

Then, I would not lightly overlook the secrecy involved in national security, that is, in military affairs, though in this field we find vast abuse. As a young Congressman and a member of the Appropriations Committee, I was one of a very small group among whom our early atomic-bomb secrets were shared. However one may feel about development of this weapon, one can scarcely deny or minimize the impact of surprise in its use.

There have been and will be real reasons for secrecy in both diplomacy and military intelligence. Yet, I must relate that every administration during which I served in the U.S. Congress—Roosevelt to Nixon—would readily hide behind the convenient shield of "national security." This is not to say that all these Presidents were equal in their easy resort to this "last refuge." Not by any means!

Let me return to the legislative branch itself. I wish to cite another combination of secret and public procedure which had an over-all beneficial result. I refer to the manner of considering the subject of deployment of antiballistic weapon systems—the ABM question, as it became known. I was chairman of a subcommittee which had the responsibility of considering this subject and making a recommendation to the Senate on it. Neither I nor any member of the subcommittee had the advantage of more than relatively elementary scientific training. Of course, the Pentagon military missile experts were ready with supporting data, but *only* with supporting data; ready, too, with scary "classified secrets" about the missile threat of the Soviet and Chinese "Communists," which were released bit by bit for maximum propagandistic effect. This was, it seemed to them and to many editorial writers, reason enough for Congress to vote billions of dollars for this new round in the armaments race.

Fortunately, there were other experts outside the Pentagon who were ready to expound ably both for and against the proposition. Congress had a unique job in ventilating the genuine differences of opinion in the scientific community on a very important, sophisticated subject.

But consider our plight on the subcommittee. We scarcely knew what questions to ask! Our need for elementary instruction in the basic science of antiballistic missiles and in the effect of their deployment on the armaments race was imperative. Was our own education a suitable exercise for public session? Who would be interested in it, or how would the public interest be served? Moreover, Congressmen and Senators are understandably reluctant to expose their ignorance.

We chose, and I think properly so, the much maligned secret executive session. There, we could ask the simple non-Senatorial questions, and engage in seemingly nonsensical but politically meaningful dialogue that served to test our judgments and eventually to whet our courage to tackle this complicated and little understood subject in public hearings and debate. During the process, deficient in acumen as it may have been, a decided majority of the subcommittee became convinced that the proposed deployment would be a grievous mistake.

It appeared to us that since those two fateful days, August 6 and 9, 1945, when American planes dropped atomic bombs on Hiroshima and Nagasaki, the United States and the Soviet Union had engaged in what was potentially the most suicidal military struggle ever known to man. Like two mad and often half-blind giants, they piled nuclear armaments on top of nuclear armaments, and together spent nearly a trillion dollars each in trying to get the better of the other. President Nixon and the Pentagon scare-mongers warned gravely of the "Communist" threat from Russia. And then there was "Red China's" nuclear missile development, which we could only counter, it was said, by deploying our own ABM weapons. We regarded all this as exaggeration at best, cited for political pressure and contrary to both fact and logic.

But how could we explain our doubts to our colleagues and to the public? Opposition to a "national defense" weapon was politically dangerous; in fact, many people regarded public opposition to any national defense proposal as downright unpatriotic, and especially so in the mysterious field of missilry. The only feasible course for effective opposition was public procedure.

Against this background of confusion and contradiction, of costly error and alarmist warnings of gross danger, the Arms Control Subcommittee took the issue to the people in public hearings. The result of that national debate—widely carried by television—was an unprecedented public involvement in a technical issue. It quickly became a hotly contested national issue. President Nixon won his go-ahead by a tie vote, but while losing the battle, we won the over-all fight. The administration has never admitted its error—no administration ever does—but the ABM project is now withering on the vine (enormous sums of money having been utterly wasted on it).

I would like now to cite an instance in which a tax loophole was initiated in secrecy, was killed in the light of public procedure, and then was revived and written into the law in the secrecy of a conference committee between Senate and House. When a bill passes each House of Congress in differing forms, it is necessary to compose these differences so an "engrossed" bill can go to the President for signature or veto. The group appointed to compromise or compose these differences is called a conference committee. On tax bills, the House conferees come from the Ways and Means Committee and Senate conferees are the senior members of the Senate Finance Committee. The version of the tax bill agreed upon by the conferees is accepted by both Houses almost without fail—an immense power in which secret procedure is dangerous to the public interest.

In 1969 the Nixon administration, in its recurring zeal to help those who least need help, was anxious from the beginning of consideration of the tax bill to cut the tax rates applicable to higher income brackets; in addition to a generous rate reduction, the administration had the effrontery to propose that the "marginal rate"—the top rate actually paid—on "earned income" be lowered from 70 per cent to 50 per cent, which would only aid taxpayers whose income was above the 50-per-cent tax bracket. A preference for "earned income" might be justified, I thought, but there could be no justification for giving such a "preference" only to those in the very high income brackets. Assistant Secretary of the Treasury Edwin Cohen had persuaded the Ways and Means Committee, meeting in secret session, to agree to this provision. When the bill was considered on the floor of the House of Representatives there was no opportunity for a member of the House to offer an amendment to strike this stark favoritism to upper-income taxpayers from the bill. The House of Representatives considers tax bills under a closed—gag—rule, meaning that no amendments are in order and thus members must vote the recommendation of the Ways and Means Committee up or down without change. (I chafed at this as a House Member.)

Upon examining the House bill in preparation for the Senate Finance Committee hearings, I found this provision the most odious of many objectionable features of the bill, and I subjected it to close exposure at the Finance Committee's public hearings. As a result, when amendments to the bill were considered, the very first amendment adopted by the Committee struck out this favoritism to the upper-income brackets. In fact, Senator Russell Long, Chairman of the Committee, seeing another tax-policy victory for me in the making (he had become sensitive about this), beat me to the punch and offered the amendment himself. It was adopted unanimously.

In the secret conference committee, however, the chairman of the conference (because he was Chairman of the Ways and Means Committee), Congressman Wilbur Mills, proposed restoration of this provision. This occurred at about two o'clock in the morning of the last night of the conference when we were nearing the end of consideration of the hundreds of issues to be settled. I immediately and vehemently denounced it as representing the crassest form of favoritism for the rich and fortunate—especially lawyers, doctors, and corporate officials who enjoy high "earned income" (salary, bonus, fees, etc.).

The discussion between Congressman Mills and me became intense—heard only by the members of the conference committee meeting in secret session. I will not undertake to state his arguments—he had none, really. Secretary Cohen made a vigorous remonstrance to the effect that "these people spend a lot of time in arranging ingenious devices to avoid high rates."

"So, rather than controlling these 'ingenious devices,' " I said, "we just give them this loophole of tax preference." I pointed out, for instance, that the chairman of the board of General Motors would receive huge tax relief. His compensation from General Motors in 1968 amounted to about $795,000, and with that amount of "earned income," so-called, the adoption of this tax cut would provide a tax cut for him of approximately $90,000 per year. And I compared that "tax relief" with the few dollars per week provided for most taxpayers. Demagogic? It was the truth.

Finally, about 2:30 in the morning, we reached an agreement which gave me most of what I was fighting for. Mills then announced that the conferees would meet again at noon that same day to sign the "conference report" (a necessary legislative step), which meanwhile would be typed into legislative form.

As we were leaving, I noticed some whispered discussion among a few members of the Committee and Treasury representatives who were sitting in on our deliberations. I unavoidably overheard Senator Wallace Bennett of Utah, a ranking Republican on the Senate Finance Committee, say to one of the Treasury officials, "Let's meet in my office."

After time for a shower, a quick nap, and breakfast, the conference committee reconvened at noon. A secret deal then quickly unfolded. Mills reopened discussion on the controversial point, and now both Senator Long, who had moved to kill it in the Senate Finance Committee, and Senator Bennett promptly and vigorously supported him. I argued as best I could—a breach of our agreement, unjustified, etc.—but the deal had been made, and another "loophole" was written into the tax law behind closed doors.

Unless the doors are opened on tax legislation, tax reform will remain an empty political slogan. Behind closed doors, the influence of the private-interest lobbies is most effectively served, and, conversely, the public interest can best be ignored. (Ironically enough, now undertaking to be law-abiding in private life, I am enjoying a certain degree of affluence that is facilitated by this very inequity.)

Fortunately, the House of Representatives liberalized its rules early in 1973 to curb and limit its secret procedures. But it has not effectively reached the most damaging secrecy in its tax-writing Ways and Means Committee, nor in the "mark-up" sessions of its Appropriations subcommittees, where the pork barrels are filled to overflowing, nor in the procedure followed by conference committees. So, the most one can say of this House reform is that it is a step in the right direction.

In the Senate, where more than one third of all committee sessions in 1972 were closed, reform has not gotten off the ground. The Congressional Quarterly reported that Senate and House committees and subcommittees operated behind closed doors 40 per cent of the time in 1972. The executive or "mark-up" (the real action or decision-making) sessions operated in secrecy 79 per cent of the time in the House and 98 per cent of the time in the Senate. These totals would likely be even higher if they included the House-Senate conference committee sessions. And it is precisely in these final legislative compromising sessions—established exactly for the purpose of composing differences between House and Senate versions of proposals that have already passed both Houses and only await approval in identical form to go to the President to be signed into law—where the greatest assaults on the public interests succeed.

Senator Long can still be expected to bring his "Christmas Tree" tax favoritisms, considered and reported by a secret committee session, to a vote in the waning hours of a Congress weary and anxious to adjourn and depart the Capitol. And more loopholes in the tax law can be jammed through in secret sessions of conference committees.

True, when our Founding Fathers themselves met in Philadelphia to draw up the Charter that founded our freedom and liberty, the very first thing they did was to close their sessions to the public and the press. Fortunately, James Madison and others kept diaries about who was what on which issue. A more democratic procedure may have served history much better, but would we have had the Constitution? Benjamin Franklin surely doubted it. "If every one of us," he said at the last session, "were to report the objections he has had to it, and endeavor to gain partisans in support of them, we might prevent it being generally received and thereby lose all the salutary effects and great advantages."

But this is 1973. What a year in our history!

How does Congress meet the unprecedented challenge of Presidential power? How does it accomplish the watch-dog function into which it is shoved by these events? Not by resorting to more secrecy in legislative and investigative processes nor by crawling further into its own cocoon of tradition and precedent.

Secrecy in the legislative process cheats the governed of their right to know, gives the concentrated special interests their maximum advantages, and affords opportunities for further encroachment of Presidential political power.

In a free society the public business must ultimately be opened to public scrutiny and must in the end be subject to public judgment.

Discussion

MR. KOCH: I serve on the Banking and Currency Committee of the House. Prior to March 6, 1973, when a new rule required all Committee Sessions to be public, there was a battle in my Committee relating to some controversial legislation. What took place in the closed session was leaked to the press—because there are no secrets, there simply are no secrets. The information that came out was that the Chairman was conducting himself in a disagreeable way. The press said so. The Chairman then said in response: "I will teach you guys a lesson. I am going to invite the press in." They came the next day. They came for two days, and they found it terribly boring, and they did not come again.

When I came to the Congress in January 1969, agencies invited the new Members to their headquarters and told us about their operations. Through these briefings they try to involve you in the agency and thus make you a friend. Maybe it is not brainwashing, but it is an attempt to fill you in. It is legitimate. At least, I thought it was legitimate—until I went. I went to a breakfast meeting in Virginia called by the CIA—a great breakfast on gold service. There were eighteen freshmen Congressmen. There were at least thirty-six agents. Richard Helms, then the CIA Director, said to us eighteen Members of the Congress, "Gentlemen, this is probably the only time you will ever have an opportunity to ask any question of the CIA. So ask." So I raised my hand and I said, "Mr. Helms, I really have two questions. How many people do you employ and what is the size of your budget?" He said, "There are only two questions I can't answer and those are the two." So I said, "Mr. Helms, are you telling me, a Member of Congress, that I can't learn the size of your budget? After all, I vote on that budget. Somehow or other I ought to be able to see it." He said, "That is exactly what I am telling you. That budget item is buried under some other items and you will not know what it is. It is passed upon by a few Members of Congress and you will never know what it is." I said, "You mean it could be buried under Social Security?" He said, "We have not used that one yet, but it is not a bad idea."

MR. GOODELL: Is it not true that the rules of the House provide that you can go into an executive session only with a public vote by a majority of the members?

MR. KOCH: That is correct.

MR. GOODELL: It would seem to me that one of the qualifications of Members of Congress is a willingness to expose their ignorance publicly. That is one of the protections we have. I think you probably agree with that.

SENATOR GORE: I gave three examples of justification for secrecy. One, genuine national security. Two, to prevent prejudice to a future court procedure. Three, to aid in exploring technical subjects so the Congressmen and Senators can become sufficiently prepared to take an issue to the people. What would we have done with the ABM hearings if we had nothing but the Pentagon appearing, giving all the reasons why it should be deployed? No one from the Pentagon would be permitted to give any reasons why it should *not* be deployed. Every person from the administration who appears before the House or Senate must support the President's position. Where would we get the opposing information? We had to go outside, and in order to become informed ourselves, we had to ask simple questions. This must be done privately.

MR. PLESSER: Senator Gore, there was something very disturbing to me in your story about the ABM hearings and the need for having secrecy. What you said, if I recall correctly, was that you had executive sessions. You determined how you came out on the issue. You said the majority came out against deployment and then you brought it to the public. What would have happened, Senator, if you had agreed with the Pentagon? What if you felt the Pentagon was doing something good, that the ABM was necessary? Then the issue would have gone through executive session and into committee. The American public would not have had the debate. I think you indicated in your comments that the ABM was beaten not necessarily by the politics within the Senate but by public support around the country. Obviously, no information was going out from the Pentagon about the ABM. No information would have gone out from the Senate about the ABM if six Senators had not decided that they disagreed with the Pentagon and were going to take the issue to the American public. Isn't the American public entitled to more of a guarantee than that?

SENATOR GORE: I think that is a valid criticism. Even so, our system can only work if leadership quality is exercised. If after executive session and exploration of a subject, a majority of the committee decides that a hearing should or should not be held, we must run the risk that their decision is right. I think you have made a valid criticism, but it is a risk our system must run.

MR. GOODELL: Wouldn't you throw the burden the other way, as they do now in the House, and require a majority vote before you go into executive session?

SENATOR GORE: Not at the preliminary session; ultimately, yes.

MR. STONE: I wanted to add to some of Senator Gore's statement about ABM and to correct some of Mr. Plesser's apprehensions.

The thing that perhaps most made ABM a public issue was completely independent of the Senate—the "bombs in the backyard" debate. The Army had decided on its own to put interceptors near cities. Scientists in Seattle and Chicago complained about the location of these sites. It became a nationwide issue overnight. Within a week of Senator Kennedy's decision to write a letter asking for the ABM decision to be reviewed, the issue jumped into full prominence.

It takes a lot of different groups, as well as some lucky breaks, to make something a national issue. Even if a Senate committee wanted to sit on an issue, it would be hard to stop it from being discussed.

MR. KOCH: I don't believe that a legislator should be shielded. Your constituents don't expect that you are an expert in everything. The fact that you go through a learning process during testimony is not going to be held against you.

MR. SCHWARTZ: As an outsider who is neither a legislator nor a government official, I think Congress comes to deal with the problem of government secrecy with its hands tied behind its back. So many of its key decisions are made in executive session. But except in defense and foreign affairs, and even there with restrictions, there is no justification whatsoever for nonpublic action by the Congress. All the arguments that are made and have been made to justify executive sessions were made when the Senate held all its sessions in secret. When the motion was made to open the Senate up to the public, the response was, "How can you do this? How can we conduct our business? How can we have our debates public? We will lose all possibility of speaking freely."

MR. GOODELL: I would like to go on record as being essentially in complete agreement with what you said.

SENATOR GORE: Obviously, the Ervin committee cannot hold a worthy public hearing if *every* American citizen who might want to testify can appear. There must be some executive procedure, some decision-making by that Committee, on who should testify, on how many witnesses there should be, on scheduling. So when you lay down the blanket rule that no private procedure is justified except in security questions, I say this is impractical. Congress cannot operate this way. You must have a functioning leadership quality in the Congress if our representative system of government is to operate.

The Secrets of Local Government

—by M. L. Stein

Of the many myths permeating our political life, none is more persuasive than the idea of open government. Americans are nurtured on the belief that their lawmakers and administrative officials are constantly in the public view—a "government of the people, by the people, and for the people."

Some of this euphoria has been dispelled in recent years by the almost paranoiac secrecy of the Johnson and Nixon administrations, the Pentagon Papers case, Watergate, and a widening knowledge of Congressional and bureaucratic concealment. In 1972 the House Committee on Governmental Operations found after forty-one days of hearings that the five-year-old Freedom of Information Act had been "hindered by five years of footdragging by the federal bureaucracy." A further chill has come in the form of intimidation of reporters through subpoena power and other pressures.

Faced with these facts, many people turn to their local government as the last bastion of freedom of information. They see in the city council, the board of education, or the zoning commission, the old-time virtue of direct access to those in power.

This may be the greatest myth of all. In actuality, local government frequently operates in an aura of secrecy and distrust of both the press and the public. Clandestine meetings, hidden records and unavailable officials are commonplace, even in states with open-record and open-meeting laws. The town-meeting tradition often has given way to backroom sessions and a private-club attitude on the part of lawmakers. In some instances, local bodies have gone to extraordinary lengths to keep out of the public view. They have met in private homes, members' offices, upstairs in firehouses, restaurants, and, in at least one case, a bank vault. If challenged, the elected officials claim they are entitled to meet on occasion in "executive session" or to schedule "work sessions" in private. In Orange County, New York, the county legislature hammered out its 1973 budget in secret conclave, because, as one member put it, "We get more work done that way."

How do they get away with it? Legally, in some states. In others, councilmen, education board members, etc., simply interpret open-meeting laws or charter regulations in their favor. Or else the officials clearly violate the spirit and letter of prevailing freedom of information laws.

Most state freedom of information laws date from the 1950s, after Sigma Delta Chi, the professional journalistic society, drew up model laws for open records and open meetings and brought them to the attention of state legislatures in a nationwide campaign. SDX's efforts were not always well received, even by newsmen. Some reporters and editors argued that the First and Fourteenth amendments were enough to enable them to keep public servants aboveboard in their handling of public affairs. Additional legislation, they felt, would provide excuses for secrecy where none existed before. Robert H. Wills, city editor of the *Milwaukee Sentinel,* charged that Wisconsin's 1959 statute had done more harm than good. Before the law was enacted, he said, he could walk into a meeting as a reporter and "nobody could throw a law book at me."

The right-to-know laws also created no little confusion and misunderstanding. Dr. Paul Fisher, Director of the nation's only Freedom of Information Center (housed at the University of Missouri's School of Journalism), noted: "What were thought to be tightly written laws shortly developed semantic leaks. Definition and interpretation became all-important, and legitimate well-meaning phrases could be twisted to close a meeting or record as well as open it. If a law specified open conduct of 'official deliberation,' who was to say what constituted an official deliberation?" [1]

So many amendments were tacked on to an Iowa freedom-of-information bill that its chief sponsor, state Senator David Stanley, caustically observed that the amendments were "cutting up an open-records bill and making it into a secrecy bill." Exemptions included appraisal reports for property purchases by governmental subdivisions, records of mentally ill persons, birth records of illegitimate children, personal student records, hospital records, police investigative reports, work products of attorneys, trade secrets, tax returns, and other documents.

In early 1973, thirty-three states had both open-meeting and open-record laws. Kentucky, Missouri, Oregon, Tennessee, and Wyoming had only open-record statutes. Colorado, Delaware, Maryland, New Jersey, Texas, Vermont, and Washington had open meetings only. Four states had neither: New York, Mississippi, Rhode Island, and West Virginia.

I Open Meetings

The laws range in effectiveness from California's tightly drawn Brown Act to an Idaho law on school boards, which proclaims that all meetings must be open to the public, "provided, however, that nothing contained in this Act shall be construed to prevent any such board of trustees . . . from holding executive sessions from which the public is excluded, but no ordinances, resolutions, rules or regulations shall be finally adopted at such an executive session."

An open-meeting law adopted by the state of Washington in 1971 is considered one of the toughest on the books. With minor exceptions, meetings of public agencies must be open, both during the deliberation stage and when a vote is taken. Any official who violates the act is subject to personal liability in the form of a $100 civil penalty, which may be sought by anyone—reporter or ordinary citizen.

The Idaho legislation is fairly typical of the working of open-meeting laws with regard to the "executive session." In many localities, officials find convenient loopholes to justify their secret deliberations. Even California's Brown Act, which limits closure to sensitive personnel matters, some parole hearings, and national-security discussions, is breached at the local level where the latter two provisions seldom apply. Dr. Allen E. Rice, an elementary education administrator in the Garden Grove Unified School District in Orange County, found numerous Brown Act violations in a 1968 study of one hundred and four California school districts.[2] Rice noted, however, that some of the abuses resulted from trustees' confusion over "conflicting court interpretations, lack of leadership from the office of California's chief state legal officer and the continual changes in the state statutes." A similar conclusion was reached four years earlier by Dr. Albert G. Pickerell, University of California (Berkeley) journalism professor, who attributed "spotty" breaches of the Act to "confusion or uncertainty as to the exact meaning of the provisions of the Brown Act" and to "a past lack of judicial interpretation which would have given weight and force to the Brown Act from the beginning." [3] The Act, which has served as a model for open-meeting laws in other states, suffered through twelve years of amendments after its original passage in 1953. The California experience lends weight to the following conclusion reached in a *Harvard Law Review* study: ". . . open meeting legislation has neither revolutionized the conduct of state and local government nor brought it to a grinding halt." [4]

Still, in states without such laws, the frequency and flagrancy of secret sessions by local agencies is much more apparent. In New York's Nassau and Suffolk counties, on Long Island, closed meetings of school boards, town supervisors, and county commissions are so common that most citizens accept them without question. The Suffolk County Human Rights Commission holds almost all of its sessions behind closed doors. In Westchester County, it's common for zoning boards to hold public hearings and then retire for private debate. The White Plains Planning Board voted secretly on one occasion to turn down an industrial firm's plea for a variance.

Its recommendation was passed to the Common Council, which held a public hearing on the matter without announcing the planners' decision.

In June 1971, New York Mayor John Lindsay directed the city's corporation counsel to insure public access to meetings of city agencies with rule-making functions. The order came after City Hall newsmen complained that the deliberations of the health agencies were shrouded in secrecy. Health Service Administrator Gordon Chase conceded the reporters' charge that, except for one session, all of the meetings of the Hospital Corporation's board of directors had been carried out in private in the past year. (The exception was in conformance with the legal requirement that the Corporation have one annual public meeting.)

The citizens of Rhode Island, another state without open-meeting or record laws, are similarly in the dark about what goes on. The *Providence Journal* scored the Fall River City Council for holding closed hearings in 1970 on alleged subversion by "local radicals" as reported in a Senate internal security subcommittee investigation. "The City Council appears to be embarked on a maneuver that threatens civil liberties and the public's right to know," the *Journal* said in a November 17, 1970, editorial. "Regardless of whether there are dangerous leftists at work in Fall River, regardless of whether some individuals may have violated laws, regardless of the validity or good sense of the committee's own investigation—regardless of all this, the people of Fall River are entitled to their own unfiltered look at their own council's study of the matter."

On March 9, 1972, the *Journal* editorially blasted the Pawtucket School Committee for meeting with the Pawtucket Teachers' Alliance "under almost cloak-and-dagger circumstances." The newspaper asserted that contract decisions were made for "rubber-stamping" at a public meeting the following week.

In Kansas City, Missouri, Mayor Charles B. Wheeler suggested last year that the City Council go into closed session to discuss two major municipal projects: the use of upcoming federal revenue sharing money and the planning of a capital improvements program. Earlier, in Webb City, Missouri, a motion was made and seconded to open long-closed meetings of the Personnel Administration Board. The motion was tabled after a member of the board, Floyd Williams, attacked the local newspapers, declaring that they were responsible for many of the board's problems. Missouri, too, is without an open-meeting law, and when, in St. Louis, right-to-know advocates won a victory after the Board of Election Commissioners decided in July 1972 to open its meetings to the news media, the action was taken with less than good grace. In its announcement of the move, the board said it was prompted "to a good extent by the fact that certain publicity seeking individuals have criticized decisions by this board solely on the ground that they were made in closed session."

A number of states with open-meeting laws are little better off than those without them. The files of the University of Missouri's Freedom of Information Center are crammed with case histories of local secrecy problems in states which have had bans against such practice for years. The difference seems to be that officials in open-meeting states spend more time seeking loopholes in the laws and in justifying their actions before the press and public. An example is the Des Moines City Council which, on April 3, 1972, held a secret meeting in the mayor's office in apparent violation of Iowa law. Mayor Richard Olson refused to say what had been discussed and expressed doubt that there had been a meeting at all.

"I don't think we held a meeting," he explained. "We had an informal discussion. If six men walk into the mayor's office, I can't tell them to get out." But according to the *Des Moines Register*,[5] three councilmen who attended said they came because the mayor's secretary had called them for a meeting in the mayor's office before the council's regularly scheduled session.

A similar case in Charlotte, North Carolina, last year ended in a court victory for a newspaperman and Sigma Delta Chi, which had sued the City Council over a meeting in the mayor's office to consider a downtown parking garage. William B. Arthur, Jr., of the *Charlotte Observer*, was ordered to leave the room after he had followed council members in. The reporter later filed suit, charging the council with violating the state's 1971 open-meetings statute. Councilmen denied they had held an "official" meeting, but Superior Court Judge Frank W. Snepp, Jr., enjoined the council from holding any private meetings, except those specifically allowed by state law, which required a public vote to go into executive session.

The Flint, Michigan, City Council also lost in court last year over its contention that it had a right to meet privately before regular sessions. Acting on a suit brought by the *Flint Journal*, Genesee County Circuit Judge Donald R. Freeman ordered the mayor and council to stop holding secret meetings, and added: "It is difficult to conceive how any hardship can be suffered by councilmen who are required to conduct business in public view. . . . The issue is not limited to the right of the press to attend and report. On a broader note, it is the right of the public to know . . . everything about that which is theirs."

Robert J. Boyle, editor of the *Pottstown* (Pennsylvania) *Mercury*, writing in *The New York Times'* Op-Ed page on March 24, 1973, described official secrecy as a serious and growing problem in his community: "School boards have been using the 'executive sessions' ploy more and more," he lamented. "The press and public are barred from executive sessions. Board members decide at these sessions what course of action to follow, and then simply approve the action at a regular meeting." (Boyle added that his City Council voted in secret to fire the police chief, and a group from the council, including the mayor, was selected to tell the chief secretly to look elsewhere for a job. He was told that it would be in his best interest to keep the decision secret. One councilman, however, discussed the action in a local bar, according to Boyle, and the *Mercury* got wind of it.)

In Oyster Bay, New York, Democratic Councilman Lewis J. Yevoli has complained that the Town Board's executive sessions have excluded him as well as the public. Yevoli said that the six other board members, all Republicans, keep him out of important discussions on town business by holding an afternoon "majority caucus" in Supervisor John W. Burke's office. Burke admitted that Yevoli has been barred from these meetings because they are for Republicans only.

Burke maintained that the board holds a "work session" Thursday afternoons at which all members can be present. But the board's information officer told *Newsday* reporter David Fluhrer that these sessions are sparsely attended or not at all because most of the councilmen maintain busy law practices. Often, Fluhrer learned, Burke speaks to the council members by telephone and Yevoli is not contacted. Yevoli can't get his resolutions before the Town Board even during its public meetings since he is unable to get a second for his proposals.

Many newsmen see the executive session exemption in open-meeting laws as the chief source of abuses. The Connecticut Daily Newspaper Association has cited a number of instances in which the executive-meeting privilege, although limited to specific matters, was frequently violated.[6] Carter White, publisher of the *Meriden Record Journal,* noted that the school board in his community had raised the salary of the school superintendent and created new school positions during the executive session, but did not make the news public until seven weeks later. A representative of Connecticut weeklies, Richard M. Diamond, publisher of the *Trumbull Times,* termed the use of the executive session as "the number-one obstacle" to the public's right to public information. In Trumbull, he said, the police commission had been meeting behind an iron door near the jail cells. Anyone seeking admittance had to wait at the door until a buzzer lock was pushed.

Virginia's Attorney General, in a 1968 opinion, confirmed a complaint by the *Roanoke World-News* that the state's new freedom of information law had a loophole so big that it tended to "defeat the whole purpose of the legislation as it affects local governing bodies." The Attorney General declared that a meeting is not a meeting when it is an "informal assemblage." The *World-News* said, the Attorney General "finds justification in a clause authorizing meetings to be closed if the purpose is a 'briefing by staff members' or concerns topics on the agenda of the public meeting. This," the newspaper continued, "is exactly what the *World-News* has complained about for many years. Governing bodies such as the old Salem Town Council and any number of boards of supervisors consistently meet at lunch, in an office or at the home of a member. There, items of the agenda were discussed and decided. When the body then met in open session, it ratified its decisions in minutes, often without discussion and without explanation to the citizen-taxpayers."

A glance at other state access statutes reveals ample opportunities for semantic fuzzing of the executive-privilege clause to give officials widespread latitude in holding secret conclaves. The Alaska law permits public exclusion "only from such portions thereof as deal with matters, the immediate knowledge of which would deleteriously affect the finances of the government unit, or that deal with subjects that tend to prejudice the reputation and character of persons."

The Delaware open-meeting statute is even vaguer, declaring, "The meetings of all boards and commissions . . . or any political subdivision thereof at which any business is transacted shall be open to the public and to . . . the press. *Nothing contained herein shall be construed to prohibit executive sessions or conferences of such boards and commissions at which no business shall be transacted*" (italics mine).

In Alaska, the decision as to what would "deleteriously affect" a council or school board's finances would obviously be made by those bodies themselves, which could interpret the phrase as they desired. They could also decide to discuss malfeasance charges against a city manager or superintendent under star chamber proceedings, explaining later that they were merely protecting the reputation of the individuals. The fact that the public has a right to know if an official is not satisfactorily performing his duties rarely enters the thinking of secrecy-minded lawmakers.

Experienced City Hall newsmen would likely regard the Delaware bill as laughable. They know that *business* is almost always transacted at private sessions. Frequently, the bulk of the give and take, the arguments, the compromises, etc., occur *in camera,* with the final decisions rubberstamped before the public. In hundreds of communities across America, this is the common way of carrying out public business. It's not asserted here that all secret meetings are excuses for skulduggery, but a commission that wants to pick the public's pocket can certainly do it more freely at a meeting in a firehouse backroom or private home than in regular chambers before an audience.

Last year, University of Arkansas students used the state's Freedom of Information Act to force the Board of Trustees to release the names of persons who received free football tickets for the past three years.[7] Subsequently, Arkansas Attorney General Ray Thornton promised to support proposals for an expanded law that would require agencies to summarize their activities in public and open their records to inspection. Handing out free football tickets may be a time-honored practice in Arkansas, but it seems clear that the trustees weren't anxious for the public to know about it.

The best open-meeting laws are those which restrict executive sessions to narrow subjects that can be reasonably defended as requiring private consideration, at least in the initial phase. An example would be a schoolteacher who had been accused of sexually molesting a student in his office. Such charges are usually brought by parents to the principal. If the accusation turns out to be false or maliciously inspired, it would, of course, cause great damage to the teacher's reputation if the facts were to be aired in public. A discussion of whether a city or school employee is physically or mentally competent to hold his job might also qualify for a closed hearing.

One of the most heartening developments for freedom of information advocates in recent years has been the Florida "Sunshine Law," which goes further than most guides in spelling out constraints on executive sessions. The rule was issued by the State Supreme Court in 1970, after the Miami City Council came under fire for holding "informal" executive sessions at which it did not take final action but from which it barred the press. The court states:

> We think that the time has arrived to declare this statement of the rule inconsistent with our entire concept of representative government as it has developed in our country. We therefore draw a sharp line of cleavage with the old rule which so often forced the public to pry open locked doors of secrecy. . . . Public records, and meetings where the public's business is conducted, should be held open

> and available to the public in the absence of some reasonable and legitimate restraint grounded on a constitutional or legislative provision or an established rule of public policy. . . . The public has the fundamental right to attend the meeting or see the records of any acts affecting their interests. . . . Any justification for secrecy must be established by the agency in a determination that the community interest is best served by secrecy rather than by informing the public.

The "Sunshine" ruling may stand as a landmark case in that its effect is to place the burden of proof on the government agency to justify denial of the public's right to know what's going on in the community. If the Florida principle catches on, it will mean that local officeholders must show that they are acting in the public's best interest when they meet behind closed doors. The idea is a long way from gaining popularity among local agencies throughout the land. Paul Fisher offered this somewhat bleak assessment of the situation:

> It is part of the folklore that citizens in this country should be able to attend, if they wish, meetings of public bodies. That isn't the fact. We define a public body with some difficulty and once we have it defined as a public body, we come up with any number of reasons why its meetings should be closed. Across the board, the states and municipalities do a much better job of spelling out when meetings won't be public than when they will be. Indeed, when they will be is, face it, much more a matter of grace than of legal requirement.

Some news organizations have learned, however, that "grace" is much more likely when officials are subjected to pressure and publicity. Indeed, a change from a closed to an open policy is usually the result of outraged howls by the media followed, in several instances, by legal action. A case in point was the suit last year by the Belvidere (Illinois) *Republican* against the Boone County Board of Supervisors, which had held a secret session to weigh the purchase of equipment for the sheriff's department. A Circuit Court judge ruled that the meeting violated the Illinois Open Meeting Act. The same judge decided that an earlier private meeting on test-borings of potential landfill sites did not violate the state law. State Circuit Judge Nelson Doi ruled in favor of a 1972 suit filed by the Hawaii Island Press Club against the County of Hawaii and the Ethics Board, which had claimed that a charter amendment permitted the board to close meetings by a two-thirds vote, declaring that sessions could be requested to be opened or closed only by a person being investigated by the board.

Lawsuits are not always necessary. In 1970, Sam Keach, managing editor of the *Robstown* (Texas) *Record,* was ejected from one of the Town Council's closed meetings. The next day, Keach ran a news story and an editorial explaining the Texas open-meeting law. He also published a front-page news item which began "City Fathers meet Monday" and ended "The meeting was adjourned"; between the two phrases there was nothing but blank space. The council subsequently opened its meetings to the *Record* and the public and they stayed open.

The Windom (Minnesota) City Council reversed a decision not to publish proceedings of its meetings in the *Cottonwood County Citizen and Reporter* after editor Ken Anderson had polled residents who overwhelmingly said they wanted them published. The South Carolina Legislature passed a freedom of information act in 1972 under constant pressure from the state's Sigma Delta Chi chapter. A compromise of sorts was worked out between the Roanoke (Virginia) City Council and local media which had complained about executive sessions.[8] The council adopted a series of guidelines defining the matters which could be discussed in closed meetings. The council also agreed to advise the mayor in writing of all items to be taken up in executive session, to announce the items in a prior open session, and to require a majority council vote before adjourning out of public earshot.

Experience has proved that a community with an aggressive, independent newspaper or broadcast station is more likely to have more open government, whatever the strength or lack of state FOI laws. Many councilmen and school-board members prefer meeting in secrecy, but they don't want the public to know about it. When a newspaper smokes out the meetings and exposes them in print, the officials are immediately forced to take a defensive position. They can't, after all, issue diatribes against the principles on which this country was founded. Media pressure has opened closed meetings in a number of communities or at least embarrassed agencies to the point where they held fewer secret ones. But even the most intense media objections will not budge some official bodies from their hiding places—particularly if the state has no open meeting statute. When an irate woman confronted a Port Washington, New York, school-board member about its frequent locked-door deliberations, he replied calmly, "We have a right to meet in executive session." He knew that the community's two weekly newspapers had not even questioned the board's secrecy habit, much less demanded that it be stopped.

Municipal agencies offer a variety of excuses for shutting themselves off from public view. The most common is that much of their time is spent on routine business that is not of public interest and, indeed, would bore citizens who sat through it. Officials usually add that this workload can be finished much more quickly if they are not interrupted by questions from the audience. They ask taxpayers to keep in mind that important matters will be acted on in open session in any event.

But other reasons are given. One Pennsylvania city official defended executive sessions, explaining, "The council has to present a unified picture to the public—one big happy family. We don't want any arguments reported." A Wyoming state representative objected to an open-meeting law because "it would do away with frank, open discussions of the problems of town councils and school boards." In Port Washington, a school-board member said that "We'd never get any work done if we held all our meetings in the open." A school-board trustee in a New Jersey suburban community put it this way: "The job doesn't pay enough for me to take the crap I know I'm going to get if we throw the whole meeting open to the public."

Some bodies, more aware of their responsibilities, limit closed sessions to sensitive personnel matters and discussions of acquisition of rights-of-way or property purchases. A few years ago a Topeka, Kansas, street commissioner refused to attend a secret meeting. He told the mayor in a letter: "One of the commission's biggest jobs is to keep the public informed about commission activity."

Gordon J. DeHond, President of the Rochester, New York, Board of Education and a State Senator, described how he resolved the question of meeting openly or privately:

> When I was elected president of the board we had executive sessions every week and public meetings every first and third Thursday. I immediately checked and found that the education law required privacy on personnel items and property acquisition only. After discussion with the board, the majority, though listing many private reservations, left it to my discretion. I immediately opened up all meetings except in the two areas limited by law. This meant staff reports as well as budget preparation were now discussed openly with the press at hand.
>
> This was the best thing I could have done. Not only did this improve credibility of the board and school district but people saw what problems really existed in running a large metropolitan government. More [news] articles and interest in education appeared and the simplistic solutions so commonly offered at public meetings diminished. . . . The idea worked fabulously.

A similarly enlightened view is taken by Jack E. Case, an official for the North Dakota League of Cities: "Some might feel that [a closed meeting] is the utopian way of conducting the public business, free of criticism or complaint. But in the end it also means freedom from public support. In short, we believe that the business of the governing board is the public's business, and members of the board have an inescapable obligation to keep the public . . . informed of their decisions and the reasons which dictated them. . . . Sooner or later you are going to need the support of that 'informed electorate' and what they don't understand they will oppose." [9]

These approaches are refreshing but not in wide acceptance. In numerous cases, the rationale offered for secret deliberations masks the true reasons: the arrogance of power, a contempt for the public's right to know, or a basic misunderstanding of the democratic process.

In many communities, agencies convene in early morning or mid-day, thereby evading both the media and the public who find the hours inconvenient. Robert M. White II, editor and publisher of the *Mexico* (Missouri) *Ledger,* and former chairman of the American Society of Newspaper Editors' Freedom of Information Committee, said: "In city after city across the nation, reporters consistently face the age-old problem of the city official, from the highest level to the lowest, who finds reasons not to reveal his mistakes, his follies, his less-than-well-done job. However, there is another side of the coin. Every newspaper and news medium in the country wishes it had the quality of staff required to dig out the misdeeds at city halls and state houses. Few of us have that much of a staff. So there is sometimes a successful kind of censorship solely because of our own inability to do that which we day-to-day try to do and to which we are dedicated."

Most dailies and weeklies have staffing problems, but it's difficult to conceal a secret meeting in a small town. Even if the location of the gathering is not known, which it usually is, an editor can normally depend on a leak or tip to point him in the right direction. What he does with the information is another thing. Although he may not have been privy to the deliberation, there is nothing to prevent him from publishing an editorial condemning the whole practice of secret government as antidemocratic and a violation of public trust. Nothing that is except, perhaps, a publisher who lacks the will and the courage to take a stand on the issue, or who may fear loss of advertising if his newspaper challenges the established order. City council, school-board members, etc., are often business owners in the community as well. There also is the publisher-businessman with no real commitment to freedom of information or free press principles. He may have inherited the paper or come up through the business and advertising sides. Some of these men hold up the banner of fearless journalism at publishers' conventions and other press forums, but in their home towns they effectively check any crusading desires their editors or reporters might have.

More than one young journalism graduate has been discouraged by the supine role he and his daily newspaper have had to take. Not only are newsmen prevented from turning the spotlight on closed meetings but they must skirt other taboo subjects besides. A chemical-plant explosion was reported in a Michigan daily, but when a reporter wanted to write a follow-up story on the plant being a continuing hazard for the community, he was blocked by the publisher's order. In northern Westchester County, New York, most of the village boards hold secret meetings without a murmur of protest from the local media. Such cravenness by some community newspapers has caused idealistic young reporters to quit the business in disgust.

Not all publishers are intimidated by the Establishment. In recent years, weekly editor-publishers in Arkansas and California have fought the right-to-know battle at a risk to their lives and property. *The New York Times, The Washington Post,* the *Los Angeles Times* and other papers have battled the government and state prosecutors who attempted to force reporters to reveal their confidential sources. The *Post,* particularly, showed both courage and journalistic zeal in uncovering facets of the Watergate case. But it is still true that while these incidents are making headlines, day-to-day secrecy remains a problem in hundreds of communities across the land. The struggle for access to official meetings is too often lost by default by the press and public.

The latter must share the blame with timid news media for the proliferation of secret government at the local level. Concerted public protest over court meetings is rare. The usual exception is when a homeowners' association or neighborhood group unites, for example, against a city council holding a clandestine session on a specific issue affecting the residents. Mass community protest condemning secret meetings on principle is virtually nonexistent—even if a local newspaper or radio station hammers away constantly on the problem. To many citizens, the right-to-know question concerns only the media and the city fathers. They do not see themselves as being involved. Indeed, it's not uncommon for some spectators to side with officials who bar the press and public from their meetings. A reporter in a small Illinois town was berated by a woman for being "nosy" when he tried unsuccessfully to gain entry to a council meeting in the mayor's office. A common assumption is that if municipal officials want to meet privately or withhold records, "They must know what they're doing. After all, they're running the city."

A survey by the Richmond *News Leader* found "little apparent public support" of the Virginia Freedom of Information Act passed in 1968 and amended in 1970. According to the study, "The public is more unaware than unconcerned about the law and its content because there is such a great variety of news sources that it does not occur to them that information is being withheld."

"The press is viewed as the antagonist in battles with politicians," said David Laventhol, editor of *Newsday*. "The politicians know this and play off the press against the public whose support they count on. The public has little understanding of the First Amendment. If we take on a local government agency about secrecy or other wrongdoing, we are often accused by people of interfering with correct process. When one of our investigative stories concerning politicians is published, we are often attacked by readers. Why are you doing this? they say."

Part of the problem may lie in the popular image of the press in general and the newsman in particular. Despite the fact that newspapers and reporters have grown more responsible (and perhaps more conservative) since the 1920s and 1930s, the stereotyped idea of the news business as being sensational and irresponsible persists. Occupational ratings by high-school students generally put journalism well down the list behind judges, lawyers, doctors, teachers, scientists, etc. Studies have shown that some people still derive their idea of newspapermen and women from exaggerated models offered by the movies, television, and popular literature. The enduring popularity of *The Front Page*, a hectic drama about Chicago journalism in the Jazz Age, is evidence that the stereotype lingers on.

The advent of broadcast news has done little to erase the stereotype and may even have enhanced it. Television footage showing scrambling newsmen thrusting microphones into the faces of newsmakers may well confirm the impression of some viewers that reporters are a band of ruffians, after all. Journalists in both the print and broadcast media, suffer from the fact that the news-gathering process is little understood by the public. In addition, the press is often blamed for the bad news it reports, a factor which made it easier for the Nixon administration to harass and vilify it.

There is some evidence, however, that the public is taking a kinder view of the press since its exposure of the Watergate affair and other secret government operations. Watergate also had the effect of easing the administration's attacks on the media.

II Access to Records

The penchant of local officials for meeting secretly is equaled only by their zeal in concealing records and data from prying reporters. Whether it be the police log or a list of building permits issued, a number of newsmen have a difficult time gaining access to them.

In some instances, the documents are made available only with the help of a court order. The Monmouth County (New Jersey) *Courier* won a legal fight in 1971 to force Middletown Township officials to reveal the records of a subdivision purchase. The weekly *Voice-Jeffersonian* in St. Matthews (Kentucky), a Louisville suburb, sued community officials last year, demanding that they give the paper access to all public records. The action followed a ruling by the city attorney that the paper could see City Council minutes, ordinances, and resolutions adopted by the council and police-court docket books. In Williamson, West Virginia, the *News* filed an action asking that the mayor and the police department be ordered to open arrest records to the newspaper's reporters. A Circuit Court judge ruled against the *News* in 1971, but an out-of-court compromise was later reached. Last year, New York City councilmen charged that public information about city employees and salaries had been "shrouded in secrecy." [10] City administration officials conceded that laws requiring publication in the *City Record* of the annual reports of city agencies and of employee salary changes had not been "fully observed" in recent years. They blamed the omission on the mayor's economy measures, denying any intent toward concealment.

When officials block access to records, newsmen cannot carry out their normal duties. A police reporter who cannot get at the police blotter is of little use to his newspaper or broadcast station. A county-court reporter checks the vital statistics as part of his job. The City Hall reporter may want to see the bids submitted for a big sewer project but finds they are not available. In each case, the public is being cheated out of information to which it's entitled in an open society.

The reasons for denial of access vary. The police chief may be feuding with the local newspaper and puts the blotter off limits to its reporters in sheer spite. A council which has awarded a sewer-building job to the brother-in-law of one of its members even though he was not the lowest bidder, isn't disposed to have the action known. Minor clerks and other low-grade employees often aren't sure of what they can and can't release so they play it safe by releasing nothing. In still other instances, hidden records hide embezzlement and other crimes.

Hostility between police chiefs and newspapers is fairly common. A running feud involving the Findlay (Ohio) *Republican-Courier* and the city's police chief has, at this writing, dragged on for months with no end in sight.[11] Chief Morris Frankhouser began a policy in October 1972 of denying the newspaper the right to inspect such information as the names and addresses of those involved in auto accidents and arrests and the names and addresses of businesses and homes which had been burglarized. Meanwhile, Frankhouser has a pending lawsuit against two *Republican-Courier* reporters stemming from their story about alleged dissension in the police department.

The Massachusetts Supreme Court last year denied the Wayland-Weston *Town Crier* a writ of mandamus which would have required the police chief to give the paper access to the police log and arrest record.[12] The decision illustrates the fact that loopholes are as prevalent in open-record laws as in open-meeting statutes. The Massachusetts open records act states that any records which are kept or are required to be kept by law shall be made public. The newspaper argued that the first part of the law meant any records kept by a municipality. Police Chief Frank O. Shaw retorted that the records in question are filed only for the town's convenience and are not required by law and therefore do not have to be made available to the press. The Supreme Court declared: "'If we adopted the petitioners' interpretation, governmental records of every nature and description would be subject to public scrutiny. . . . we are convinced that while the legislature has liberalized access to governmental records since the enactment of the first statute defining 'public records,' it has at no time broadened the statutory definition to cover, in effect, all records kept by public officials, regardless of whether they contain entries made pursuant to a requirement of law."

The question of police records being made public lies in a gray area. The news media generally take the position that they should be disclosed and have fought in and out of court for access to them. State open-record laws do not include police logs or arrest records among the documents to be shown to the press and public on demand. The *St. Louis Globe Democrat* found this out when it pressed police for information about a rape suspect a few years ago.[13] Officers balked at the request, referring the newspaper to the St. Louis County prosecuting attorney, who said; "Police chiefs don't have to tell you or the public a dammed thing. It's their prerogative to handle a case the way they want. There's nothing in the statute that says you or the public have to know a thing about police investigations. Police records are not public." But if the Missouri records law does not specify police files, it does state that: "Except as otherwise provided by law, all state, county and municipal records shall at all reasonable times be open for a personal inspection by any citizen of Missouri, and those in charge of the records shall not refuse the privilege to any citizen." The language, which is similar to that of most open-record acts, does not appear to exclude police data.

The city attorney of Bay City, Michigan, did not think that his state's record law gave the police any kind of exemption from public scrutiny. Last year he ruled that the City Commission had erred when it ordered the police to withhold the names of victims or complainants in crimes at their request. According to the city attorney, such names are part of the police record, which newsmen have a "general right of access to and inspection of."

Disputes between the media and the police appear to be on the rise. This can be partly attributed to the fact that a new breed of young editors and reporters are staffing newspaper and broadcast stations. They are less likely to be intimidated by police news blackouts and also prefer to keep their relationship with officers on a professional level. Thus, they are able to probe more deeply into alleged police corruption than the traditional police-beat reporter, who was usually on a friendly, first-name basis with the lawmen. The racial and political turmoil of the 1960s produced a hardening of attitudes between police and the media. As police were criticized for their sometimes brutal handling of hippies, war protesters, and minority group members, they became increasingly defensive and hostile in dealing with the media. The culmination came during the 1968 Democratic Presidential Convention in Chicago, where police beat up a number of reporters and photographers. In recent years, police have restricted news in a number of American cities, including Fremont, California, New York City, Minneapolis, and San Francisco.

Access to other kinds of records, notably welfare rolls and personal-data files, is also a source of contention between local officials and the media. The clash over welfare records reflects a split between the press and public, which demand their availability on the grounds that public money is involved, and welfare bureaucrats and some civil libertarians who contend that disclosure would be an invasion of privacy. William K. Babel, editor and publisher of the weekly *Enterprise & Journal* of Orange, Massachusetts, expressed the first point of view: "Welfare operation has been one area of government spending that has operated in great secrecy. For the idea has long persisted that it would be embarrassing to reveal publicly the names of welfare recipients and how much they receive. . . . Yet this is public money that is being spent and in astronomic proportions. And we are not allowed as citizens to know who gets welfare aid, how much they get, or anything about the circumstances of their cases. . . . Why should government persist in the Puritan idea that this is an area that must be kept secret and private and free from the public eye?" [14]

The conflict over welfare files remains unresolved in most states, including those with open-record laws. The laws do not specify welfare data, thereby throwing the issue into litigation when disclosure is demanded. Pennsylvania's Commonwealth Court, in a historic decision, directed the State Secretary of Welfare to open the state's welfare rolls to inspection by the *Philadelphia Inquirer.*[15] The unanimous opinion ended a year-long battle between the newspaper and the state over access to the names and addresses of welfare recipients. The *Inquirer's* executive editor, John McMullan, hailed the ruling as a "victory for the people of Pennsylvania," and added: "We are gratified at the court's reinforcement of the principle that governmental operations in a democracy must be conducted out in the open rather than in bureaucratic secrecy. The bona fide welfare recipient has nothing to fear from our scrutiny of the rolls. We are interested only in the abuses that have caused the costs of welfare to skyrocket."

Disputes over personal data files generally occur at the federal and state levels (Army, FBI, state police, etc.), but there are local counterparts. Professor Arthur Miller of the University of Michigan Law School testified before a Senate subcommittee that files on political activists are maintained by police departments in most major cities.[16] Miller noted that New York state's Identification and Intelligence System had confidential files on 4 million people—only half of whom have criminal records. Some light was shed in Chicago in 1972 when the police department, which had been under strong criticism for alleged hostility toward blacks and Latin Americans, turned over its files of police brutality charges for review by the Chicago Human Relations Commission.[17]

The *Des Moines Register* reported (August 12, 1972) that a secret group of undercover policemen had been operating in nine Iowa cities for nine months with the stated objective of gathering data on organized crime, police corruption, and narcotics peddling. The surveillance activity, the *Register* said, was paid for with $373,000 in federal money from the Law Enforcement Assistance Administration of the Justice Department, which dispenses funds for the federal anticrime program. According to the newspaper, the project was so secret that even the Iowa Crime Commission didn't know what the group was doing.

III Secrecy by Gag Rule

Reporters collect much of their information by interviewing governmental officials. Getting a story often requires talking to the mayor, police chief, district attorney, city manager, etc., or their subordinates. Access to meetings and records doesn't always give the newsman all the facts he needs. So explanation, interpretation, and additional details must be obtained from knowledgeable sources. When these sources aren't allowed to talk for publication or broadcast, the information flow is quickly clogged up. Administrators and departmental chiefs may order their underlings to tell the press nothing, arrogating to themselves the sole right to make official statements—if any are made at all. Case histories show that gag rule is practiced quite freely in local government.

Honolulu Mayor Frank Fasi denied *Star-Bulletin* reporters access to his office and department heads for what he termed the newspaper's attempt to discredit his administration. Cheyenne Mayor James Van Velzor last year ordered all city departments to clear all press releases with him before handing them out. The edict, the Mayor explained, "is not an attempt to censor or suppress the news. This is so we have proper coordination." In Hartsville, South Carolina, the Town Council passed a resolution that it must approve any town news before it was distributed to the media. Censorship? Not according to Councilman P. H. Beattie, who said the move was merely to insure that what was printed about Hartsville was correct. The resolution came after the Florence *Morning News* ran a story which claimed that drug arrests in Hartsville had increased 900 per cent from 1970 to 1971.

The San Francisco County Sheriff's Department also found what it felt were good reasons for its muzzling of employees last year.[18] An order by Undersheriff Reuben Greenberg prohibited "any statement to the press or any other representative of the news media regarding any incident in the county jail, court or other place or situation." Greenberg asserted there was nothing new about the gag, citing a section of the department's rules allegedly barring statements to the press by rank-and-file employees. Greenberg added that the regulation also was meant to keep office workers from giving out names and addresses of deputies to everyone who called.

"We have to protect our men from any released inmate who might attempt to settle a score," he explained. "We intend to continue our cooperation with newsmen. It's just that we want to beef up a professionalism that has been absent from the department in the past."

Milwaukee Journal reporters must work downward from the mayor's office when they cover City Hall. Mayor Henry Maier has been feuding with the *Journal* since 1967 after a dispute on civil rights issues, and on December 17, 1971, Mr. Maier announced that he would no longer answer questions from the two daily newspapers, the *Journal* and the *Milwaukee Sentinel,* and the WTMJ television and radio stations, all owned by The Journal Company.[19] The *Journal* editor, Richard Leonard, said, however, that Mr. Maier's blackout has not extended to other City Hall departments to which *Journal* reporters have regular access. The newspaper's City Hall men, Lawrence Lohmann and Joel McNally, reported no difficulty in covering the Common Council, committee meetings, and hearings, even when the Mayor was participating. "There's been no change in any city department except the Mayor's office itself that I know of," McNally said. "People let the Mayor go his way and they go their way."

Despite the above examples, local gagging of city employees would appear to be far less of an access problem than that of meetings and records. Enterprising reporters usually have inside contacts who will leak information on a not-for-attribution basis, however riled by the press their bosses may be. In addition, almost every City Hall or school administration has disgruntled staff members who will go out of their way to thwart administrators. A foolproof gag order is wishful thinking on the part of its originator. To enforce it he would have to keep tabs on his staff twenty-four hours a day. Then, too, such regulations are often lifted voluntarily when the administrator discovers that he doesn't have time to function as his own public relations agent and attend to his regular duties as well.

IV The Public Interest

There is ample evidence that local government carries on much of its business in secret, even in states where laws forbid or restrict the practice. So far, the fight against closed meetings and records has been waged almost entirely by the more courageous and tough-minded elements of the communications media. There has been little help from the public, which, for the most part, is either apathetic or actually sympathetic to the government.

Newspapers and broadcast stations should join in efforts to get the public on their side of the issue. Our democratic heritage notwithstanding, most people are simply not aroused over the fact that they are being denied the right to watch their elected officials conduct *public* business. The antipress climate generated by the Nixon administration undoubtedly has contributed to public hostility toward the media and an indifference to their disagreements with local politicians on access. There's also the "You can't fight City Hall" attitude which has seeped through our society. Finally, vast numbers of people are ignorant of their rights and their leaders' obligations.

As experts in communication, newspapers and broadcasters are ideally equipped to swing the public to their point of view. They can, for example, launch a public-relations campaign that would define clearly what their readers have at stake in the access issue. Editorials and interpretive articles could be reprinted for distribution to schools, parent-teacher groups, local action organizations, and the business community; speakers could be made available to explain the problem at community gatherings.

If the news media want public support against the encroachments of federal, state, and local governments on the First Amendment, they've got to go out and get it. At the same time, they can help their cause by increasing efforts to be fair and accurate in presenting news. The aloofness which has characterized the news industry for many years is an unaffordable luxury in the 1970s. Readers can no longer be written off by being offered a letter-to-the-editor—or even an Op-Ed page. The media must make a hard sell if they want the public's help in breaking down the doors of secrecy in government.

Meanwhile, efforts should continue to obtain passage of right-to-know laws in states without them and to strengthen those already on the books. As pointed out earlier, some open-meeting and open-record laws are weakly drawn and subject to easy circumvention by local officials. Contrary to the cynicism displayed by some newsmen toward these statues, they do make it harder for politicians and administrators to bottle up news. As Henry Stasiuk, managing editor of the Newark (New Jersey) *Star-Ledger*, put it: "The open meeting law may not be perfect but it gives us leverage. We can raise hell about a secret meeting and know we've got the legal right to do so." Most of all, perhaps, newspapers and broadcasters should be unrelenting in efforts to put public activities under a spotlight. The public may come around, freedom-of-information laws might become stronger, but there's no substitute for hard-nosed reporters and editors who will blow the whistle on any elected official who tries to do public business in private.

V Discussion

MR. GLASSER: I think it is important to say that what Professor Stein has told you is pervasively true at every level. Practically every local institution which people experience, from the time they enter school when they are six or seven years old, plays a large role in creating the patterns of cultural acceptance which I think makes a Watergate or Pentagon Papers case possible. The pre-eminent examples of that are school boards and school systems. They function with all the habits of official lawlessness, noncompliance, official secrecy, and noninformation that we have talked about on a larger scale the last few months.

People are compelled to attend these institutions throughout their childhood and youth. They learn the political habits which will later form the basis of their behavior as adult citizens. It is not surprising that people think the President is above the law. All of us go to school and learn that the school principal is above the law. All of us learn that every day. A few years ago, a school student asked me if it was true that it was against the law for the principal to suspend a girl for wearing slacks in the winter. I said yes, there is a judicial decision about that. He said it happens all the time in his school, and could he have a copy of that decision? Information being a weapon, I gave him a copy, and he went and mimeographed three thousand copies—no revolution is complete without a mimeograph machine. He went in front of the school and distributed those copies, whereupon he was suspended for distributing seditious literature. The student, not yet then a radical, pointed to the part of the social-studies textbook about James Madison, freedom of speech, and John Peter Zenger. The principal was not impressed. Then the student showed him the decision, and said it was the law. The principal said, "I don't care what the law is, I run my school the way I see fit."

If I have heard that once about a principal, I have heard it a hundred times, and we have heard it also from welfare institutions, housing agencies, sanitation departments, and police departments. It is endemic in all of these institutions.

People subject to these institutions—and the schools are critically important here—learn very quickly that you say one thing, you subscribe to a set of ideals, but you act in another way. People learn that if you step out of line and go against the rule of man, never mind what the rule of law says, you get zapped. They learn that very quickly. I think they learn to internalize that so that they never step out of line. People in positions of power are able to go along unchecked, and it is rare when a person does not go along. Those habits are learned early.

The question of school suspensions in every major city in New York State is vexing and disputatious. In New York City a few years ago, we did a study of one hundred fifteen school suspensions in which we represented students who came off the street to us. We found out that in every single one of them there were several violations of the Board of Education's own bylaws.

We published our study. It ran in the press. The *Times* published an editorial no less outraged in tone than any it has run on Watergate. We raised the question, and the *Times* raised the question, of the other fourteen thousand suspensions that occur annually in New York City. Are they all in violation of the law too? We wanted information about them. The Board of Education never answered. It does not answer letters, it does not answer us, it does not answer *The New York Times*, it does not answer anybody. Nobody needs to answer because nobody is accountable to anybody. That is a pattern learned quickly.

What is happening to most of those kids who are out on the streets, those fourteen thousand kids? They have few options; if you are black and poor and don't have a high-school diploma these days, your options are to get on welfare or escape into drugs. If you are more together and competent, and you have some skills, you turn to crime or the Army. That's about it. And this problem permeates the crisis in our cities. The welfare problem, the drug problem, the school problem, the unemployment problem—all of these are partially related to the fact that kids are not finishing school because of suspensions about which we cannot get any information. This problem is referred to in the literature and the press as a "drop-out" problem, which is to say a student's problem. But in fact it is a *push-out* problem. That is what the schools are doing, illegally. The language defines our reality; the language we read in the press determines the way we look at the problem by calling it a "drop-out" problem. The possible political responses, once legislators start to look at the problem, are already determined. The institution means to control the words it uses to describe the problem, because to do so is to control the solution.

Hannah Arendt wrote a book about the Eichmann trial which was subtitled *The Banality of Evil*. I think we might well begin to look at the banality of secrecy and the banality of official lawlessness. What is terrifying about official lawlessness and official secrecy is not that it is an aberration, but precisely that it is routine.

MR. MARTIN: I served in state and local government in both the legislative and executive branches. I would like to distinguish between open records and open meetings. There may be virtue in having a system that affords the opportunity to meet in public, to meet in something less than public, and to meet in secret.

MR. STEIN: What I have found in communities with secret meetings is that the open meeting is simply an opportunity for the board members to rubber-stamp whatever they have decided on in secret. This is a common practice. It is done every day. Do I see a justification for closed meetings? I do. An example is if a teacher, let us say, were accused of a morals charge in connection with a student, and this was simply the result of an hysterical mother. Certainly I think that teacher would be entitled to have the charge, at least initially, heard in a closed session. But the point is that school boards and city councils simply don't confine it to those special issues. They discuss everything in secret and they do it all the time.

PART TWO

— OPEN GOVERNMENT

Administering the Freedom of Information Act: An Insider's View

—by Robert L. Saloschin

About ten years ago, when my children were in the public schools, the members of our elected county school board got into a dispute about a very searching questionnaire which had been administered to some of the older students. According to the newspapers, certain board members said this questionnaire invaded the privacy of the students' families, but other members said it had been prepared at Princeton and was a bona-fide instrument of educational research. I was actively interested in school affairs at that time and I became curious which side was right. So I telephoned the office of the School Superintendent and asked to see a blank copy of this controversial questionnaire. The answer was a firm bureaucratic no. There was no Freedom of Information Act for me to turn to, but I told the Superintendent's office that I thought it would be easy to get resolutions adopted by various PTA's with appropriate publicity, demanding the disclosure of this questionnaire as a matter of legitimate interest to the parents, taxpayers, and voters. After a short delay, they changed their minds and gave me a copy. I discovered when I read it that both sides were right—the questionnaire was obviously a sincere project in educational research and also a serious invasion of privacy. In addition, there had been little if any reason for resisting my request to see a blank copy of it, although no one should have seen the completed questionnaires unless the students' anonymity was protected.

These days about 90 per cent of my work involves the Freedom of Information Act, including the counseling of federal agencies on how the Act applies to requests for access to their records. I sometimes remember my skirmish over that school questionnaire, and I hope it helps me to see the problems of governmental withholding of information from both sides.

The Freedom of Information Act gives anyone the right to see any agency records, unless they come under specified exemptions, with a right to sue the agency if access is denied, and with the burden on the agency to justify a denial. Most of the legal problems under the Act involve the applicability of the various exemptions to an infinite variety of records and of circumstances pertaining to them.

I Experience under the Act

After a decade of effort sparked by the news media, the Act was passed on July 4, 1966; it became effective exactly one year later; and it now appears as Section 552 in Title 5 of the United States Code. The Act was reprinted with explanations in the Attorney General's Memorandum of June 1967, which was issued by Attorney General Ramsey Clark after exhaustive consultations with, among others, the Congressional committees which had reported this legislation plus media organizations supporting it.

A basic feature of the Act is the provision for decentralized administration: each agency acts upon requests for its own records. This is probably wise, but it creates a need for coordination, which the Justice Department tries to meet. On March 10, 1972, Ralph Erickson, then head of the Office of Legal Counsel in the Justice Department, testified at the Moorhead hearings and gave a comprehensive report on the Justice Department's role in administering the Act, detailing the work of our Freedom of Information Committee in counseling other agencies. On May 8, 1973, the present head of OLC, Assistant Attorney General Robert G. Dixon, Jr., testified on legislative proposals in this field and described recent steps we have taken to improve administration of the Act.

We have now had almost six years' experience in administering the Act. While this may seem like a lot, it is not really a great deal because the Act can touch almost everything the government does or knows about, and its full ramifications will take years to develop.

But six years of experience is something. There are now reported court opinions in more than fifty cases under the Act, although only one has reached the Supreme Court, and there are more than seventy-five FOI cases pending in the courts. There have been extensive hearings by Congressional committees, especially Chairman Moorhead's 1972 hearings. The Justice Department's Freedom of Information Committee was created at the end of 1969 to provide speedy and informal consultations with agencies planning to issue final denials of requests for their records in order to screen such denials and reduce unnecessary litigation. This Committee has reviewed approximately two hundred contemplated final denials and has responded to several times that many inquiries from agencies seeking preliminary advice.

It would be interesting to discuss how the Act relates to other fields of information law, such as pretrial discovery, executive privilege, the security classification of documents, and the law of intellectual property. I would particularly enjoy discussing freedom of information in its cultural context, relating it to developments like the computer, and to the traditional yet changing values and roles of individuals and institutions in our society. I suspect that the ultimate application of some of the exemptions in the Act, like some clauses in our Constitution, may be shaped and perhaps should be shaped by a deep understanding of critical and complex aspects of our civilization. For example, what we mean by privacy will affect our reading of the 6th exemption, and how we view the process of policy-making and decision-making will color our understanding of the 5th exemption. But instead of exploring these questions, I shall confine myself to some fairly firm tentative conclusions, based upon the experience of the Justice Department.

First, however, let me comment on the data base of these conclusions. We are dealing with day-to-day problems under a statute regulating access to billions of records, handled by millions of past and present federal employees, in hundreds of activities and programs conducted by dozens of agencies. Statistics can be misleading in this field, except to indicate the almost infinite variety of the potential problems. Although our office probably sees more situations than either the courts or Congressional committees, we nevertheless see only a fraction of the action. We find ourselves encountering unforeseen and often difficult problems at an undiminished rate. But there are some things we are relatively sure of, and for convenience I will put them in question-and-answer form.

1. Is the Act having a substantial effect? Unquestionably, yes, even if so far it is not so much as some people would hope. Agency after agency now makes available records previously withheld, and this trend will continue.

2. Are the effects of the Act beneficial? This may seem to some to be a strange question, but it is worth asking. The benefits probably outweigh the detriments, although a really thorough appraisal of either would require exhaustive study and sophisticated judgment. For example, it is almost impossible to determine the true economic costs of the Act. Benefits can be expected, even if they are hard to measure, where an agency is prone to questionable performance, for the Act tends to keep it on its toes. Apart from this, the Act may help to keep all agencies from becoming too insular in their outlook. And, naturally, benefits flow to private persons, either as requesters or as members of the public, when they obtain valuable information.

The other side of the coin is that the Act has few restraints on abuses, since the purpose of the request and its burden are generally irrelevant. Accordingly, the Act serves not only Ralph Nader and news media concerned with the public's right to know, but it also serves defense contractors seeking to resist the renegotiation of their excess profits, and corporations resisting regulation to reduce the lead in gasoline. In other words, requesters use the Act for their own ends—good, bad, or indifferent. The chief detriments, apart from the unmeasured costs to the taxpayer, are probably the potentially adverse effects upon individual privacy and upon the effective discharge of certain vital government functions. The task of good administration is to try to maximize the benefits and minimize the detriments.

3. Is the Justice Department, and particularly its Freedom of Information Committee, a force for greater withholding or for greater disclosure? Agencies are asked to consult the Committee only when they contemplate a final denial, not if they grant access. We advise against denial in roughly a third of the cases we screen, and we indicate that a second third are highly uncertain. We also remind the agencies that an exemption does not require them to deny but merely gives them that option.

4. How can access to government information be further improved? Are amendments to the Freedom of Information Act necessary? From our vantage point in the Justice Department, the basic obstacle to improved public access is not the Act. Although some of the wording may be clumsy, the courts have generally resolved legal doubts in favor of disclosure. Similar pressures for disclosure, whether or not the law requires it, come from Congress, the press, and others. It is increasingly clear that where access is still inadequate, the primary need is not to change the law but to improve agency compliance with its letter and spirit.

I am not thinking primarily of deliberate noncompliance, because such instances are rare. I am talking about the quantity and quality of the effort that goes into the processing of requests for access. This naturally varies from agency to agency and from time to time. But this is where most of the real opportunity for solid improvement lies. It will take time, money, effort, and understanding to upgrade this processing. It does not generally lend itself to mass-production methods.

Let me put it in another way. Anyone who is seriously concerned with unwarranted secrecy in government and seeks constructive improvement in this field should realistically face the facts of agency life. Less than ideal compliance has various causes. It is often due to organizational problems, changes in structure or personnel, or the fact that an agency does not have the money or the qualified staff to handle its freedom-of-information work load on top of its main mission and regular functions.

And we must remember that the regular functions of government agencies have become much more complex. Gone are the days of the old Lighthouse Service, which kept the lights burning. Gone is the CAA, which kept the airways operating. Its present-day successor, the FAA, and for that matter almost all federal agencies, have in recent years been confronted with a greatly expanded series of complex and interrelated public concerns which demand better solutions than every before. You will recognize these concerns: environmental impact, energy crisis, a shifting world power structure, inflation, balance of payments, equal opportunity, metropolitan planning, and others that have not yet fully emerged.

Agencies must deal with these matters in the face of an information explosion and a popular revolution of rising expectations. Superimposed on this burgeoning situation is the Freedom of Information Act, creating a new field of administrative responsibility. The field grows as the public becomes increasingly aware of it, and yet no appropriations have ever been made to administer the Act. The work created by the Act, which is often complex and time-consuming, has simply been additional work for existing staffs, usually performed on a squeeze-it-into-your-regular-work basis. When a massive request is filed, and when further such requests are expected, how do agency employees react?

An agency employee who is indifferent to his job would probably not care who browses through agency files. Most employees, however, take their jobs seriously and tend to identify with their assignments, their agency, and "their" files. As a citizen and a taxpayer for whom these employees work, I am glad they identify with their missions, and I imagine most people would probably agree. But there is a side effect. Any freedom-of-information request that hits the employee's in-box is likely to take time from his regular work. The employee's approach may also be affected if the requester projects himself as an adversary. In these circumstances, some doubts about granting access may be resolved against release, especially in view of the natural fear of creating a bad precedent. Similar attitudes can also be found in nongovernmental organizations.

The most practical way to meet this situation is to provide better guidance, training, and help for agency staffs. Oversight from all the sources in and out of the government which now provide it has been and can still be a useful prod, especially if it is informed with a regard for the problems that confront the agencies, as well as those that confront requesters. In other words, agency personnel will give greater recognition to the public's right to know when it is reconciled with respect for the importance, complexity, and dedication of their regular work—work which was also mandated by Congress. With enough qualified personnel, we can provide more leadership in training, research, guidance, and review, and the agencies can process requests more quickly without sacrifice of quality, all of which will generally upgrade the administration of the Act.

On June 26, 1973, Attorney General Elliot Richardson, testifying in a joint hearing by three Senate subcommittees on various aspects of government secrecy, announced four actions being taken by the Justice Department to encourage better administration of the Act:

> — First, we will request the Civil Service Commission to include freedom-of-information material in its executive training and legal training programs and to assist us in arranging for inclusion of similar material in other programs for training government personnel.
>
> — Second, we will conduct an interagency symposium on the Freedom of Information Act before the end of this year, to emphasize the need for improved administration and to provide wider sharing of problems and ideas. This symposium will involve two-way communications as well as direct presentations, and we plan to invite the participation of Congressional and private speakers.
>
> — Third, we will promptly institute discussions with the Administrative Conference of the United States, the Civil Service Commission, the Office of Management and Budget, and perhaps other agencies, seeking their assis-

tance in launching a comprehensive study of how the executive branch can better organize itself to administer the Act, both within and among the agencies. This study will cover staffing, budgeting, training, and meeting the need for research in the application of the Act to major areas like government procurement, regulatory programs, law enforcement, and computerized records. It will cover the extent to which desirable improvements should be effected by legislation, executive order, or departmental orders. It will take account of inputs from outside the executive branch, and it is designed to point the way to sound and relatively permanent improvements, including greater speed of processing, greater uniformity, and greater disclosure. Our objective will be to have this study launched within ninety days and completed within one year, with reports to be furnished to Congress.

— Fourth, I will immediately remind all federal agencies of this Department's standing request that they consult our Freedom of Information Committee before issuing final denials of requests under the Act. In this connection, I will order our litigating divisions not to defend freedom-of-information lawsuits against the agencies unless the Committee has been consulted. And I will instruct the Committee to make every possible effort to advance the objective of the fullest responsible disclosure.

II Information and Democracy

Freedom of information fits into the overriding goal of permitting our free society to survive. The importance of an informed public in a democracy is obvious. It should be equally obvious that knowledge is power, at least to the extent the holder can utilize it. To preserve a free society, power must be diffused among the different branches and levels of government and among individuals and private groups, with safeguards against undue encroachments by any public or private entity. Thus, to preserve the position of individuals and groups outside of government, it may be important that the government, when it holds recorded information about them, sometimes be permitted and if necessary encouraged to protect their privacy and autonomy. These considerations generally underlie exemptions 4 and 6 in the Act.

If we look at our history, for example at the Alien and Sedition Acts or the Army-McCarthy hearings, we have some reason for confidence that encroachments involving information control can be checked by the Constitution and by our institutions before they go too far. But if we look at world history, there is another threat to a free society at least as serious as encroachment by one branch of government upon the others, or upon the private sector. This less conspicuous but perhaps more insidious threat is the erosion of governmental effectiveness. The great revolutions of this century, which did not advance the cause of civil liberties, in Russia, Germany, and China, were due not so much to governmental encroachments on freedom as to the growing inability of those governments to perform the jobs their people relied upon them to do. Therefore, the Freedom of Information Act, while advancing the public's right to know, should not be administered in a way that renders the government ineffectual in combating tax evaders, corporate monopolies, organized crime syndicates, airline hijackers and terrorists, and so forth. Similarly, the government's ability to represent and protect the nation in a complex and dangerous world may be impaired, if the entities with which we must cooperate, negotiate, or compete all know far more about our strengths and weaknesses than we know about theirs. Such considerations generally underlie the 1st, 2nd, 5th, and 7th exemptions in the Act.

These are generalities. The most they can do is suggest the need for balance and a broad perspective. They are no substitute for the thorough and sophisticated case-by-case approach that should be given, staff time permitting, to some of the difficult controversies that arise under the Act. Where there may be a real conflict between legitimate competing interests, and there often is, the best chance for satisfactory solutions requires, in addition to balance of approach, the will and the resources to give sufficient attention to the particular facts and circumstances of each dispute.

III Discussion

MR. KRONFELD: I want to dispose of one of the red herrings that often comes up in a discussion of the Freedom of Information Act. The Act was not designed to invade privacy, aid organized crime, destroy the U.S. patent system, or give aid and comfort to enemies at home or abroad. If the Act worked well, it would only scratch the surface of government information. I also don't particularly care who brings actions under the Act, whether they be Grumman Aircraft, Bristol Meyers, or the Center for the Study of Responsive Law. Large corporations hire very effective counsel. Some of the major and most effective cases have been brought by large corporations. These cases have a carry-over effect into the public interest sector.

The intent of the Freedom of Information Act is that all government information is public, unless it can be withheld, under one of the nine exemptions, as a discretionary matter. The discretionary authority exists to invoke the exemptions. It does not require denial of information.

Many agency officials feel that their own regulations are superior to the U.S. Code. I will often call an agency and say I saw a regulation printed in the *Federal Register*, and it is a regulation which contravenes the Freedom of Information Act. They say, well, that's our regulation. Some of the agency officials just don't understand that regulations are not the law, that the Code is the law.

The overriding problem with freedom of information is that the career civil servant, the bureaucrat, is really incapable of understanding the intent of the Freedom of Information Act. These individuals view information as a capital asset. They are operating a program, they think they are doing a good job. Their information is capital, and they hate to disburse their capital by releasing it. A lot of education has to be done within the agencies. One thing we might think about is legislating sanctions for illegal withholding of information.

We have to look at the Freedom of Information Act as a possible block to the efficient administration of government. It was not designed to promote efficiency in administration. We should not view it as such. It was designed to get the information out, even if that impedes the function of government. Providing information is as much a part of the regular activity of a government official as the operation of his program. It is not secondary.

MR. PLESSER: Over the past year I have been litigating more than fifteen cases under the Freedom of Information Act and have been involved in a couple of *amicus* briefs. I think I represent about twenty per cent of Mr. Saloschin's Freedom of Information Act cases. I agree with Mr. Saloschin that where access is still inadequate, the primary need is not to change the law but to improve compliance by the agencies with the letter and the spirit of the law. One of the great frustrations I have had is radiating court decisions into agency regulations and actions. The courts have been overwhelmingly favorable to access to information. But, still, we almost have to sue each agency on each issue. The Federal Trade Commission, which has recently become fairly enlightened about information activities, came out with a set of regulations about six months ago in which it was said that administrative staff manuals and manuals to field inspectors about how they are to do their job are confidential. There have been three major cases decided on that issue. One has been affirmed in a very strong decision after the FTC situation. I called up the General Counsel of the FTC and I said, "Are you aware of these cases, because your regulations are obviously not following the case law?"

The General Counsel put me off and a staff attorney called me a day or two later, and said they had considered those cases, but they were not going to change their policy on the basis of three cases. In effect, he was saying to me that if I wanted those manuals from the FTC, I was going to have to sue the agency.

MR. GILLERS: In planning this conference, I got to talk to a fairly well-known investigative reporter in Washington, and he told me a story about his use of the Freedom of Information Act. He said he had been after certain information contained in a periodic publication of the Department of Health, Education, and Welfare. After much stalling on HEW's part, and after he threatened to go to court under the Act, he finally got HEW to agree to release the series, but at the same time that they did so they began to omit the information he wanted from that series. He had to go about looking for where the information was now located and to try to get that new publication.

MR. PLESSER: This is an argument we receive all the

time from people, especially when we are looking for inspection reports. If an inspector knows his report is going to be published, he will eliminate some of the most useful information in it. Obviously, that is one danger in allowing access to information—that the information you get will be censored in a way that it wasn't before.

MR. WELLFORD: I have one brief example of what Mr. Gillers is talking about. We went to court a couple of years ago to get access to reports by inspectors of conditions in meat plants. After two years' delay and about ten thousand dollars of legal costs—we had to pay for it—we did get access to those reports. For about six months, the information was not very useful. The other day I was over there looking at the fruits of our victory, and I found the whole system by which those reports were made had changed. Instead of having long-hand descriptions by the inspectors of what was wrong with the plant, the inspector now simply fills out a form in which he basically says pass or fail. So now it is all pretty useless to us.

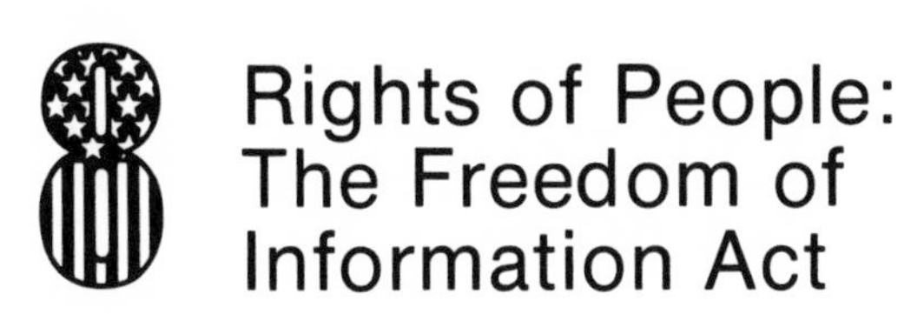

8 Rights of People: The Freedom of Information Act

—by Harrison Wellford

In a democratic government, information, especially timely information, is the currency of power. The relationship between free access to information and responsible government is direct. Excessive secrecy blocks the citizen's ability to hold officials accountable. It discourages citizen participation in government and destroys popular sovereignty. Congress has been slow to aid public access to information. As late as 1967, the Senate Judiciary Committee found that although "the theory of an informed electorate is vital to the proper operation of a democracy, there is nowhere in our present law a statute which affirmatively provides for that information." [1]

The 1966 Freedom of Information Act was designed to remedy this oversight. For the first time, it established the right of the average citizen, not just a party directly affected by a government decision, to learn what his government is doing. According to the Attorney General's memorandum interpreting the Act, its goals were that "disclosure be the general rule, not the exception, and that individuals have equal rights of access; that the burden be on the government to justify the withholding of a document, not on the person who requests it; that individuals improperly denied access to documents have a right to seek injunctive relief in the courts, that there be a change in Government policy and attitude." [2]

Since 1967 the Freedom of Information Act has brought great advances in public access to government information, but for the most part the beneficiaries have not been the average citizen, the press, or scholars but organized interests with the legal and lobbying resources to develop special relationships with federal agencies. The great majority of the cases brought under the Freedom of Information Act have been by private corporate interests which use the Act as a substitute for discovery. The second largest litigant class under the Act is the public-interest community. The press has used the Act rarely, and the average citizen, without a Washington-based organization to back him up, has used it hardly at all.

While legal victories by these organized interests have often benefited the general public, they have not led to substantial reforms in government information policy which would help the average citizen in his requests for information.

This is not what Congress intended in passing the Freedom of Information Act. In deliberate contrast to the public-information section of the Administrative Procedures Act, which aimed to improve the equity and efficiency of the administrative process, the Freedom of Information Act aimed at improving the electoral process by helping to create informed voters. The Act specifically permits "any person" to request government records, not just those special interests "properly and directly concerned" with an agency action, as under the Administrative Procedures Act. As Charles Koch recently concluded, "This change in language indicates a shift of emphasis from providing access to citizens directly affected by an agency action to establishing a more informed electorate—an opening of the bureaucracy to any interested citizen." [3]

This purpose of the Act—to protect the right of the average citizen to learn what his government is doing—was expressed eloquently by Attorney General Ramsey Clark in a memorandum summarizing its provisions:

> If government is to be truly of, by, and for the people, the people must know in detail the activities of government. Nothing so diminishes democracy as secrecy. Self-government, the maximum participation of the citizenry in affairs

> of state, is meaningful only with an informed public. How can we govern ourselves if we know not how we govern? Never was it more important than in our times of mass society, when government affects each individual in so many ways, that the right of the people to know the actions of their government be secure.[4]

In 1973, when an excessive regard for secrecy and the crimes committed in its name have tainted the highest levels of government, these words have a truly prophetic ring.

I Problems in Enforcement

Unfortunately, it takes more than mere words on paper to change years of ingrained habit and most federal agencies continue to have a two-pronged information policy—one toward organized groups, chiefly regulated industries but increasingly public-interest groups with legal resources, and one toward the individual citizen. There are three primary reasons for this policy: reliance on the courts to enforce the Act, the costs of gaining access to information, and the delay in answering information requests. Fundamental to each of these problems is the lack of internal bureaucratic incentives to obey the Act, exemplified by the agency's failure to organize the processes by which data is indexed, stored, and retrieved to speed data to the citizens who request it, and by the agency's tendency to stretch unjustifiably the exemptions from disclosure permitted by the Act.[5]

Judicial enforcement. Usually, only organized interests have the financial resources to obtain judicial review of an information denial and to pay search fees and photocopying charges if the request is granted. The only sanction for a public official who wrongfully withholds data is repudiation in the courts. The official knows that when he denies information to a special interest, the basis of that denial is likely to be tested. Often, the mere threat of legal action makes information available that originally had been denied. The government's fear of being sued is understandable because the courts, for the most part, have interpreted the Act liberally. Of ninety-nine cases decided by the courts between 1967 and 1971, the government's refusal to release information was sustained in only twenty-three cases.[6] The Center for Study of Responsive Law has won thirteen of fifteen cases challenging information denial.

Litigation, however, is a luxury few citizens can afford. It is therefore critical that successful plaintiffs in a Freedom of Information Act case, at the court's discretion, be allowed to recover reasonable attorneys fees and other litigation costs. Even the simplest freedom of information case will cost in excess of $1000, a sum which practically guarantees that few cases will be brought by private citizens. The government now loses the great majority of these cases decided by the courts. If the courts had discretion to charge the government for the attorneys fees of deserving plaintiffs, the government might be more likely to take only its strongest cases to court. Such fees should be assessed against the specific agency that denied the information.

Delay The average time for initial action on an information request is thirty days, and on appeal fifty-five days. Similar delays occur when a denial is taken to court. A statistical analysis of thirty-three Freedom of Information Act suits filed in the United States District Court for the District of Columbia found that the federal government takes an average sixty-eight days to file any responsive pleading in a case. It takes an average one hundred sixty-seven days before a case is decided by the courts.[7] For the press, a delay of three months before it knows whether it will get the information defeats the purpose of requesting the information in the first place. It is no surprise therefore that of one hundred fifty to two hundred cases which have been filed under the Act, only four have been brought by newspapers or individual reporters. These delays are equally discouraging to the citizens whose desire for information is not buttressed by an economic interest.

Agencies should be required to respond to information requests in a finite period of time. Proposed amendments to the Freedom of Information Act would limit the period in which an agency must make a final determination on an information request to twenty days. Other amendments would eliminate the delay of the now obligatory internal agency appeal of an initial denial. The adoption of some limit is critical.

The costs of access Another problem area is the practice of charging citizens for the "search and copying fees" incurred by the government in making information available. These "user charges," as they are officially known, have been justified at various times by the government on the grounds of economy and as a means of discouraging "frivolous requests." [8] While both these grounds may seem reasonable on the surface, the Act provides no guidelines for the application of user costs by the agencies. As early as 1968, a year after the Act took effect, the House Committee on Government Operations found that agencies were abusing their discretion over fees, abrogating "to themselves more power in the handling of public information than the law intended." [9] In leaving this minor housekeeping function to the discretion of the agencies, Congress surely did not intend for them to create toll gates on the citizen's access to information.

The Administrative Conference found that copying charges range from 5 cents a page at the Department of Agriculture to as high as $1.00 a page at the Selective Service System. A charge of 25¢ a page is common. Clerical research charges vary widely, from a low of $3.00 per hour at the Veterans Administration to as much as $7.00 an hour at the Renegotiation Board. The Department of Agriculture requested prepayment of $85,000 in one instance and $91,840 in another for access to documents in its pesticide division.[10]

On May 2, 1972, George Shultz, Director of the Office of Management and Budget (OMB), finally tried to curb this abuse of search and copying fees by sending a directive that fees "should not be established at an excessive level for the purpose of deterring requests for copies of records." But in January 1973, OMB, with its tail between its legs, told the House Government Operations Committee that it would not enforce the earlier directive and was permitting agencies to charge what they wished.[11]

Not only do these charges vary widely from agency to

agency, but they are also often applied in a discriminatory fashion. There have been frequent complaints from citizens who have been charged search fees and photocopying costs for information which an agency made freely available to its regulatory clients. These "user" charges should be made uniform, low in cost, and subject to waiver in certain cases.

Computerization of records: a shield for secrecy? Automation of data storage and retrieval through computer systems has important implications for freedom of information. In the late 1960s and early 1970s, basic decisions about computer systems have been made, vital software programming which controls access to automated files has been created, and manual records have been destroyed, all without any effective oversight by Congress, the press, or public-interest groups.

It is critical that Congress address the public-access issues of computerization before it is too late. It is very costly and disruptive to make major changes in computer systems once they have been designed in a particular way. These systems are now designed to serve the managerial needs of agency administrators, not the disclosure needs of the public. Even when a citizen finds computerized data programmed to meet his request, there are serious problems of cost. According to James Kronfeld, Special Counsel to the House Government Operations Subcommittee, it is a common practice for agencies to charge for the time required to locate information on computer tape, plus $5.00 per page for the print-out of the data. Agencies charge up to $75–$80 an hour for computer time.

The application of computer technology to government record-keeping is an inevitable and welcome development. Properly designed, it can reduce the cost and time required to meet public requests for information. Improperly designed with narrow concepts of bureaucratic efficiency or secrecy in mind, it can render futile the efforts to strengthen the Freedom of Information Act.

Agencies should be required to give public notice when they plan to introduce a new computer system, and to provide Congress and the public with an impact statement on the

Freedom of Information Act implications. Public advisory committees should be established in each agency to give guidance on ways in which the computer system can be designed to advance the goals of public access.

II Public Access to Internal Memoranda

Internal agency decision-making should be opened to public review after certain time limits. Despite the disclosure purposes of the Freedom of Information Act, Congress made a major exception for the internal memoranda generated by government decision-making. Exemption 5 of the Act states that its disclosure requirements do not apply to "inter-agency or intra-agency memorandums or letters which would not be available by law to a party other than an agency in litigation with the agency." The purpose of the exemption was twofold. Agency witnesses convinced Congress that a free and frank exchange of ideas necessary to effective decision-making would be inhibited if agency personnel were forced to operate in a fish bowl. Disclosure of internal memos, it was argued, would make staff members cautious and timid, fearful that they might be made a scapegoat for an unpopular decision. The District of Columbia Court of Appeals expressed this view in *Ackerly* v. *Ley:* "In the Federal Establishment, as in General Motors or any other hierarchical giant, there are enough incentives as it is for playing it safe and listing with the wind; Congress clearly did not propose to add to them the threat of cross-examination in a public tribunal." [12]

The second purpose of the exemption was to prevent premature disclosure of agency decisions. According to the Attorney General's "Memorandum on the Freedom of Information Act." Congress never intended to require the release of internal memos if premature disclosure would compromise agency objectives.

There is, nevertheless, a strong public policy in making the basis of government decisions available for public review. It might be argued that the "statement of reasons" accompanying agency decisions, and the right of judicial review, give protection against arbitrary decision-making even when internal memos are not disclosed. But these protections, even if they are adequate, do not operate for "inaction" decisions—decisions to do nothing or do nothing now. These are the most common decisions made by agencies. When an agency decides not to investigate or not to prosecute, it rarely justifies its action publicly. Indeed, the public rarely learns that an action was considered. Even if agencies could be persuaded to issue opinions on no-action decisions, public review of bureaucratic discretion would still be incomplete. As Kenneth Culp Davis has pointed out, discretion is exercised not merely in final dispositions of cases but at each interim step. These interim decisions are far more numerous and sometimes just as important as final ones. "Discretion is not limited to substantive choices but extends to procedures, methods, forms, timing, degrees of emphasis, and many other subsidiary factors." [13]

Perhaps because public checks on bureaucratic discretion are so limited, the courts have been reluctant to grant a blanket exemption for internal memoranda. In a case brought by the Consumers Union,[14] the courts made a distinction between internal memoranda conveying factual material, which it said should be made public, and those conveying policy, which it said should remain exempt. In a second case, arising in the District of Columbia,[15] the court refined the exemption further, holding that only the opinion portions of internal documents could be withheld from the public. This decision left the agencies with the administratively messy task of gleaning the factual sections from otherwise exempt policy papers.

No one is very happy with this state of affairs. Separating fact from opinion in individual memoranda is hardly a task for clerks. It requires the attention of policy personnel, taking them away from more substantive duties. As a result, requests for internal papers are probably subject to more delay than requests for any other items under the Freedom of Information Act. Citizens feel that too few internal papers are made available, while bureaucrats feel that if any more were made available, their decision-making would grind to a halt.

What is to be done? Several remedies have been proposed, from establishing a blanket exemption for all internal memos to abolishing the 5th exemption altogether. The case for making all internal papers public has some attractive features. Ralph Nader has argued that staffs are less likely to recommend "insupportable or otherwise politically inspired or campaign-fund inspired statements if they know they have to be justified in the open sunlight." [16] Charles Koch, a lawyer with the Federal Trade Commission, concludes that the necessity for protection of internal memoranda is overstated. "The decision-making process as a whole may benefit from criticism of the internal work product or the decisional process which resulted in an official decision." [17] Staffs are likely to do a more careful, unbiased job if they realize that their work product is going in to the public record. Perhaps the prospect of disclosure will stiffen their backbone in resisting the pressure of special interests who, without disclosure, are the only ones who know of their role.

Opposed to this view are the "fish bowl" and "premature disclosure" arguments. Release of internal memos on pending decisions might hamper an agency's enforcement procedures and allow special interests to zero in on individual staff members whose policy views they dislike. If all staff memos were released, there would also probably be an immediate depreciation of their value. The written memos would begin to resemble press releases, sensitive policy advice would be delivered orally.

A middle ground is to establish a statute of limitations, say two years, after which internal memos would be made public. The courts would still have authority to protect certain classes of information, e.g., where release would affect national security, law enforcement, and personal privacy, but the perpetual protection of documents merely because they are internal would no longer be allowed. The present case law allowing release of factual internal documents would continue to give citizens limited access to internal memos during the two-year period.

III The Secrecy Bias of the Agencies

The Freedom of Information Act has permitted access to categories of data that were previously closed to the public, except when officials selectively leaked them to the press. Investigative files, for example, must now be opened to public view except when to do so would prematurely disclose a government case, compromise confidential sources, or seriously infringe personal-privacy rights.[18] Even the correspondence between an agency and the subject of an investigation must now be released, although the exceptions also apply here.[19] The courts have expressed a strong policy interest in helping the public learn how the agencies are carrying out their responsibilities, even at the risk of adding to their administrative burdens. As the Fourth Circuit Court of Appeals said in *Wellford* v. *Hardin:* "The Freedom of Information Act was not designed to increase administrative efficiency, but to guarantee the public's right to know how the government is discharging its duty to protect the public interest."[20]

While the courts have used the Act to open new categories of information to the public, day-to-day access to the data depends on the attitudes of the agency officialdom; there the picture is darker.

In the 1966 hearings on the proposed Freedom of Information Act, spokesmen for federal agencies and departments were overwhelmingly opposed to its major provisions. This view persists today. As the hearings by the House Committee on Government Operations clearly point out, the federal bureaucracy's original hostility has tainted its implementation of the Act. The Committee concluded in 1972 that in a number of significant instances "an entrenched bureaucracy is stubbornly resisting the efforts of the public to find and pry open the hidden doors which conceal the Government's business from its citizens."[21]

This comes as no surprise. As early as 1967, the Attorney General's "Memorandum" emphasized the critical importance of a basic change in government attitude toward public information if the Act were to be effective.

In a few agencies, such a change is now evident. The Federal Trade Commission has come a long way since that day in the summer of 1968, when it refused the staff of the Center for Study of Responsive Law access to its organization chart with the preposterous claim that it was an internal memorandum and therefore exempt under the Act. The information policy of the Environmental Protection Agency under the leadership of William Ruckelshaus was a great advance over the policy of predecessor agencies. The same may be said to a lesser extent of the Food and Drug Administration under the guidance of its former general counsel, Peter Hutt.

Strong public policy considerations support the disclosure of test data on food, drugs, cosmetics, pesticides, and industrial chemicals. Knowledge about the long-range effect of chemicals is so limited that every available resource must be tapped in decisions about their use. In the words of the court in *Soucie* v. *David:* "The public's need for information is especially great in the field of science and technology, for the growth of specialized scientific knowledge threatens to outstrip our collective ability to control its effects on our lives." [22] Decisions by EPA and FDA to make more of this safety-testing data available to the public have brought outside scientists into regulatory decision-making, making it more difficult for these decisions to be made on extra-scientific grounds.

The sodium nitrate food additive petition is a good example. In 1972, FDA, after much delay, provided Dale Hattis, a Stanford graduate student, with all the safety and functionality data it had collected on sodium nitrate, a preservative and coloring agent which under certain conditions can be converted to a carcinogen in the body. Hattis presented FDA with a seventy-eight-page analysis detailing its errors, including the fact that the manufacturer had submitted no test data to FDA before getting his petition approved. Peter Hutt acknowledged Hattis's work as "an important service" and added, "We must simply learn to pay the price of the public criticism that inevitably attends this type of analysis in order to obtain its benefits." [23]

Despite these bright spots, most observers of government information policy, judging by the recent House hearings, feel that public access to information continues to be burdened by bureaucratic intransigence, and that changes in administrative procedures or amendments to the Act will not matter. In the positive cases of the FTC, FDA, and EPA, strong pressure from leaders at the top—Kirkpatrick, Hutt, and Ruckelshaus—was necessary to begin a shift away from traditional patterns of secrecy. Such leadership is rare. As for the other agencies, most public-interest lawyers would agree with William Dobrovir, a Washington attorney who has handled many freedom-of-information cases, that "unless there is a fundamental change in the attitude . . . of government officials, either by process of education or . . . some kind of court sanction, I do not believe the Act is going to be administered." [24]

While everyone complains about agency sabotage of the Act, there has been little attempt to understand the incentives for secrecy which exist in the culture of bureaucracy. The bureaucracy's secrecy bias is not the result of a conspiracy between the permanent government and special interests. It reflects instead a reality of the organizational process: disclosure of information to the public threatens standard operating procedures and priorities of the agency and often the careers of the disclosers. This fear of public disclosure afflicts both political appointees at the top management level, who fear they will be embarrassed or "second-guessed" if confidential information is made public, and middle- and lower-echelon staff who fear for their job security and advancement if information they release leads to embarrassment.

A major reason for the Food and Drug Administration's timidity in implementing the law, according to Peter Hutt, has been concern that release of information on which decisions are based would permit dissatisfied critics to engage in endless second-guessing of the agency. "Rather than risk the expenditure of substantial resources in public debate of this nature, with possible attendant increase in public confusion and loss of Food and Drug Administration prestige, it was easier to maintain the confidentiality of the underlying information and simply avoid the debate." While this justification for secrecy obviously cannot stand before Congress' mandate for full disclosure, the attitude it represents is endemic to large organizations and cannot be legislated out of existence.

Release of information not only threatens the agency's public image but also the bureaucracy's control over information going to the top administrators. Such control is a primary source of the permanent government's power. Rodney Leonard, a former administrator of USDA's Consumer and Marketing Service, an agency which for many years has had one of the most parsimonious information policies in government, describes this attitude: "I discovered during my service in the Department of Agriculture that many officials and employees of the Department seek to minimize the information made available to the public in order to shield their decisions and actions from questioning, and frequently to cover up mistakes and misjudgments in the administration of public programs. In a very real sense, the administrator lacks information and analysis . . . which are not clothed in the self-interest of agency bureaucracy." [25]

The fear of disclosure at the lower levels of bureaucracy is not so much the fear of an embarrassing disclosure as of retaliation from superiors for release of something which conflicts with the official agency policy. Many officials, from assistant administrators to inspectors on the line, regard requests for information as a trial of nerves that will jeopardize their careers if a superior concludes they have said the wrong thing. The fear is evident when an official refuses to be interviewed alone and insists on having an attorney or his superior present; when he asks a stenographer to record verbatim what is said; when he writes copious memos to his files and reports to his superiors on every request for information and every visit from the public.

An example of the plight which these self-protective practices can create for top administrators occurred in the USDA in 1971 during the controversy over restricting the carcinogenic hormone, diethylstilbestrol, in animal feed. The key issue was whether residues of the hormone were turning up in U.S.-inspected meat. As late as August 1971, Assistant Secretary of Agriculture Richard Lyng specifically assured House and Senate Committees that no residues were present, effectively quelling demands by Senator William Proxmire and others that DES be banned. Unknown to Lyng, however, USDA's laboratory services division had been detecting residues for several months but had not reported them to their superiors, presumably because the findings contradicted a long-standing

Departmental policy that DES was safe.

The DES data were kept secret until September 30, 1971, when Peter Schuck, a lawyer with Washington's Center for Study of Responsive Law, asked Dr. Kenneth McEnroe, the USDA's meat-inspection chief, to confirm or deny rumors of the findings. Dr. McEnroe emphatically denied the rumors, then calling Mr. Schuck up twenty-four hours later to apologize. To his surprise, he had found upon checking that the rumors were correct. Dr. McEnroe's superior, Assistant Secretary Lyng, then wrote Senator Proxmire apologizing for his Department's "inexcusable error" and promising a thorough investigation of this "gross malpractice." The USDA's misstatements fueled Congressional efforts to ban the feed additive. A bill banning DES passed the Senate but died in the House.[26]

Public officials, even when discussing the most trivial or mundane issues, frequently insist on anonymity as a condition of cooperation. Fred Bruning, a columnist for *The Washington Post,* recently confronted this attitude when seeking information for a column on the handicrafts of the American Indian. He called an official of the Indian Arts and Crafts Board of the Interior Department. After getting some data on the popularity of Indian art work, Bruning asked the man for the correct spelling of his name. The Interior official replied apologetically that he would like to oblige but it was against agency policy to have the names of staff members mentioned in articles. When Bruning insisted, the man said he would check with his superior. There was a short silence and he was back on the phone. "No," he said, "I'm sorry. There's been a policy decision. . . ."

For many reasons, requests for information from an agency's special-interest constituency are far less threatening than those from citizen groups. In part, this is because industry representatives have time to develop friendships with agency personnel; more significantly, it is because industry does not request information which threatens the agency's self-image as an aggressive, independent protector of the public interest. Those who are regulated are less likely to complain to Congress or the press about enforcement failures, conflict of interests, or political compromises of the regulators, since they often benefit from this malfeasance.[27] Release of embarrassing information to citizen groups, by contrast, may lead to Congressional hearings, General Accounting Office investigations, and adverse press comment which darken the agency's public image and jeopardize the careers of its upper staff.

In trying to understand the psychology of secrecy in the government bureaucracy, we should not overlook the territorial imperative of bureaucrats, the instinctive belief, as one Civil Service Commission lawyer has described it, that "they own their desks and they own their file cabinets and they own the papers that are in them." There is nothing uniquely federal about this attitude. In virtually no other institution except the federal government are employees expected to open their files to outsiders. Such obligations to the public obviously do not exist in private business, nor do they operate generally in state and local government or the Congress. It is little wonder, then, that many federal officials have to be "reprogrammed" if they are to observe the spirit as well as the letter of the Freedom of Information Act.

One major reason the bureaucratic attitude—"when in doubt, withhold"—is so entrenched is that it is rooted in legal self-protection. An official is held individually accountable under criminal statutes for releasing trade secrets or other confidential commercial information but faces no sanction at all if he illegally withholds information from the public. The Federal Food, Drug, and Cosmetic Act and the Federal Insecticide, Fungicide, and Rodenticide Act, for example, contain specific confidentiality requirements, which along with the general federal confidentiality statute, 18 U.S. Code, Section 1905, make a public official criminally liable if he releases commercially valuable information. Senator John McClellan of Arkansas has recently proposed a new criminal code which extends even further the scope of disclosure for which a public servant can be sent to jail. Under McClellan's proposal, a federal employee would be criminally liable if "in violation of his obligation as a public servant under a statute or rule, regulation or order under such statute, he knowingly discloses any information which he has acquired as a public servant."

On the other hand, the public official who illegally refuses to release information is subject to no civil or criminal penalty. A recent case in the Office of Economic Opportunity illustrates this double standard. The OEO suspended Rudy Frank, one of its employees, for allegedly releasing confidential information on the salaries of teachers at a day-care center operated by a private corporation under contract to the OEO. Frank then sued the OEO under the Freedom of Information Act to force the OEO to make the day-care salaries public. Faced with the lawsuit, the OEO gave the "secret" data to Frank but refused to lift his suspension.[28]

The OEO's action has an unmistakable Kafkaesque flavor. The agency punished an employee for releasing "secret" information which it conceded is "public" when challenged by a lawsuit. Ronald Plesser, Mr. Frank's attorney, argues that instead of punishing Frank for disclosing what turned out to be public information, the OEO should suspend or terminate those officials who suppressed the documents in the first place.[29] The natural tendency of a federal official faced with administrative or criminal sanctions if he incorrectly releases data is to keep records secret if there is any doubt that the documents are public.

Granted that freedom of information often conflicts with these self-protective attitudes, how can we create incentives for openness in bureaucracy which will counter its secrecy bias? One proposal is to create incentives for implementation of the Act through the budgetary process. At the present time, a major cause for delay in meeting information requests is the fact that information retrieval is "added on" to the work load of officials assigned to operational duties. A great many information requests have policy implications that cannot be resolved by the lower echelon. With a request for investigative files, for example, the agency must sift the file for data which might result in premature disclosure of its case, often a sophisticated task requiring professional skills. In other words, resources for handling information requests must be subtracted from substantive agency missions. If agencies were given specific appropriations for public information work, implementation of the Act would improve.

These public-information funds would encourage the agency to reorganize its information system with the goal of reducing the discretionary factor. Now, most agencies respond to information requests on an *ad hoc* basis, with little screening of information in advance of requests. Each agency should have a public-information center, where public and exempt information would be indexed for public review. The index of withheld documents should include the reasons the agency considers them exempt under the Act. This system would have many advantages. By forcing the agency to specify reasons for withholding documents, it creates incentives for release (the citizen could still sue if he felt the information should not be exempt). Most important, it forces the agency to make most of its policy decisions in advance of a request, thereby reducing delay.

Requiring the government to pay attorneys' fees and court costs for successful plaintiffs under the Freedom of Information Act would create another incentive for compliance. The GAO is virtually certain to criticize any agency which pays out large sums to compensate citizens wrongfully denied information. Agencies will want to avoid this criticism. Finally, I would suggest that administrative appeals from information denials not go through the agency initially refusing access, where self-protective instincts may smother them, but to an independent agency with special expertise, such as the Administrative Conference of the United States.

IV Discussion

MR. SHATTUCK: I am sure that I don't have as much to offer as the Nader engine room on the Freedom of Information Act, but I would like to add a few things to what Mr. Wellford has said. I am not sure I agree fully that the difficulties with the Freedom of Information Act have to do more with the noncompliance of agencies than with the problems inherent in the statute itself. I think Mr. Wellford has taken the position that we are dealing with a bureaucratic problem here. But in some respects we are dealing with a problem inherent in the statute. Before I describe a couple of ways in which that is true, let me underscore the bureaucratic difficulties that he has been explaining and describing.

One example comes to mind immediately, which illustrates the self-protective attitude of the agencies. We requested on behalf of a client some trial procedures to be used in parole-board hearings—a short two-page procedural statement of the way parole-board hearings would be conducted. There was no claim that the material was exempt; the question was whether the parole board was an agency within the terms of the Act. We had long negotiations by letter and by telephone with the parole board, which ended up with the person on the other end of the phone saying, "Well, we're really ready to give you this material, but we can't figure out how we should get it to you." I suggested that it might simply be put in an envelope and stuck in the mail. Another three or four weeks passed before they were able to decide who in fact would put it in the envelope and stick it in the mail. I think to this day the parole board has not confessed to being a government agency within the terms of the Act.

A second administrative snag not found within the Act is the way the "need-to-know" requirement has been brought in. The Act clearly provides that the public—*any* member of the public—has a right to information which is nonexempt under the Act. But in some cases where a "need to know" has not been demonstrable, we have had difficulty, and in some cases where a clear "need to know" has been shown and no claim of exemption has been made, we have also had difficulties.

The government is not even-handed in granting access to controversial but nonexempt files. We have a number of cases where information in the hands of the government has been used to manipulate the truth about certain incidents. In one case now pending, a teacher at Smith College requested FBI file information concerning the Alger Hiss case. To be sure, that probably is one of the most controversial cases of our history, but the Hiss files have, in fact, been shown to persons who have been willing to write favorable stories about government's handling of the Hiss case, but they have been denied to the Smith teacher.

A number of ways in which the Act itself is deficient are in its exempting provisions, particularly the "national security" exemption. This exemption makes it virtually impossible to inspect classified information. It has had exactly the opposite effect from what the Freedom of Information Act is supposed to do. It has been used to authorize the executive branch to classify indiscriminately, and in applying the Act the courts will not second-guess the classification.

In the *Mink* case—the first Supreme Court decision on the Freedom of Information Act—Justice White, who wrote the majority opinion, denied access to classified materials. Nevertheless, he pointed out that Congress clearly has the power to adopt different provisions in the Freedom of Information Act, provided the courts can conduct secret inspection of these materials. In fact, exemptions are now pending to provide for *in camera* inspection. That is absolutely vital if the first exemption is not to be too broad.

MR. MARTIN: If Mr. Wellford really means what he said, then the Act was drafted and passed to serve the needs of the average citizen. Maybe that is the trouble.

I don't think you really believe that, Mr. Wellford. That is arm-waving. The average citizen probably has no interest in getting government information. It seems to me that to talk in this arm-waving fashion about the problems under the Act really does not advance the cause of discreetly identifying the problem areas and trying to deal with them.

We have problems in the federal government in finding information, for whatever purpose, not because of a paranoid unwillingness to disclose on the part of the bureaucracy, but because very often the information sought is scattered through any number of offices in a large bureaucracy. In some instances, where one is trying to learn about something across the board, it takes a great deal of time, it takes time to be sure you are getting a full and accurate reply. I think the delays that we ourselves encounter, and I don't know why it would be any different for public inquiry, are the product of the desire of civil servants to make sure that they are providing accurate, reliable, and complete information.

I don't mean to say that there are not problems, but to start off a discussion and to attack the problem as though you have a government from which you cannot get information is not very helpful.

Go to England—try to get information out of the British government; go to other countries; and then perhaps, having had that experience, come back to the issue of getting information out of the federal government.

MR. WELLFORD: I think that if I was arm-waving, you are arm-waving as well. You are creating a straw man here, I am not suggesting that the only purpose of the Freedom of Information Act was to help the little old lady in Dubuque get information. That is not what I said. I am talking about the interests of citizen groups, the interests of public-interest groups, the interests of business associations, a vast galaxy of organized groups, particularly in the environmental field, who are constantly trying to get information from the government.

The fact is that as long as there is a discretionary content to requests for information, that is, as long as there is going to be policy decisions made, the government's attitude is going to be important. I am not saying that we have it worse here than a scholar in England trying to get information from Parliament. I agree the information resources available to citizens in other countries are probably much smaller than ours. I have spent four years dealing with federal agencies virtually every day, and we have to think about ways to build bureaucratic incentives to change their attitudes.

MR. WESTIN: There are many incidents in which agencies take the view that, in order to protect confidential information, you are the last person who should ever have the right to inspect a file about yourself. I am not hopeful that the courts will act swiftly enough on this.

MR. CALLEN: I am grateful to Professor Westin for saying this now. What often happens is that one does not even know that one is under a cloud. It may happen that you want a higher security clearance. The agency will stall and delay on the basis of some kind of record in the file, and it simply won't answer your question. It will hope you will go away, that you will stop applying. If you keep insisting and say, I want to know, am I getting clearance or not? they will say to your superior: "Go to the fellow and tell him to withdraw his application. See, it's better that way, so we don't have to say something against him." And very often you will go away because you do not want to have a bad record. If you persist and say you want to know, then yours goes to the security people and tells them you want to go through with it. They say, "Well, we are denying clearance, but we can't say why because we are protecting him. We are protecting him by not disclosing what he has done." So you never know.

A person should have the right under the law to expunge, a right to face witnesses, a right to put stuff into the record, and the right to see for himself what is in that file about him.

DR. WIESNER: We are contending with two separate problems: one, the protection of the individual and his civil liberties, and, two, the information a citizen needs to be a citizen in a democracy. This second has been an aspect of information access legislation that has troubled me most. The exemptions permitted are generally for the most important pieces of information a citizen ought to have in order to know how to run his government. Frequently, when I worked in the government, I would ask myself why a piece of information was "top secret" when it was clear that it was known to the Russians. It was obvious that it was being kept from the United States public so it would not know what was being done by their government in their name. The fact that we were bombing Cambodia must have been known to the Cambodians.

In my view many of the most decisively wrong policy errors of the last twenty years which exacerbated the cold war and led to many other bad decisions would probably not have been made if Congress and the people had been told even a small amount about the quality and character of the information these decisions were based on.

Undoubtedly a case can occasionally be made for keeping some information back, but by and large we have done this excessively, and continue to do it excessively, and it is my own view, having thought about the matter for more than a decade or so, that if we had the choice between complete openness—with the cost that means in the technical and military fields—and the kinds of policies we have had, the country would be better served by complete openness.

Pressures on the Press

—by David Wise

When five men, wearing rubber surgical gloves, were arrested inside the Democrats' Watergate headquarters in June 1972, John N. Mitchell, the campaign director of the Committee to Re-Elect the President, announced that the suspects "were not operating either on our behalf or with our consent." Soon after, Mr. Mitchell resigned his $60,000-a-year post, in order, he said, to spend more time at home with his family.

During the Presidential campaign, in case the voters had begun to suspect otherwise, Ronald L. Ziegler, the President's press secretary, a man of great resiliency, declared: "This administration does not condone or tolerate, and no one in the White House condones or tolerates, political sabotage, espionage, and that type of activity."

That comment was perfectly clear and should have ended the matter, but four days after President Nixon's election, the President's Special Counsel, Charles Wendell Colson, journeyed to Kennebunkport, Maine, where quite possibly he thought no one was listening, to denounce The Washington Post. *The* Post's *coverage of the Watergate affair, said Mr. Colson, was "unconscionable" and its impact was to "erode somewhat public confidence in the institutions of government." Mr. Colson indignantly took issue with the implications of the* Post's *news stories. "The charge of subverting the whole political process," he said, "that is a fantasy, a work of fiction rivaling only* Gone with the Wind *in circulation and* Portnoy's Complaint *for indecency."* [1] *Shortly thereafter, Mr. Colson, like so many of his friends, departed the White House at least partly under a Watergate cloud then—relatively speaking—no bigger than a man's hand.*

I The Press in the Middle

The Watergate tragedy *has* had elements of fantasy. Who could believe, until the story finally unfolded, that men entrusted with power had engaged in such wide-ranging and total corruption of the American democracy? Who could have believed that the White House would encourage criminal acts in the name of "national security"? In a novel, the plot would hardly be credible: a dispatch case containing $700,000 in cash for the President's election campaign secretly flown to Washington in a private aircraft; hypodermic needles being jabbed into the backside of the wife of the Attorney General of the United States; former top-level CIA and FBI operators caught in what—and we have Mr. Ziegler's word for it—was certainly a "third-rate burglary attempt." A Watergate conspirator flying out to Denver in a red wig to interview Dita Beard, she of shredded memo fame. The President's personal attorney skulking about in the wings paying off political saboteurs. Mr. Mitchell announcing that he participated in discussions of illegal bugging of the Democrats while the chief law-enforcement officer of the United States. The Vice President of the United States announcing his "full confidence in the integrity" of the President. The Director of the FBI resigning after it was reported that he had destroyed key evidence on the instruction of the President's most trusted aides. The attempted theft of medical files by White House agents in the Daniel Ellsberg case. The mass resignations and the President who knew nothing about Watergate.

The wiretaps on White House aides and newsmen approved by the President and Henry Kissinger. The secret plan approved by the President, for burglary and opening of first-class mail, although he was warned, in writing, that breaking and entering was "clearly illegal." Testimony that the counsel to the Finance Committee to Re-elect the President had suggested to the Attorney General of the United States that American citizens be kidnapped and taken to Mexico during the Republican National Convention of 1972. And the deep involvement of both the FBI and the CIA in the Watergate affair.

Small wonder if reporters in Washington assigned to cover Watergate—and one wishes more of them *had* been assigned during the summer of 1972—might have slipped into fantasy, as Mr. Colson charged. The problem is, what can a fellow believe in this sort of a situation? The reporter conscientiously trying to gather the facts and pass them on to his readers has a rather difficult task. He has no way to determine which officials of the government, if any, may be telling the truth. The result is understandable confusion. He could, of course, turn to Higher Authority, the President himself. On June 22, 1972, in his first public comment on the Watergate, President Nixon assured us that Mr. Mitchell and Mr. Ziegler "have stated my position and have also stated the facts accurately. . . . The White House has had no involvement whatever in this particular incident."

Then, on August 29, in another press conference, at San Clemente, California, President Nixon sought to lay the Watergate matter to rest once and for all.

"Within our own staff under my direction," the President said, "Counsel to the President, Mr. Dean, has conducted a complete investigation of all leads which might involve any present members of the White House staff or anybody in the government. I can say categorically that his investigation indicates that no one in the White House staff, no one in this administration, presently employed, was involved in this very bizarre incident."

So it is easy to see why the liberal, Eastern press goes astray. If it would just stick to reporting what the President and other officials of the government say, there would be no problem. At least there would be no problem with the officials of the government.

Bizarre indeed, and frightening too, but the Watergate scandal does illustrate some of the enormous problems faced by the news media in attempting to report about the government in the pressure cooker of Washington. For the press, no less than any other institution in our society, operates in a highly charged political environment. There is a natural tension between the press and the government, for when reporters attempt to tell the truth about what the politicians are up to, the politicians don't like it. This activity may lead to a Pulitzer prize, but as we have seen in recent times, for the reporter it may also lead to a grand-jury investigation, arrest, indictment, and jail. It is no longer necessarily so that the truth shall make you free; it may make you unfree. If this is inconvenient for the press, it is even more ominous for the public, which must depend on the press for the information upon which to base intelligent decisions about politics and government.

Pressures on the press, in short, may be highly hazardous to the health of our democracy and to the survival of the Republic. And that is not fantasy.

The danger exists despite the special position of the press in the American constitutional system. With foresight and vision that seem astounding some two hundred years later, the Founding Fathers—with a little help from their friends—added the First Amendment to the Constitution. There was a practical political reason: they had to promise a Bill of Rights in order to get the Constitution ratified by those big, Eastern liberal states. The result was language designed to try to protect the press and the people from their elected and appointed leaders. As the late Justice Hugo Black phrased it so beautifully in the disagreement over the Pentagon Papers: "In the First Amendment, the Founding Fathers gave the free press the protection it must have to fulfill its essential role in our democracy. The press was to serve the governed, not the governors. The Government's power to censor the press was abolished so that the press would remain forever free to censure the Government. The press was protected so that it could bare the secrets of government and inform the people. Only a free and unrestrained press can effectively expose deception in government." [2]

But how free is the press today?

I shall attempt in this chapter to profile government pressures on the press, and the relationship of those pressures to the Constitution and the law, particularly in the area of news reporting about national security information and foreign policy. Secondly, the chapter will discuss political pressures on the press, which are equally formidable, but operate, in part, outside the legal framework. And it will discuss the general role and responsibility of the press.

In the age of the nuclear warhead, the computer, the data bank, and the wiretapper, the power of the government to control information, to conceal truth, and to shape information to fit government policy has reached unprecedented levels.

At the same time, the public's need for information has never been greater, because in the nuclear age, the stakes are higher than before. Government can secretly take action and make decisions that lead to total war. (In the words of a recent *New Yorker* cartoon, "This has been a test. Had this been an actual emergency, you'd probably never know what hit you.") A political democracy presupposes an informed public with access to information, both sufficient and accurate, on which to base its vote at election time and its opinions about public affairs between elections.

Consequently, the public's need for knowledge has been increasing at the very time that government control over information, and government secrecy and deception, have also increased. It has become more difficult for the press to bare the secrets of government and inform the people.

Partly this is so because the Constitution and the First Amendment are imperfect instruments for the protection of the press, and of the people, who necessarily depend on the press for their information. As Charles Evans Hughes pointed out so clearly more than half a century ago, the Constitution is what the judges say it is. And the judges change. The Supreme Court also operates in a political environment, and the Court is, after all, a branch of the federal government. It was the four

Nixon appointees to the Court, for example, who made possible the 5–4 majority ruling against Earl Caldwell, and it is hardly accidental that the issue of newsmen's privilege has come to a head during the Nixon era.

Although the First Amendment provides that "Congress shall make no law . . . abridging the freedom . . . of the press . . ." the language is an absolute that has become highly qualified. It is true that, under *The New York Times* v. *Sullivan* rule, it has become increasingly difficult to libel public officials, but the theater in which one may not shout fire has, of late, become crowded with the strangest assortment of patrons—newsmen jailed for protecting their sources or consorting with Indians, journalists yanked off public television because they had apparently offended the same wonderful folks who brought you the Watergate, local broadcasters told to censor network news, and a former high CIA official who—unlike a number of Presidents of the United States—has been enjoined by a federal court from writing a book.

Then there is the special problem of television. Since the Founding Fathers, despite Benjamin Franklin's scientific accomplishments, were unaware of the cathode-ray tube, they did not design the First Amendment to cope with the peculiar problem of television. Because it would not do if television stations broadcast willy-nilly, and interfered with one another, Congress in its wisdom empowered the Federal Communications Commission to regulate the air waves in the public interest, convenience, and necessity. Today some 45 million Americans watch the nightly news on the three networks each weekday evening; television news, and not the printed word, apparently has the greatest impact on the consciousness of most Americans. There are in America, according to the 1970 Census, more households with television sets than with bathtubs.

But the extent to which the First Amendment protects television news and television is not at all clear, for it depends on how loud one believes *Red Lion* roars.[3] The result is an anomaly: the medium with the greatest impact is the least protected from government interference with its message.

Although not regulated by a government commission,

newspapers and other forms of print media are hardly free of government pressures, particularly when they report on foreign policy and national security.

In exposing political corruption, the activities of organized crime, or the activities of radical groups, the journalist, it is true, faces the hazard that he will become the target of official investigators demanding to know his sources. There is no *law* against investigative reporting, however.

There may or may not be a law against reporting information relating to the national defense, depending upon how one chooses to interpret the espionage statutes. In any event, if we do not have an Official Secrets Act at the present time, that oversight by the Framers of the Constitution may be remedied by contemporary political leaders with presumed greater wisdom.

II Legal Sanctions

There are basically two kinds of legal sanctions that may, or might, be taken against the press for reporting about national security, and about war and peace—the very subjects that matter most to citizens interested in life and survival. One is prior restraint by the courts to prohibit publication of objectionable news. The other is subsequent punishment for breaking the law.

Until the Nixon administration sought to protect the American public from the Pentagon Papers, the classic case dealing with prior restraint was *Near* v. *Minnesota.*[4] A vicious Minneapolis scandal sheet, the *Saturday Press,* charged that a Jewish gangster controlled gambling, bootlegging, and other forms of racketeering in the city of Minneapolis and was paying off the cops. The city, the newspaper charged, was in the hands of "ganefs." The Minnesota gag law gave the state power to shut down any "scandalous and defamatory newspaper, magazine, or other periodical." Acting under this statute, a state court enjoined the newspaper from publishing. The United States Supreme Court reversed, 5–4. Chief Justice Hughes, in delivering the opinion of the Court, did not address himself to the substantive question of whether the city of Minneapolis was, or was not, in the hands of "ganefs," and instead quoted Blackstone: "The liberty of the press is indeed essential to the nature of a free state; but this consists in laying no *previous* restraint upon publications, and not in freedom from censure for criminal matter when published." Chief Justice Hughes said it was accepted that the chief purpose of the First Amendment was to prevent "previous restraints upon publication," such as had existed in England when the press was licensed. The Minnesota statute, he found, was "the essence of censorship."

Had Chief Justice Hughes stopped there, the decision would have been tidy, and it might have deprived us of the drama of the Pentagon Papers case, but he did not. He went on to say that "the protection even as to previous restraint is not absolutely unlimited." Prior restraint of the press, he said, might be acceptable in "exceptional cases," and in the area of national security he named three: "No one would question but that a government might prevent actual obstruction to its recruiting service or the publication of sailing dates of transports or the number and location of troops." These were the major "*Near* exceptions." Boiled down, they meant that the government may not be able to stop newspapers from printing information which it claims endangers national security—but it can try.

In June 1971 it did. The government, in seeking to suppress the Pentagon Papers, argued that the *Near* exceptions were illustrative, not exclusive, and it charged that further publication by the *Times* of the Pentagon history of the Vietnam war would cause "grave and immediate danger to the security of the United States." The government lost, but it also won. Because it did succeed in preventing *The New York Times* from publishing for fifteen days while the matter was argued in the federal courts, which was, after all, an effective form of prior restraint. Three other newspapers were restrained from publishing the papers. No one could remember when the government had succeeded before, through court action, in preventing newspapers from publishing information about foreign policy which the government found objectionable.

No more than *Near* did the Pentagon Papers case settle the question of prior restraint. The government is free to try its luck again at any time. And the press is well advised to keep this in mind, particularly when it is writing about "ganefs" in high places. Indeed the government did try again in 1972 when the CIA successfully enjoined the publication of a book about intelligence by one of its former employees, Victor L. Marchetti. Alfred A. Knopf wants to publish Marchetti's book, but under the permanent injunction of a federal court, Marchetti must submit in advance to the CIA, to be censored by it, anything he writes about intelligence "factual, fictional, or otherwise," which means in plain English that he cannot even publish a spy novel without the government's permission. It is, of course, a special case, since Marchetti signed a secrecy agreement before he left the CIA, but it seems doubtful that a person can sign away his constitutional rights, and the case is some indication of which way the wind is blowing.

In June 1971, during the period when the Nixon administration had succeeded temporarily in preventing publication of the Pentagon Papers in the *Times* and other newspapers, the President's Director of Communications, Herbert Klein, held a background session for reporters. In it, he said the question of whether the *Times* had endangered the nation's security was of less concern to the administration than permitting a precedent that would encourage future leaks. Since at that very time the administration was arguing in court that publication of the Pentagon Papers would cause grave and irreparable injury to the Republic, Mr. Klein's comments shed a good deal of light--perhaps more than he would have wished—on the political reasons for prior restraint.

When we turn to the question of subsequent punishment of the press for printing information which the government finds disagreeable, the matter gets a good deal more complicated. We must start with a brief discussion of the complex and often misunderstood classification system and its relationship to the espionage laws.

"As the law now stands, there is no connection between them. Security classification is a purely administrative system, unrelated to the criminal law. The classification of a document determines the precautions to be taken in handling it. The higher the classification, the more stringent the physical precautions required (e.g., locking up in safes), and the more restrictive the rules about who may have access to the document. Classification does not determine the sanctions taken for unauthorized disclosure." The quotation is from a 1972 study of the British Official Secrets Act by a committee appointed by the Home Secretary and headed by Lord Franks, but the words describe the situation in the United States as well.[5]

The classification system in the United States is not a law, nor created by a law, nor is it, as a general rule, a violation of law to read or possess or publish a classified document or even to mimeograph classified documents and pass them out in Times Square. The classification system was created by executive order of the President and it applies to employees of the United States government in the same sense that an executive order dealing with three-day holiday weekends applies to federal employees. It no more governs the activities of ordinary citizens, or of journalists, or scholars, than does a National Park Service directive about Smokey the Bear. The laws of the United States are still made by the Congress, and simply because a bureaucrat decides that a document is secret does not necessarily make it so, even if he marks it with an impressive-looking rubber stamp that says SECRET.

Why people outside the government, with the possible exception of Jack Anderson, are afraid of classified documents is not entirely clear, but they are, and it has more to do with psychology and the mystique surrounding classification than the law. The system of classification that we accept as the normal, everyday facet of government power in the 1970s has in fact been with us only since 1951. On September 24 of that year, President Truman issued the first executive order on classification, creating a secrecy system for civilian departments. Before that, only the armed services and the military departments had used classification stamps. Truman's order allowed any agency of the executive branch to classify national security information. Two years later, President Eisenhower replaced Truman's order, and Eisenhower's order, with some amendments by Presidents Kennedy and Johnson, provided the basic classification framework for almost twenty years. On March 8, 1972, President Nixon issued a new Executive Order, No. 11652, effective June 1, 1972, replacing its predecessors. Since the classification system is the subject of Chapter 2, it will not be discussed here in detail. Suffice it to say that the executive order continues to provide for three levels of classification, "Top Secret," "Secret," and "Confidential," and permits, in fine print, the creation of all sorts of special classifications even beyond "Top Secret," dealing with intelligence matters and codes. The executive order contains an elaborate system for downgrading and declassification, designed to create the appearance that official documents will in time be released to the public while preserving the option of the government to keep them secret.

Under the Espionage Act of 1917, and its amendments, the government can prosecute someone for the unauthorized use of "information relating to the national defense." The existing law, however, with certain narrow exceptions, does not bar disclosure of "classified information" as such. Therefore, when the government seeks to prosecute a spy, a leaker, or a newspaper reporter under the espionage laws, it must first prove that a particular classified document falls within the ambit of the statute. It is not enough for the government to show that the document was stamped with a classification mark. The Supreme Court indicated as much in 1941 in the *Gorin* case.[6]

With two exceptions the law, therefore, does not concern itself with classified information. The exceptions are these: Section 798 of Title 18 of the United States Code, which was added to the espionage statutes in 1951, does bar the publication or unauthorized use of "classified information" about codes or communications intelligence. And the Internal Security Act of 1950 prohibits government officials from handing over "classified" information to a foreign agent or member of a "Communist organization." Otherwise, the law does not mention classified information.

The fact that the espionage laws have not, at this writing, been used to prosecute reporters does not mean that the government may not, at some time, give it a whirl. There have been some attempts. In 1942, the *Chicago Tribune* published a story about the Battle of Midway. It gave so many details about the Japanese fleet that Washington feared the Japanese would realize that the United States had broken its code. The Attorney General announced that a federal grand-jury investigation would be held to determine whether the newspaper had violated the Espionage Act. The Navy decided it did not wish to testify before the grand jury, and, as a result, there was no prosecution. Three years later, the FBI arrested the editor and coeditor of the magazine *Amerasia* and four other persons and confiscated about 1700 government documents, many of them classified, that it had found in the magazine's office in New York. All six persons were arrested on charges of conspiracy to violate the Espionage Act, and this appears to be the only case where the government *arrested* journalists for allegedly violating the spy laws. However, indictments were returned only against three of the six defendants, including one journalist, the editor, on lesser charges of conspiracy to steal government documents. So again, there was no *prosecution* of the press under the espionage laws. After the Pentagon Papers were published, the government displayed great interest in the activities of Neil Sheehan, the *Times* reporter who had obtained them, and a federal grand jury in Boston appeared to be exploring the possibility of indicting him under the Espionage Act or for theft. As long as the espionage laws are on the books, the government may be tempted to use them against reporters, who, if not spies, are often regarded by the government as at least equally pernicious a group.

The espionage laws have served, and do serve, to inhibit the press in covering national-security affairs, because their existence implies their potential use against newsmen. Most reporters have usually been cautious about accepting or quoting from classified documents (partly because they have not understood that, as a general rule, the act of stamping a document with a classification label is not a barrier to its publication). But a jury *might* find that publication of a particular classified document is a crime under the espionage laws. So the possibility of prosecution for reporting and publishing information "relating to the national defense" is always present.

The Boston grand jury that investigated Neil Sheehan was well publicized, and its inquiries cannot fail to have had a chilling affect on the press as a whole.

Nevertheless, secrets *do* get published, and the more authoritarian American minds have long looked wistfully across the Atlantic to England, where the Official Secrets Act helps to keep the press in line. Under Section 2 of the British Official Secrets Act of 1911, it is an offense for a Crown servant or government contractor to make an unauthorized disclosure of information which he has learned about in his job, and it is equally a crime to receive such information. The effect is to bar publication, since a reporter who breaks the law by receiving unauthorized government information would reveal his crime by publishing it. The British Act covers all kinds of records and information, in any form, written or verbal, regardless of whether the information applies to the national defense. It covers all servants of the crown, a policeman no less than a Minister.

The Act is reinforced by a "D-Notice System," a peculiarly British institution. D-Notices are issued by a joint press-broadcasting-government committee, and they serve to remind the editor that a piece of information, or a category of information, may well fall within the restrictions of the Official Secrets Act. In effect, the D-Notice tells the editor that he is free to publish but had better not.

The United States, with no Official Secrets Act, must limp along with prior restraint and attacks on the press in the style made famous by Spiro T. Agnew (before his conviction for income tax evasion). But these are poor substitutes, and the pressure for a U.S. official secrets act has mounted in recent years. Under present law, in order successfully to prosecute a reporter, the government may have to prove a number of things, among them, that the information published does in fact relate to the national defense, and that the reporter acted in bad faith or with guilty knowledge in publishing it. That is to say, that he had reason to believe that the information could be used "to the injury of the United States or to the advantage of any foreign nation. . . ."

Since the determination of whether a reporter has violated

the spy laws must be left to a jury—a notoriously unreliable group of people—the government has long been tempted to eliminate the middle man and make guilt for publication automatic. The British Act embodies the principle of automatic guilt for disclosure of government information, and this principle is what the Nixon administration would substitute for the First Amendment in America.

Early in 1973, the administration, dissatisfied with existing statutes, introduced what amounts to a virtual Official Secrets Act for the United States. Buried in the lengthy revision of the federal criminal code proposed by the White House and introduced in Congress are proposals that would make it a federal crime to disclose "classified information," thus neatly welding the entire classification system to the espionage laws for the first time. Under the Nixon proposal, an official who had disclosed "classified information" to an unauthorized person—even if the information was improperly classified—would be guilty of a felony, and so would a reporter or editor who received "national-defense information" and failed to return it to the government promptly. Taken together, these provisions are close enough to Section 2 of the British Official Secrets Act as to be almost indistinguishable from it.

This latest effort to impose secrecy in America had its roots in 1966, when Congress appointed a Commission on Reform of the Federal Criminal Law; former governor Edmund G. Brown of California was named chairman. The Commission submitted its lengthy recommendations in 1971. Then in November 1972, the staff of the Senate Subcommittee on Criminal Laws and Procedures, headed by Senator John McClellan of Arkansas, drew up its own bill to revise the criminal code. It contained a provision making it a federal crime to reveal "classified information." Senator McClellan wanted Senator Sam Ervin, Jr., of North Carolina as a cosponsor, and Senator Ervin's staff, alert to the implications of this language, negotiated the words "classified information" out of the bill as part of the price of Ervin's support. The language was changed to "national-defense information," which was an improvement, but the phrase was still very broadly defined.

Four months later, the White House version of the bill was

introduced. One section would make it a crime for a government official to give "classified information" to a person not authorized to receive it. Under this section, a person who receives such information cannot be prosecuted as an accomplice, a provision that at first glance would appear to exempt the press. Other sections, however, would make any person guilty of an offense if he communicates "information relating to the national defense" to an unauthorized person, or possesses such information and fails to deliver it "promptly" to the government. National-defense information is very broadly defined to include even foreign relations. And, clearly, these sections would apply to the press.

Under the *Caldwell* decision, reporters would be unable to cite the First Amendment as grounds for refusing to name the sources of such documents or information. Since a reporter who published "information relating to the national defense" would already have revealed his crime by the act of publication, he might not be able to cite the Fifth Amendment and fear of possible self-incrimination if asked to reveal the source of his documents. And since reporters or others who receive information are excepted from prosecution as accomplices under the section dealing with "classified information" they could not claim the Fifth Amendment under this section, either.

It is, therefore, a neatly drawn package, designed in the first instance to make it a crime for government officials to leak unauthorized information; second, to inhibit reporters from printing it; third, to force newsmen who do publish to reveal their sources of national-security information. Because the proposed law makes no mention of bad faith or guilty knowledge or intent, the government would not have to prove this key element in a prosecution of a newsman or of his source. By making it a crime for an official to disclose classified information to an unauthorized person, the administration embraced the concept of automatic guilt, for by a mere administrative act—stamping a document "Top Secret," "Secret," or "Confidential"—disclosure would become a crime under the law. The punishment is designed to be rather discouraging to reporters and sources: fifteen years in jail and a $100,000 fine if the offense is committed during wartime or a "national-defense emergency," whatever that is. Seven years and $50,000 in other cases. Three years in jail and a $25,000 for minor infractions. The *pièce de résistance* is that it would not be a defense to prosecution under the section dealing with classified information to prove that the document in question was "improperly classified." In other words, a bureaucrat could stamp *anything* with a secrecy label—and disclosure would be a crime.

Such legislation would of course give the government total control over information, instead of, as is now the case, only partial control. Its passage would mean the effective repeal of the First Amendment, and the early arrival of 1984 in time for the American Bicentennial. What is truly shocking about such legislation is not its terms and its provisions, which are totalitarian, but the fact that the legislation could have been drafted and proposed at all. For it reveals a quality of mind that should be truly frightening to anyone who respects truth and values freedom.

III Pressure on Sources

Closely related to the question of whether the press can constitutionally be prosecuted for publishing national-security information is whether or not the government can take legal sanctions against those who provide reporters with this information—i.e., their sources. Although Daniel Ellsberg was technically no longer in the government at the time of the Pentagon Papers case, this was precisely the political issue involved in his prosecution. Ellsberg was clearly the biggest leaker that Washington has seen in modern times, a superstar of leaks, and something, as the President's Communications Director himself pointed out, had to be done.

Now, if one admires the Weberian model of efficient bureaucracy, one can argue that the orderly conduct of public business requires that action be taken against a leaker. Weberian or not, the Nixon White House employed a team of "plumbers" to plug leaks to the press. There are at least two problems with prosecuting leakers, however. First, if only *un-*

authorized leakers are punished, then the press and public become captive of the authorized leak. And who is to decide whether a leak is authorized? At what level of authority can an official decide, without specific permission from his superiors, to leak certain information, whether classified or not, to the news media? Since group leaks, known as "backgrounders," are as much a way of life in Washington as the annual Cherry Blossom Festival, it is difficult to see who shall draw the line, bell the cat, and draft the indictments.

Second, former Presidents and lesser officials often write their memoirs after putting the burden of public service behind them, and frequently their works include information from classified documents that they had foresightedly removed when they left Washington. The government officials then profit from the sale of classified information in book form. As I have written elsewhere in this connection, "To put it simply, the classification system has been used to deprive the American people of vital information, which is then later sold to them by political leaders whom they elected or by appointees of those elected leaders. But the same information is denied to Americans when it is current, when it might be pertinent to the opinions they hold and the manner in which they express those opinions at the ballot box." [7]

It seems morally and logically difficult to justify the prosecution of government officials who leak secrets as long as Presidents and other officials are free to publish those same secrets in memoirs and to collect royalties. Nevertheless, even as the law now stands, it is possible for the government to prosecute newsmen, and their sources, for publishing or disclosing information which the government contends relates to the national defense.

Moreover, in the Ellsberg trial, the government in effect put forth some novel and ominous legal theories, namely, that the government owns not only classified documents but the information contained in them, and that it is a crime to steal the information. In addition, the government invented a new crime nowhere defined in the law—interference with its right to control the dissemination of classified information. If indeed the government owns and controls "information" in the abstract, it is not hard to see how the press, too, could be prosecuted for "stealing", i.e., publishing, such information.

These and other constitutional issues raised in the Ellsberg prosecution were never reached, since all charges against Daniel Ellsberg and Anthony Russo, Jr., were dismissed by the judge. He acted because the government admitted it had wiretapped Ellsberg's conversations, and admitted as well that burglars in the employ of the White House had broken into the office of Ellsberg's psychiatrist in search of medical records.

But there remains a growing threat, implicit in the prosecution of Daniel Ellsberg and actual in the arrest of reporter Les Whitten, of sanctions against newsmen for alleged theft of government information. Section 641 of the U.S. Code, Title 18, designed to prevent civil servants from taking home paper clips, may be used to jail reporters who possess classified documents or publish the information contained in them.

Prosecution of journalists under existing espionage or theft statutes, or under any new secrets act, would, in time, very likely destroy American democracy.

And here we are at the heart of the matter. I maintain that *the right of the press to report about the government and the activities of the government cannot be qualified consistent with the First Amendment.* The moment that reporters are prosecuted or prevented from publishing certain kinds of information about the government, the press is no longer free. It is censored and regulated. And this would surely happen if the government had the power to declare that broad classes of information relate to the national security or national defense and that it is a crime to publish such information. Once the government controls the definition of national security, there is no limit to what information it may decide falls within this category. The national security or the national interest is always a political term, defined differently at various times by different political parties, leaders, and administrations. Everything affects the national defense.

And governments have always been concerned about leaks. It is irritating to officials to see information contained in documents—especially documents that have been stamped with a secrecy label—turn up in *The New York Times.* Usually, however, official secrets turn out not to be secrets at all, but official embarrassments. The rationale for secrecy is that the American people must be denied certain information in order to deny it to foreign adversaries. More often than not, however, just the opposite is true—the information denied to the American people is well known to other nations.

For example, in April 1965, when President Johnson ordered the U.S. combat role in Vietnam kept secret, it was indeed kept secret from the American people for two months. It is hardly likely, however, that the Viet Cong or the North Vietnamese were unaware that the Marines were shooting at them. Similarly, the American role in the secret war in Laos was scarcely a secret from the Laotians. So in fact, the secrecy and deception are injuring only ourselves.

I do not overlook the requirement that government keep certain things secret at certain times. Nor do I deny that from the government's point of view, and even from the public's point of view, it may be necessary to balance the requirements of a free press against the needs of secrecy and security. But to concede that rights may be in conflict is not to concede the power of censorship to the government. The press may have no constitutional right to know everything the government is doing, and to publish it, but I contend that it does have the right to publish what it can find out. Once information escapes from government hands, it is out. As Professor Thomas Emerson of the Yale Law School has put it so well, "A cat in the bag cannot be treated in the same way as a cat outside the bag. Once the information gets outside the executive—once the executive loses its control for any reason—the information becomes part of the public domain." [8]

This does not mean that the press must print everything it learns. In a free society, the press should also be free not to print. Such instances ought to be extremely rare, because normally disclosure and public debate is the far healthier course in an open society. But the important consideration is that the decision not to print or to delay a story be left up to the press and not imposed by the government. The press can listen to a government official's plea that a story not be printed, it can weigh his arguments, and make its decision. That is called freedom. Anything less is called censorship.

IV A Newsman's Privilege?

There are other ways in which the government can place pressure on the press by placing pressure on its sources. This is what is really involved in the issue of newsmen's privilege. Press subpoenas and grand-jury investigations are a subtle form of prior restraint in that they discourage potential sources from ever talking to reporters in the first place. Forcing newsmen to talk about their sources would seem to be an obvious abridgment of freedom of the press within the meaning of the First Amendment, and four Justices of the Supreme Court thought so, but five did not, and we have a democracy in all things, including the Supreme Court. In its central finding, the majority opinion of the Court in the *Caldwell*, *Branzburg*, and *Pappas* cases seems at worst disingenous and at best obtuse. The Court held that the public interest in law enforcement outweighed the burden on a free press resulting when "reporters, like other citizens, respond to relevant questions put to them in the course of a valid grand jury investigation or criminal trial." The Court added: "This conclusion itself involves no restraint on what newspapers may publish or on the type or quality of information reporters may seek to acquire, nor does it threaten the vast bulk of confidential relationships between reporters and their sources." [9] This is an amazing and remarkable statement, in that confidentiality of sources goes to the heart of the news-gathering process. It does affect the nature of the information that a newspaper may publish, because, while it may not limit what information reporters "seek to acquire," it does affect what information they get.

Defenders of *Caldwell* have sought to comfort us by pointing to Mr. Justice Powell's concurring opinion, in which he reassures us that "no harassment of newsmen will be tolerated." If a newsman believes that a grand-jury investigation "is not being conducted in good faith, he is not without remedy."

One man's harassment is another man's law enforcement, and to rely on the good faith of federal, state, and local prosecutors not to harass newsmen is to leave the First Amendment in rather shaky condition. There is in all of us at least a bit of Walter Mitty, and Mr. Justice Powell's words conjure up a picture of a reporter hauled before the grand jury, pointing his finger righteously at the DA and declaiming: "You, sir, are not conducting this investigation in good faith!" Whether the newsman in such circumstances would receive Justice Powell's "appropriate protective order from the Court" may be left to the imagination.

Since the First Amendment has proved inadequate as a newsman's shield, in the aftermath of the adverse decision in *Caldwell*, there have been Congressional hearings and renewed attempts to pass legislation to protect newsmen from naming sources. This has raised a very real concern that a bill spelling out protection for the press carries with it the implication that the press does not now enjoy such protection under the First Amendment—hence that a qualified shield law will actually limit the power of the press. However, there are numerous instances where legislation is used to reinforce and protect rights already contained in the Constitution. What immediately comes to mind is the public accommodations section of the Civil Rights Act of 1964, which spelled out the right of all Americans to stay at a motel or eat in a restaurant, even though that right might reasonably be assumed to have already been protected by the Fourteenth Amendment. Similarly, the Voting Rights Act of 1965, permitting suspension of literacy tests in certain areas and the appointment of federal examiners to register blacks in the South, reinforced what the Fifteenth Amendment had already provided. The analogy may not be perfect. But if the times, and the whims of political leaders, seem to require protection for newsmen, the law can be phrased in a way that is, on balance, reinforcing rather than limiting. A second objection, the problem of defining journalists under such legislation, is tricky but not insurmountable. Once the definitions are established, it could be left to the courts to determine whether a particular individual fell within them.

There are those who argue that a reporter's willingness to go to jail is the ultimate protection he can offer his source. But this is hardly a solution when the number of instances in which reporters have been subpoenaed has increased markedly, and where the political environment is hostile to the press. Willingness to go to jail is not an index of freedom in a democracy. At least it shouldn't be.

While strong arguments can be made both for and against a shield bill, on balance such legislation seems necessary and desirable in the present climate. The desirability of shield legislation may really be viewed as more of a political than a constitutional question. In the best of all possible worlds, a shield law would not be necessary. The First Amendment already protects newsmen, in theory. But if journalists are going to jail, they are not being protected in fact. In these circumstances, shield legislation appears at least temporarily necessary. The purpose of a shield law is not to establish a special privilege for newsmen but to insure that the protection already implicit in the First Amendment is actually afforded them. Obviously, a favorable First Amendment decision by the Supreme Court on newsmen's sources would be the most desirable remedy. In the meantime, a shield law would seem better than no protection at all.

Government pressure on the press is not limited to prior restraint, subsequent punishment, subpoenas, and other forms of legal action. The government employs a wide range of tools in applying political pressure to the news media.

Senator Ervin has called the Nixon administration the "most repressive" toward freedom of the press and other rights since the administration of John Adams. The administration's effort to discredit the press in the eyes of the public began with, but was not limited to, Spiro Agnew's attacks on network commentators in November 1969. Ronald Ziegler solemnly assured us then that the Vice President spoke for himself, although Mr. Ziegler said, the President's speechwriter, Patrick Buchanan, had drafted Mr. Agnew's speech. Many other high officials spoke out against the news media, and their names have since become increasingly familiar: H. R. Haldeman, L. Patrick Gray III, Richard Kleindienst, Kenneth Clawson, Charles Colson—the roll call of statesmen could go on. The President himself criticized the television networks for their insufficiently optimistic coverage of the invasions of Laos and Cambodia.

The drumfire of criticism by the administration, aside from its sheer therapeutic value to the officials concerned, appears to have had at least three purposes: to cast doubt on the credibility of the press in order to divert public attention from the credibility of the government; to intimidate the press and make it more cautious in its judgments of the administration's actions and policies; and to build and consolidate political support among those segments of the public that share White House attitudes toward the news media.

The natural reaction of many members of the press to such criticism is to minimize its importance on the grounds that the press can take care of itself. But it is not that simple: concerted and sustained criticism of the press by the highest officials of the federal government has ominous implications. It is a form of pressure designed to weaken a constitutionally protected institution; if successful in the short run such a policy would increase executive-branch control over information. But in the long run it is even more dangerous, because the people depend on the press for their information about government, and if they are encouraged not to believe the press, their disbelief is bound to reach back to the government itself. In this circle of disbelief, no one wins.

There are other political means by which the government places pressure on the press. These range from barring a *Washington Post* society reporter from White House functions to a wholesale attempt to dictate the content of public television. When *Newsday* wrote a critical series about the President's closest friend, Charles "Bebe" Rebozo, its White House correspondent did not get a seat on the plane to China. The newspaper was even unable to get a repairman through the White House gate to fix the correspondent's typewriter in the press room. The White House reporter for the *Los Angeles Times*, whose copy offended the since-disgraced palace guard, somehow did not draw as many "pool" assignments to cover the President. A CBS correspondent was investigated by the FBI, and the President's assistant, John Ehrlichman, asked the network whether it might consider transferring the CBS White

House correspondent back to Texas. The President's Telecommunications Director threatened television stations with the loss of their federal licenses if they fail to correct "bias" in network news programs. The list of such examples is much longer, of course.

Developments in the Watergate scandal have once more demonstrated the central and indispensable role of the free press in America. The people have learned that the government they elected was run by a gang of corrupt men and criminals. Those responsible for enforcing the law were breaking it; those chosen to provide moral leadership were providing amoral leadership. The would-be destroyers of the press have themselves been destroyed. The terrible truths that shook America in the spring of 1973 would not have been brought out into the sunlight without the press, and particularly without two tireless young reporters and a great newspaper that had the courage to support them.

These cataclysmic events may tend to overshadow the past, to make us forget the years of harassment of the press by the shattered Nixon administration. We should not forget. The temptation to repress, restrict, and blame the news media will remain a continuing danger.

But perhaps the agony of the Watergate, and the revulsion over it, will finally make our political leaders understand, once and for all, that lying and secrecy have no place in a democracy. Perhaps it will mark an end to deception and a beginning of a time of truth and decency.

V Discussion

MR. LEWIS: I think Mr. Wise is too optimistic when he says that we don't have any connection in this country between the classification system and the criminal laws. In fact, the case against Mr. Ellsberg was an attempt—a brazen attempt, a serious attempt—to make exactly such a connection. One of the charges against Ellsberg and Russo was that they had been involved in a conspiracy to defraud the United States by impairing its lawful government function of controlling the dissemination of classified government studies. That is the language of the indictment. There, without any statute whatsoever supporting the notion that violation of the classification system can be criminal, was an attempt to make it so. Indeed, the entire Ellsberg prosecution was an attempt to give the United States an Official Secrets Act of the British kind without even the safeguard of having to pass it through Congress first. So I am even less optimistic, if possible, than Mr. Wise on that point.

I will note in passing my disagreement about shield laws. I do not think we ought to have newspaper shield laws, for two reasons. First, I doubt that any shield law likely to pass will do more good than harm. Any shield law that could actually be enacted would turn out to be more injurious than no shield law, would take more away than it would give. Second, I don't think it is rationally possible to classify who should benefit from a shield law. I personally do not want to benefit from a shield law that does not help people who work on underground newspapers, or Ralph Nader, or others who might not qualify for the formal designation of journalist. I don't want to begin drawing lines about who is a journalist, because I think that is dangerous.

One comment I would make generally is that I am against euphoria on behalf of the press—euphoria even about Watergate. Very few newspapers or newspapermen worried about Watergate in the summer of 1972 or did any real work on it: fewer still did any effective work. We did hold the 1972 election on a fraudulent basis. It was not only the fault of the press, but the fault of the flabbiness and corruptness of Congress and some of its members—corruptness not in a monetary sense, but in their unwillingness to look into something vitally important to the coming election. The laziness of the press had something to do with this.

Even now the press is insufficiently sensitive to a lot of things that ought to worry us a great deal. It is insufficiently sensitive, for example, to the wiretapping that we now know Henry Kissinger not only condoned but inaugurated—of members of his own staff. It is insufficiently sensitive to the attempt in the Ellsberg case to create an Official Secrets Act by judiciary. I doubt that there are many editors in the country who know about the *Marchetti* case. It is an astounding proposition: that if you have worked for the CIA, you cannot write a book afterward that mentions or deals with it without first submitting that book to the CIA for clearance. I would not have thought that the Constitution or the First Amendment was something you could swear away by signing a piece of paper. But so the Court of Appeals held, and the Supreme Court declined to review it.

Not only the press but the public in this country, until quite recently, could be said to have had an insufficient sense of outrage. The press is only helpful if what it says interests people.

MR. SYLVESTER: I find Mr. Wise's paper rather commonplace newspaper talk: the government is being hard on him. Well, that is our business. I don't care how hard they are. Our job is to fight back and get the news anyway. Pressures on the press are not new. To those of us who covered the McCarthy hearings, the most terrible pressure you were under then was not from the government but from the large proportion of people in this country who were McCarthyites. If you simply wrote your stories using only the transcript of the hearings, you were vilified in a way that I have never seen newsmen vilified since. The pressures are constant. They come from government, they come from outside government, they come from groups of people. But if you can't take pressure you don't deserve to be in the business.

Mr. Wise referred to Mr. Agnew, who capitalized on a tremendous distrust in our business throughout the country. This is a distrust which has been building over a number of years.

You can talk to your friends or strangers, almost anybody who has been reported on by the press. They will tell you, rightly or wrongly, that they were misrepresented, that the story was not right. The newspapers never get anything right. We know in our business that that is not true, but there is a tremendous distrust of newsmen, and it goes back a number of years.

I doubt very much if the government could be as successful as it is in harassing us, in bringing pressure to bear, if there was not such a widespread distrust of the press throughout the country. I think there always will be distrust. It is now at its height. Possibly Watergate will change that. Maybe people will begin to see that there is some truth in us.

So far as shield laws are concerned, it seems to me that we as newspaper people are putting our heads right in the lion's mouth. We are asking a special privilege when special privileges are something we as newsmen and newspapers, and television and radio news media, should be utterly against. It is true that when a newspaper truck backs up and blocks traffic in the middle of the city, it is violating traffic laws, but it doesn't get fined. We do take special privileges. Let us not take this one.

MR. STEIN: I, too, would like to feel that the First Amendment is shield law enough. However, the alternative, as I see it, to not having a shield law is more newsmen going to jail. I was a practicing newspaperman for almost seventeen years and I was fortunate in not having gone to jail, but I talked to Peter Bridge, who did, and he did not find the experience at all enjoyable. The atmosphere calls for a shield law. I don't think there is any alternative. I would favor a shield law that provides for absolute immunity. Any other shield law would not even be worth discussing. I fully conceur with Mr. Wise that the First Amendment should be buttressed with a very strong and absolutely unassailable shield law, or we are going to see more journalists in jail.

MR. LEWIS: Would your absolute strong shield law cover Professor Samuel Popkin of Harvard, who went to prison for contempt for refusing to disclose to a grand jury possible contacts or sources in connection with the Pentagon Papers cases? Would it cover Ralph Nader if he were investigating a government agency and declined to give his sources? If it did not cover those people, I agree with Mr. Sylvester. I don't want to have an advantage over them.

MR. STEIN: No, I think it wouldn't cover them. That would pose almost insoluble problems. Mr. Nader is capable of taking care of himself. So is Mr. Popkin. I think the limits of journalism must be defined. I can see that it is a weakness, but there is a business or profession called journalism which has practitioners who are accredited, who are recognized. This would have to be defined. In spite of this definition problem, I still would move very strongly for a shield law, particularly in light of our current situation.

MR. SCHWARTZ: I would agree with Mr. Lewis. It is very hard to be overoptimistic in this area, but I would caution against taking an opposite point of view. I am speaking primarily of the law. We overlook the tremendous progress that has been made in this country in the First Amendment area, particularly in freedom of the press. I would say without any fear of contradiction that the press is freer in this country from investigation and criticism of government than in any other country in the world today. Our British visitors are amazed at the leeway which the law gives our press. If we compare the law today with what it was in earlier times, we would have to conclude that tremendous progress has been made.

The people who voted the First Amendment into the Constitution approved such things as sending a newspaper reporter to jail for printing that if, during a Presidential visit, when a twenty-four-gun salute went off, the wad of the cannon had landed in the President's backside, it would have been an improvement. The reporter was sent to jail and there was no protest at the time.

We have had in our history newspapers suppressed, issues confiscated, editors sent to jail. These things would be unthinkable today. Think of the progress in areas such as libel, where the Supreme Court has so expanded the right of newspapers to comment on public officials and matters of public interest.

One thing which is never mentioned is the tendency of the press, which is a business in this country, to conglomerate and to go into other businesses, particularly businesses that depend on privileges from government.

How many newspapers that also own radio or television stations have investigated concentration of ownership in public media?

MR. WESTIN: Congressman Robert Drinan made the comment the other day that all over the country prosecutors are looking at what Congress and the state legislatures will do if a shield law is not passed. The clear message to prosecutors will be: Congress does not think reporters ought to have immunity and you can bring them up before the grand juries, and call them before other proceedings, because the *inaction* of Congress is a signal that you should not be given statutory protection. It seems to me that first we must answer the question whether judicial or legislative protection is where we should place our primary reliance. Some may have noticed an article by Joe Califano in the *New Republic* arguing that the Supreme Court decisions are not really as unpromising as they appeared. He said in the long run we can count on the federal courts to take Justice Powell's remarks in the *Caldwell* case and extend protection to newsmen in specific situations. Maybe we would have more trouble with Congress, and Califano suggested we ought not to go the legislative route. I don't agree with that. I don't believe the problem is that hard when you try to clarify and act on it.

The definition of whom should be covered: I agree that a privilege only for the press would be incorrect because another stream of development has been taking place in the American public community. That is a growing concern for privacy of research of both the investigative reporting and the scholarly type—into social-research topics, drugs, alcoholism, student activism. In these areas, legislative exemptions from penetrating confidential and research relationships have been written into recent federal legislation. There is public support for recognizing that if legislation is to be written, it should be comprehensive. It should cover not only the press, but be broad enough to cover all to whom confidential information is given in the expectation that it will be held in confidence.

The government has the burden of making out a case, in grand-jury proceedings or at a trial, through its own evidence, rather than going back to the easier procedure of calling people up and extracting information from them. To summon the journalist or the investigator and require him to make the government's case under penal sanction is a frightening shift in the government's investigative or adjudicative job. The answer to Mr. Lewis is, yes, it would be wrong to single out the press. We need a comprehensive privilege which covers more than the press. It should include the investigative journalist and professional researchers in the academic community.

On the scope of the privilege, I think we should distinguish between the investigative phases of our criminal-justice system and the adjudicative phase. We should give an absolute privilege in the investigative phase, before legislative committees and grand juries. In the adjudicative phase, at trial, the defendant has a Sixth Amendment right to exculpatory evidence. There, we should allow the defendant to compel the testimony of a reporter or researcher, where that is necessary to the defense.

MR. CLARK: What Mr. Westin says strikes a chord with me. The distinction between journalists and other researchers is propagated by self-interest. It is not a real distinction.

MR. MARSHALL: We should not let this subject go by on the premise that only newspapers are involved. Television, which is an important news media, is not nearly so protected from pressure, including government pressure, as are newspapers. Mr. Wise refers to the *Red Lion* case. The *Red Lion* case is ambiguous, I suppose, but to some extent it says that the First Amendment does not apply to television news. That would seem to me to be an important decision.

MR. EMERSON: It is a mistake to interpret the *Red Lion* case as saying the First Amendment does not apply to radio and television. On the contrary, I would say that *Red Lion* applies the First Amendment in a double way to radio and television. The decision makes a distinction between radio and television operators when they express themselves—and there the First Amendment fully applies in the traditional way—and the fact that radio and television facilities, because of their scarcity, must be made available to other viewpoints. In this second connection radio and television stations act in the capacity of trustees, or agents, for other persons. To that extent, they can be required to broadcast certain material. Where they are broadcasting for themselves, they are protected by the usual First Amendment rules.

If through cable television or other technical advances, there is as much access to radio and television as there are to printing presses, then I think the second aspect of *Red Lion* would not be applicable. But until that time comes, I think the

Red Lion case was correct in opening up access to radio and television.

MR. MARSHALL: I realize the *Red Lion* case is based on scarcity of air waves, but you could say that *The New York Times* is a scarce item too, or *The Washington Post*. There are more television stations than newspapers in most cities.

MR. EMERSON: But there are more printing presses than there are wave lengths. I agree, incidentally, that any scheme of government regulation, such as is involved in licensing systems for radio and television stations, gives the government an enormous amount of pressure which can be exercised in an informal way. So I have no doubt that radio and television are subject to much greater pressure than the press. But that is a somewhat different question.

MR. RANSOM: It may sound too elementary, but we are talking about power, and the distribution of power. The issue before us is the power to get hold of and dispense knowledge. I am operating on the premise that knowledge is power in our system, and the system will not work, will break down, will be destroyed if any of the main institutions of our system use this power in an unrestrained fashion. We have discovered, to our amazement, that the Presidency has been using secret power in an unrestrained fashion. I am sure the Presidency will be punished. It will be punished by the press; it will be punished by Congress. In the past, Congress has been guilty as an accomplice of McCarthyism, using the press to exercise power in an unrestrained fashion. Senator McCarthy was ultimately punished. The press often abuses its power when publishers, editors, journalists, and columnists become so involved in the political process that they are manipulating it and going beyond the rights they hold and the freedoms they hold and, in so doing, abuse their responsibility. The unrestrained use of power on the part of any of our major institutions—President, Congress, or the press—will destroy our system.

MR. SALOSCHIN: I wonder if I could comment on that briefly from a lawyer's viewpoint. I think the last comment was particularly significant in terms of the preservation of a free society, which to me means a society in which power is diffused.

When we discuss subjects as we have discussed them here, like executive privilege and classification, we discuss power granted under the Constitution to this or that branch of government. But there are types of power, and very effective types of power, other than legal power. That is, to get things done in our society—or to prevent things from being done in our society—the movers are not necessarily the people who hold legal power. I have the legal power to start a steel company, but I assure you I don't have the practical power to do it.

In a society with an information explosion, the power to be able to select objects for attention becomes critical. Those institutions which disseminate information can shape the thinking of the public and focus the attention of the public.

This is a tremendous power, which does not reside primarily in government. When, as Mr. Sylvester says, this power has fallen to institutions which are fewer and fewer in number—and I am referring to the fact that twenty years ago we had seven or eight major newspapers in New York, and now we almost have a monopoly—we should be concerned. What are the techniques in our society of guarding against the possible abuses of monopoly power?

We regulate, but I don't think any of us wants to regulate, except for air waves, and even that gives us real problems. So we can't effectively rely on regulation. What can we rely on, then? We certainly don't want censorship. We have a king-sized problem here, and we have got to do something about it.

MR. DORSEN: I have a comment that follows from that and also the point Mr. Ransom made. Did Mr. Agnew do something wrong when he made his famous speech in Des Moines, and some of his other speeches, criticizing the press?

He was subjected to criticism by many of us and many people we would regard as our constituency. But isn't it a fact, as many here suggest, that the press should be responsible? If government believes that the press is being irresponsible, is it wrong for a high official to say so and say so the way he did? I am not talking about governmental discrimination against particular news media or newspaper people, but *speech*. Is there another way for the government to fight back if it honestly believes, as I take it Mr. Agnew and his friends did, that the press was being irresponsible?

MR. FRIEDMAN: I think there is a big difference between expressing disapproval of what the press says and the use of compulsory process against the press. In the brief *The New York Times* submitted to the Supreme Court in the *Caldwell* case, it indicated that in less than two years there were some sixty-five subpoenas served on the press.

Vice President Agnew made another speech, which was not widely reported, in which he expressed his disapproval of certain song lyrics that seemed to indicate an approval of smoking pot or taking dope. Immediately thereafter, the FCC issued a regulation against that kind of song.

MR. MARTIN: I don't see how Mr. Lewis can seriously suggest, if there are genuine problems, that we not try to fashion laws to deal with excesses against journalists. To react to the law as though it were a kind of all-or-nothing technology which either solves everything or fails to solve everything is not helpful.

MR. LEWIS: I couldn't agree more with Mr. Martin's dislike for all-or-nothing solutions. Indeed, that is precisely why I am against the shield law. I think questions like that have to be left to time and the judicial process to work out. I do not believe in trying to engrave into a statute a permanent law. It is not something that you can change every year or with every case that comes up. There is not time for Congress to pass a new shield law every year. Professor Schwartz said rightly that we had made great gains in the First Amendment and the freedom of the press. Most of those gains have come through the judicial process. One of the examples he gave was in the area of libel, and the case that brought about the change was the Supreme Court decision in *New York Times* v. *Sullivan*. It was not an act of Congress. I can assure you that if you had tried to get Congress to pass a law establishing what *New York Times* v. *Sullivan* established, you would have been laughed at. Further, *New York Times* v. *Sullivan* and later cases created a freedom for criticism of public officials or of people involved in public events, not for the press alone, but for everybody. That is the way I think the rule ought to be, not for the press alone.

MR. GILLERS: We have been talking about the press as an adversary of government and as a vehicle for information to the people. It has happened that the press has served as an appendage of government. It has received information that may be newsworthy, but has chosen not to print it. To what extent should any quality other than newsworthiness be a determinant in an editor's decision to print or not print a secret that the editor has gotten from a government source?

MR. SYLVESTER: "Newsworthy" is a very slippery word and I can hide behind it any number of different ways.

—by Ernest Fitzgerald

I Birth of a Whistle Blower

"Mr. President," the intense young Senator said, "I have introduced in the Senate today a bill to make it a violation of law for any officer of the federal government to dismiss or otherwise discipline a government employee for testifying before a committee of Congress." After more introductory remarks, he summarized the need for his bill for his colleagues in the Senate chamber: "It is essential to the security of the nation and to the very lives of the people, as we look into these vitally important issues, that every witness have complete freedom from reprisal when he is given an opportunity to tell what he knows.

"There is too much at stake to permit foreign policy and military strategy to be established on the basis of half-truths and suppression of testimony.

"Unless protection is given to witnesses who are members of the armed services or employees of the government, the scheduled hearings will amount to no more than a parade of yes men for administration policies as they exist."

The young Senator's name was Richard Milhous Nixon. The date was April 26, 1951. Senator Nixon was concerned about the fate of dissident witnesses General Douglas MacArthur and Admiral Denfeld, who were at odds with President Truman. Senator Nixon, along with cosponsoring Senators Taft, McCarran, Wherry, Schoeppel, Bricker, and Joseph McCarthy, was seeking to strengthen the law protecting Congressional witnesses, 18 U.S. Code 1505. The law then provided a $5000 fine and a five-year term for persons convicted of violating the law. Senator Nixon's amendment would have made any adverse action taken against a government witness within one year after his Congressional testimony *prima facie* evidence of criminal retaliation in the absence of "misfeasance, malfeasance," etc., on the part of the witness.

Senator Nixon's amendment did not pass, but 18 U.S. Code 1505 has remained part of the United States criminal code, and over the years Mr. Nixon expressed ever-increasing devotion to law and order. Accordingly, a reasonable and trusting person might have expected Mr. Nixon to remain a stanch advocate of unfettered truth-telling by government employees after he was elected President. This same reasonable person might have expected a freer flow of previously suppressed information from President Nixon's administration, via Congressional witnesses, even if their testimony was embarrassing, that is to say, whistle blowing.

The Nixonian attitude toward candor was especially important to me, because I had been guilty of the bureaucratic crime of giving embarrassing Congressional testimony just after Mr. Nixon's first election but before he took office. On November 13, 1968, I testified on military procurement problems before Senator William Proxmire's Subcommittee for Economy in Government. In my job as Deputy for Management Systems in the Air Force Secretariat, I knew a good deal about the status of the Air Force's big weapons systems' procurement projects—to much for my own good, as it turned out. Senator Proxmire's interest that day was focused on the giant C5A transport plane which Lockheed Aircraft Corporation was building for the Air Force. The C5A project was the Pentagon's model procurement program, and was described by its enthusiasts as "a miracle of procurement." Actually, the project had suffered disastrous technical problems and huge cost overruns from its inception, but the Pentagon and its contractors had concealed the problems by the Big Lie technique. Senator Proxmire asked me if the miracle of procurement was, in fact, not a miracle at all, but instead would overrun its cost estimates by $2 billion. I waffled a little in giving a long Pentagonal answer. Translated from bureaucratese, my answer was "maybe." It was enough, though. I had committed truth. When the reporters closed in on me in the big Senate hearing room, I knew I was in big trouble.

Professionally, the roof fell in on me immediately. Invitations to major business meetings in the Pentagon dried up. Instead of keeping track of the big weapons programs—the C5A, the F-111 fighter-bomber, the Minuteman missile, and the like—I was asked to look into food-service costs in the mess halls and into the construction of a bowling alley in Thailand. My boss's military aide, or "weenie," as they are called in the trade, was dispatched to disinvite me to official and semi-official social functions on the grounds that my presence would be "embarrassing." My career tenure as a civil servant, which theoretically protected me from arbitrary dismissal, was revoked without explanation just twelve days after my testimony before Senator Proxmire's Subcommittee. My immediate boss asked associates to stop working with me.

My testimony threatened the impending bailout of Lockheed. What *The Wall Street Journal* later called "the artful rescue of Lockheed" was even then underway, and by spilling the beans, I complicated matters. Senator Richard Russell of Georgia, Chairman of the Senate Armed Services Committee and soon to be Chairman of the Appropriations Committee and President Pro Tem of the Senate, was Lockheed's chief patron in the Congress. Lockheed's Marietta (Georgia) plant, which was assembling the C5A, was the largest employer in the state. Senator Russell was distressed at my testimony, and so informed the Secretary of the Air Force, Dr. Harold Brown. Secretary of Defense Clark Clifford, a big-time Washington fixer for giant corporations, also passed the word that he was "very displeased with Mr. Fitzgerald."

Responding to all these signals from on high, the Air Force's personnel bureaucrats, led by Harold Brown's administrative assistant, John Lang, prepared a long memo outlining the three best ways to get rid of Fitzgerald, including one which the memo frankly described as "underhanded."

With all these troubles, I was naturally hopeful that things would change with the replacement of the Johnson-Clifford regime by the fresh new Nixon-Laird administration. Things did change. They got worse. The downhill slide of my Pentagon career accelerated. The new Secretary of the Air Force, Robert Seamans, falsely accused me of security violations in secret testimony before Mendel Rivers' House Armed Services Committee. Secretary of Defense Melvin Laird implored his subordinates in writing to find ways to "thwart or amelioriate" criticisms like those of the C5A scandal. Apparently, the thought that he might "thwart or ameliorate" criticisms through reform never crossed Mr. Laird's mind, and when he and the rest of the Nixon administration adopted as their own the scandals they had inherited from the outgoing Democrats, my days in the Pentagon were numbered. Having decided to continue the Pentagonal thefts, it was only prudent to get rid of troublesome, whistle-blowing watchmen. Since I was among the noisiest objectors to stealing in the name of defense, it seemed a good idea to do me in thoroughly, as an example to other potential truth-telling tightwads in the Pentagon. *The Washington Post*'s Bernard Nossiter, commenting on this tactic, recalled Voltaire's remarks on the execution of Admiral George Byng: "It is good, from time to time, to kill an admiral, in order to encourage the others."

In the predatory, parasitic federal bureaucracy, simple firing of a nonconformist is viewed as an inadequate deterrent to good stewardship. The dissenter must be utterly ruined, then hounded for the rest of his life if possible. As Admiral Hyman Rickover has said, "If you must sin, sin against God, not against the bureaucracy. God may forgive you but the bureaucracy never will." Having decided to make an example of me, the Pentagon intensified its organized high-level badmouthing campaign, led by the mendacious Secretary of the Air Force, Robert Seamans. Hoping to find some factual support for the charges they were already circulating, the Air Force unleashed its Office of Special Investigations (OSI), headed by General Joseph Cappucci, to probe my private life for defamatory material. Investigative departments of giant military contractors I had offended were also drawn into the act. In fact, it was through the inept bungling of the contractor gumshoes that I first learned of the dirt-digging attempts. One of my friends, a former military gumshoe, was approached by an old Service buddy, retired and working as an investigator for a West Coast contractor. The contractor investigator told our mutual friend that his firm, in concert "with the DOD" (Department of Defense), was finally going to "get Ernie." A joint investigation was under way to establish my 1) relationship with women other than my wife, 2) overuse of alcohol, 3) use of drugs, or 4) homosexual contacts.

Since I was too busy and too poor to have serious problems with items 1) and 2) and had never been attracted by items 3) and 4), I wasn't too worried about the gumshoes digging up significant facts in their efforts. However, I knew enough of the ruthlessness and lack of morality of the dominant bureaucrats to recognize that the rascals were perfectly capable of fabricating incidents, so I passed word among my friends that I would like to learn more about the dirt file being assembled on me. Eventually, with the help of Senator William Proxmire, Congressman William Moorhead, and some brave OSI agents, I learned that a nationwide investigation (with file number—HQD 24–12052) had been authorized. The snoopers didn't find anything noteworthy in my sex life or drinking habits, but they did manage to flush anonymous informants T-1, T-2, T-3 and T-4, who were willing to provide some juicy gossip. To add to Dr. Seamans' false security charges, the Ts' accused me of the heinous crime of working late in the Pentagon (it made my fellow bureaucrats feel guilty in their early-afternoon stampede out), and of being a threat to the Republic because I was a "penny pincher" as evidenced by the fact that I drove an old Rambler automobile. The Ts' also passed on a rumor that I was guilty of conflicts of interest in connection with the business operations of the industrial-engineering firm I had headed before going to work in the Pentagon.

General Cappucci was troubled only momentarily by the fact that the conflict-of-interest charges didn't stand up under investigation. He simply discarded those investigative reports which cleared me of the charges. At the same time, the anonymous gossip was retained in the official dirt file, which supposedly supported the charges that I was guilty of security violations and conflicts of interest.

Even though Dr. Seamans had to back away from his lies about security violations when confronted with them in public, and the conflict-of-interest charges were proved groundless, the bureaucratic hatchet men were not even slowed in their organized campaign to bad-mouth me in the business community, in the Justice Department, on Capitol Hill, and in the White House. Assistant Secretary of the Air Force Spencer Schedler, fresh from his triumphs as an advance man for Vice President Agnew, and his military aide, Colonel Dudley Pewitt, were dispatched to the White House to spread the smear charges. Messrs. Schedler and Pewitt had the misfortune to encounter an honest man, Clark Mollenhoff, a Pulitzer prize-winning investigative reporter, who unaccountably had been appointed special counsel to President Nixon. When the Pentagon pair tried to sell him their slanderous stories, Mr. Mollenhoff challenged them to put the charges in writing so that actions appropriate to the alleged crimes could be started. When Messrs. Schedler and Pewitt refused to make their charges official, Clark Mollenhoff made his own investigation, which convinced him that I was one of the long list of people he had seen smeared by the Pentagon bureaucrats to cover up and divert attention from their own bungling and malfeasance. Mr. Mollenhoff tried to persuade President Nixon to intervene to keep me from being fired, but got only ridicule from Presidential advisers Haldeman and Ehrlichman for his troubles. At the time, late 1969, Mr. Mollenhoff thought President Nixon was personally receptive to the suggestion that I be promoted rather than fired.

However, the military and civilian bureaucrats and their big-contractor partners continued to demand my scalp, and after many adventures I was finally fired.

After leaving the Pentagon, I learned the true price of whistle blowing to the embarrassment of the powerful military spending complex. The punishment for such deviant behavior is to be outlawed, particularly in professional relationships with and responsible employment by either big business or government. The Pentagon is far and away the world's major customer and dispenser of patronage. Every large manufacturing company, every big bank—in fact, every major commercial institution in the country—has an interest in staying on the good side of the Defense Department. So do practically all big colleges and universities as well as other subdivisions of government. Therefore, all such organizations try to avoid associations with people marked as unacceptable by the Pentagon. My status as a Pentagon-designated outlaw automatically made me an outcast with major institutions having an interest in getting along with the military spending complex. Before going to work for the Air Force, I usually had more management-consulting work than I could handle. Afterward, I was completely cut off from the type of work I had done in my pre-Pentagon days.

Nevertheless, I was extremely fortunate in having the support of influential businessmen and Members of Congress. A group of businessmen not dependent on Pentagon spending sponsored a nationwide speaking tour for me. I received an attractive contract to write a book. Senator William Proxmire and Congressman Wright Patman arranged for me to work part time as a consultant to the Congressional Joint Economic Committee. Later, Congressman Jerome Waldie helped me obtain a contract to assist the House Post Office and Civil Service Committee. My appeal to the Civil Service Commission protesting my illegal firing and related court actions were conducted without cost to me by the American Civil Liberties Union and attorneys John Bodner, William Sollee, and John Bruce. Most important of all, I have been sustained throughout my difficulties by the unwavering moral support of my family, my friends, and by total strangers who are just plain sick of lying, stealing, and corruption in government.

I should quickly point out that I was extraordinarily fortunate in the amount of support and help I received after being outlawed by the Pentagon. Most Pentagonal pariahs are absolutely ruined. Over the years, I came to know many of these outcasts. The indignities, personal tragedies, and financial disasters visited upon these people should arouse even the most complacent citizen. The people hurt most severely by being outlawed are specialists who have been intensively but narrowly trained to function as parts of large, complex organizations. When such people are suddenly excluded from employment in large organizations, their specialized skills are not salable, and many of these unfortunates are reduced to working at strange jobs well below their capacities or to living on welfare or the charity of friends and family. Oftentimes the brutal, total ostracization permanently damages the personality of the victim. Quite understandably, some outlaws become obsessed with the injustice done them, and become their own worst enemies.

II Other Cases

A few cases of punishment inflicted for whistle blowing, for nonconformance with the amoral bureaucratic expectations, will illustrate the problems faced by most whistle blowers who oppose the big spenders in the Pentagon. One military contracting officer, cast out after a long and successful career for refusing to approve some particularly outrageous give-aways disguised as contract changes, was reduced for a time to working as an itinerant dishwasher.

Another case involved two officials of a government employees union local. These two men became concerned that their employer, a military procurement agency, was knowingly accepting faulty helicopter parts. At the time, accidents were causing more casualties among helicopter crews in Southeast Asia than enemy action, and some helicopter-maintenance specialists blamed faulty parts for many of the accidents. Working-level civil servants who tried to correct the situation were overruled by their superiors, and, in frustration, took the dispute to their union local. The local passed a resolution calling for corrective action and sent it to Congressmen and other high government officials. Those responsible for accepting the bad parts went unpunished, but the two union officials found themselves in deep trouble with their military superiors, and both were eventually fired. However, before they were fired, one of the union officials was found beaten nearly to death on the military reservation where he worked. The victim claimed he recognized his assailants, and tried to press charges. The courts ruled that the alleged assailants, government security officers, were protected from prosecution under the doctrine of absolute immunity, and the case was dismissed. Both the union officials impoverished themselves in futile efforts to get justice through the courts, and are still struggling to build new lives for themselves.

Then there was the case of John McGee, the Navy fuel inspector who uncovered massive, highly organized thefts of petroleum products in Thailand. Armed with irrefutable documentation and tape recordings of threats and warnings from his supervisor aimed at silencing him, John McGee blew the whistle on one of the biggest and most systematic thefts of the sordid Southeast Asia war. Due to faulty or missing records, the General Accounting Office reported that they could not document the total magnitude of the thefts, estimated by John McGee at one half of all the petroleum products shipped into Thailand by our military. The GAO was able to verify that at least 5.6 million gallons of fuels and lubricants were stolen in Thailand during 1967 alone. Investigators blamed the thefts on bribery, forgery, and the laxity of government officials.

Were John McGee's superiors reprimanded, fired, or prosecuted for the thefts? Was John McGee commended and promoted? The answer is "no" to both questions, of course, and it is a measure of our acceptance of government corruption that no one would guess otherwise. John McGee's superiors continued to prosper, while McGee was relieved of his responsible assignment, shipped home in disgrace, and assigned to a do-nothing job in a Washington suburb; the Navy and the Civil Service Commission meanwhile conspired to wreck his career. He was denied a routine, in-grade pay raise, and the Navy started action to get him fired on the basis of records falsified by the personnel bureaucrats. This plan was headed off only by exposure of the spiteful and illegal scheme and by the vigorous intervention of Senator Proxmire. Still, John McGee was made to suffer further. He was transferred from his do-nothing job near Washington, where his case continued to draw press and Congressional attention, to another do-nothing job in Pensacola, Florida, where, it is hoped, the embarrassing situation, including McGee himself, will just fade away. McGee has tried to find other, more honorable work, but as usual, no one seems to want a whistle blower on the payroll. So he continues to live in isolation, with his fellow civil servants afraid to associate with him and his military superiors harrassing him constantly.

To me, the saddest whistle-blowing case is that of Kenneth Cook, who was an Air Force weapons analyst. Mr. Cook, a mathematician and physicist with a long and excellent record of incisive evaluation of advanced weapons proposals, was ruined because he refused to alter his devastatingly accurate study of a useless and expensive secret weapon favored by his military bosses. Using the cruellest of all techniques to get rid of Mr. Cook, the Air Force declared him mentally incapable of carrying out his duties. The Civil Service Commission allowed this ruling to stand in spite of contrary evaluations by civilian psychiatrists *and* by the Air Force's own top psychiatrist, who could come up with nothing more damaging than the statement that Mr. Cook was a "perfectionist" and "relatively inflexible" in defending his views. I had personal knowledge of the proposed boondoggle which got Ken Cook in trouble, and in my opinion it would have been impossible to be too "inflexible" in opposing the idiotic scheme.

Nevertheless, Ken Cook got the ax, and having been declared mentally incompetent, however casually, he found himself not only unemployable but also without apparent legal recourse. The ACLU tried to help Ken Cook through legal channels but without much success. Although the legal bases are unclear and in dispute, it appears that until recent rule changes, a command doctor, not necessarily a recognized psychiatrist, could unilaterally and arbitrarily declare a government employee mentally incompetent. No formal evidence was needed, just a statement by the local doctor. Worst of all, the government's position, supported by many judges, is that there is no recourse to such a ruling beyond a review by the Civil Service Commission, the usually compliant servant of the executive branch agencies.

Kenneth Cook, already in his fifties when railroaded out of the Air Force, chose to fight the injustice done to him through legal and political means. Meeting indifference or even hostility from the politicians and government agencies, Mr. Cook persisted in his fight for years though reduced to poverty. When he fell behind on the taxes on his home in New Mexico, his property was auctioned off at a tax sale. After payment of past-due taxes and the exorbitant costs of seizing and disposing of the property, this poor man received 57 cents for a home in which he had more than $10,000 in equity.

Until that time, Ken Cook had retained his determination, his competence (he did valuable volunteer work helping to debunk the ABM), and a realistic, practical outlook regarding his chances for redress. However, the day he showed me the absurd check for 57 cents in payment for his home, he broke down and cried. He was never the same afterward. He continued going through the motions of fighting his case, but with deepening despair and ever more crushing poverty. While petitioning his government for redress, he subsisted on one meager meal a day. Unable to afford any sort of transportation, he trudged many miles every day between his bare room and the various Congressional offices and government agencies which should have been interested in helping him but were instead destroying him.

Finally, in January 1973, sick, ragged, and embittered, Kenneth Cook dropped dead in a Washington department store. Fifty-nine years old at his death, Ken Cook looked seventy-five. His entire estate amounted to $7.32, found in his pocket when he died.

As an illustration that retaliation against whistle blowing in the military-spending complex is not confined to government employees, consider the case of Henry Durham. During nearly twenty years of devoted employment at Lockheed Aircraft Corporation's Marietta plant, Henry Durham had risen from an hourly stock chaser to a middle-management position in which he had charge of several production control departments. Mr. Durham became increasingly disturbed at what he later called "the disastrously rotten management" of the C5A program by Lockheed. His initial concern was that his company would suffer as a result of bad management and shoddy work. Among other things, Henry Durham reported to his bosses that airplanes were being moved from one assembly station to another with thousands of parts missing but with production and inspection records falsified to show the missing parts installed. This practice not only helped conceal shortcomings but also facilitated an unchecked flow of money to Lockheed for progress payments and partial completions of contract work.

By late 1969, Defense Department auditors concluded that Lockheed had already been paid $400 million more than they had coming under terms of their contract. In concert with Lockheed, the Pentagon decided to ignore the overpayments and even to authorize more money to conceal the outrage, and to brazen out the affair at an extra cost to the taxpayers of at least $1 billion.

In this climate, Henry Durham's employers weren't the least interested in cleaning up the problems he had brought to their attention. In fact, once Lockheed was assured of reimbursement of their costs no matter how high they went and no matter how poor their product, *Henry Durham* became the problem, not high cost or poor performance. After being rebuffed by Lockheed management up through the Chairman of the Board, Henry Durham left Lockheed. He then began writing letters to politicians, from President Nixon on down, imploring them to stop the waste of public money at Lockheed. He made the same appeal to major newspapers all over the country, supporting his charges with documentation and offering more to any interested party. Of the dozens of letters Mr. Durham wrote, only those to Senator Proxmire and Morton Mintz of *The Washington Post* elicited significant responses. Senator Proxmire invited Henry Durham to air his charges before the Subcommittee for Economy in Government, and Morton Mintz visited Durham's home in Marietta, Georgia, to examine the evidence. On Sunday, July 18, 1971, the *Post* published a long article on Durham's charges, which were also carried in the Atlanta papers. Local reaction in Marietta, an Atlanta suburb, was immediate, vicious, and shocking. The Durham home came under virtual siege. Automobiles cruised slowly by with the cars' occupants shouting threats and insults. The telephone stayed busy with profane, threatening calls. Angry Lockheed partisans promised to kill Durham and his family and to burn their home. One caller even threatened to disfigure Durham's teen-aged daughter, saying, "You have a pretty daughter now, but she won't be pretty long."

Signs appeared in Lockheed's Marietta plant urging the inmates to "Kill Durham" and "Kill Proxmire." However, it was reliably reported that Lockheed Board Chairman Daniel Haughton wrote a letter asserting that such proposals were against company policy.

At Senator Proxmire's request, the FBI investigated the threats against the Durhams. The danger was genuine, and federal marshals were assigned to protect the Durham family around the clock.

Although the constant presence of the marshals provided a measure of physical security, the Durhams' troubles with the community continued. The threatening phone calls went unabated even when the angry callers were told that federal marshals were listening on the extension. The family became outcasts in the community they had lived in for twenty years. In an unparalleled act of journalistic irresponsibility, the local newspaper further incited Durham's depraved neighbors by labeling him "Public Enemy Number Two." (Senator Proxmire was already Public Enemy Number One to these good Georgia Christians.)

Henry Durham's wife, Nan, was a devout and energetic worker in her local church, where she had taught Sunday School for many years. When Henry Durham's charges were publicized, other church workers told Nan Durham that they "understood" that she wished to discontinue her Sunday School teaching. The Durhams' preacher, cold and aloof, refused to support or even to comfort the family in their difficulty. In anguish, Nan Durham wrote to Billy Graham, whose gospel ministry she had long admired and supported. After a long period of silence from the Reverend Dr. Graham's camp, without even a note of acknowledgment, Mrs. Durham wrote the great revivalist another letter, sharper and more insistent than the first. After another long delay, one of Reverend Graham's assistants mailed Nan Durham some Bible tracts.

Even though Henry Durham's charges were accurate and well justified, he too had great difficulty getting responsible work afterward. One of his superiors at Lockheed had assured Durham he would be blackballed if he aired his grievances after leaving the company. Apparently, this promise was kept.

III Protecting Whistle Blowing

The list of horror stories could go on, but the point is made: whistle blowing, especially in opposition to Pentagon rip-offs, is a losing proposition. The price for the whistle blowing, the savage retaliation by the spending establishment, is simply too great to be borne alone by the whistle blower and his family. And yet, there is little hope that information regarding official thefts and other malfeasance can be made public if the culprits are protected and the whistle blowers are destroyed. The federal bureaucracy, like any other society, is steered by an operative rewards and punishment system. The key word here is "operative," because the *de facto* standards of conduct are polar to official statements of policy.

Consider, for example, the "Code of Ethics for Government Service." Don't laugh. There really is one, though the conjunction of "ethics" with "government service" may today seem unreal. The Code of Ethics is official, having been adopted by the 85th Congress as House Concurrent Resolution 175. It starts out by affirming that "Any person in Government should: Put Loyalty to highest moral principles and to country above loyalty to persons, party or Government department." The Code goes on in this vein and concludes with the admonition to "Uphold these principles, ever conscious that public office is a public trust."

All in all, the Code is a noble document, expressing exactly what the taxpayers should expect of people on their payroll. But really, given the Nixon administration's emphasis on "team-playing" (even in covering up crimes), is it reasonable to ask public servants to adhere to the Code? Clearly, the rewards and punishment system demands that federal employees behave counter to the Code if they are to prosper. For that matter, what political leader, conservative or liberal, even talks about upholding "principles" these days? The most frankly admired quality is something called "pragmatism." Most of the people I hear praised as "pragmatic" would have been described as "unprincipled" by my grandmother.

Moral and behavioral standards being what they are, it simply makes no sense to expect working-level public servants to bear the brunt of carrying out policies opposed by their superiors. If the public really expects ethical behavior and good stewardship from its employees, the rewards and punishment system must be set right. It citizens expect to get a free flow of information needed for intelligent self-government, then the individuals conveying that information must be able to survive doing their duty.

In the problem area I know best, conveying information to Congress, it would appear that federal government employees already have strong legal protection. Taken together, the right to petition Congress, the expression of Congressional intent in the Code of Ethics and the sanctions of 18 U.S. Code 1505 seem adequate on paper. The problem is enforcement. When I was fired from the Pentagon, Senator Proxmire demanded that the Justice Department do its duty and enforce 18 U.S. Code 1505. Summing up a strong statement, he said: "Now we know a crime has been committed. The provisions of this statute have been clearly violated. We know the victim is Ernest Fitzgerald, and we know an attempt was made to obstruct a Congressional hearing. It is therefore the duty of the Department of Justice to identify the perpetrators of the criminal acts and to take the necessary action against them whoever they may be." When, predictably, nothing happened, Senator Proxmire issued a series of even stronger statements, culminating in his demand that the Justice Department "apprehend the felons in the Pentagon."

Therein lay the problem, of course. In the course of my firing, the Air Force functionaries had slyly implicated Secretary of Defense Melvin Laird in the illegal act. Was it reasonable to expect Attorney General John Mitchell to put Melvin Laird in jail? For that matter, would Attorney General Robert Kennedy have moved against Secretary of Defense Robert McNamara under similar circumstances? Not likely.

The prospect of 18 U.S. Code 1505 functioning as intended became even more remote in my case when President Nixon took personal credit for firing me. Clark Mollenhoff, returned to his more appropriate role as a newsman, pinned Mr. Nixon down with questioning at a news conference on January 31, 1973, and under pressure the President admitted that he had personally approved my firing. "No," he said, "this was not a case of some person down the line deciding he should go. It was a decision that was submitted to me. I made it, and I stick by it."

In the consternation that followed, Presidential press agent Ronald Ziegler was sent to explain that the President "misspoke" in describing his role in my firing. Deservedly, no one believed him.

If it seems unreasonable to put the Secretary of Defense away for five years for punishing a whistle blower, what about the President? We are so far reverted to feudal distinctions regarding who is subject to the rule of law that no one even uttered the disrespectful thought that the President himself appeared to have broken the law.

The irony of this episode is the compelling evidence that *Senator* Nixon and his 1951 cohorts had President Harry Truman very much in mind in seeking to strengthen the law protecting Congressional witnesses.

So, unless some protection can be formulated against felony high in government, I do not think public employees carrying bad news can expect much help from law-enforcement agencies. As a matter of fact, the clamps on information flow will be screwed down tighter than ever if a recent Attorney General has his way. In Senate testimony on April 10, 1973, Attorney General Richard Kleindienst stated that the President was within his rights to block Congressional demands for any document within the executive branch as well as testimony of any of the two and one-half million federal employees.

So much for 18 U.S. Code 1505, for the Freedom of Information Act, or any other law inconvenient or distressing to the sovereign.

Turning to more practical remedies, I think government employee whistle blowers might be helped somewhat by laws which facilitate civil damage suits against high government officials who interfere with or retaliate against employees for carrying out their duties. The prospect of personal loss might deter reckless actions where unenforced criminal laws do not.

There are many things which Congress could do to help matters if the majority were so minded. Of all measures Congress might take, judicious application of the power of the purse would be most immediately effective. In each of my horror stories of disaster inflicted on conscientious employees, the underlying problem was too much money for government agencies. Congress should interpret punishment for acts of good stewardship as proof positive that the agency involved has too much money. They should cut the offending bureaucrats' budgets sharply, and keep cutting until healthy, honest, and open attitudes are present. This would also put in proper perspective some of the asinine moral agonizing feigned by those who wonder about "loyalty" to one's organization. In practically every Pentagon case I can think of where competent whistle blowers were put down, the legitimate ends of the organization coincided with the whistle blowers' aims, rather than with their detractors'.

How was our military capability improved by the Thailand fuel thefts which John McGee tried to stop? The big winners were the thieves, the bribe takers, and, of course, the oil companies whose sales were increased. Ken Cook's opposition to secret weapons boondoggles could only help the effectiveness of the Air Force. Again, those who stood to gain were the bureaucratic promoters of useless programs and the contractors who got most of the loot. Similarly, the best interests of the Air Force were not served by concealing the C5A problems, by deliberately funneling excess money to Lockheed, or by conspiring to accept airplanes that shed parts and did not perform properly.

If the Pentagon were really faced with stretching scarce resources, it might even seek out people of the whistle blower bent. I wouldn't go so far as to suggest that the Pentagonists would ever willingly rehire me, but surely they could bring themselves to use the likes of John McGee, Ken Cook, and the honest helicopter-parts inspectors.

In the final analysis, though, any genuine improvement in the climate for doing right must be based on grass-roots indignation and action. This is true even with respect to Congressional action. People who lament Congress' lethargy really expect too much, in my opinion. Where the electorate sits back and expects leadership, it would be lucky to get representation. If the roar from the home folks is loud enough and genuinely threatening to their representatives' tenure, Congress will sometimes act to protect whistle blowers. A good example of a partial victory for the good guys was the recent restoration to duty of Gordon Rule, the Navy procurement specialist who got in trouble for criticizing Litton's shipbuilding bailouts and the appointment of Litton executive Roy Ash to oversee the transactions. The Pentagon was even more stupid and heavy-handed than usual in handling the exile of Gordon Rule to a meaningless job. The publicity given the affair was exceptional, and the ensuing uproar convinced Congress and the Pentagon that a small retreat was in order, at least until the annual budget was safely approved.

From the personal standpoint of the cast-out whistle blower, public support, to be effective, must be direct and tangible. If the victim chooses to fight his dismissal, he needs legal help and lots of it. On his own, no ordinary citizen could afford to hire the amount and quality of legal assistance needed to take on the federal bureaucracy successfully. As of May 1973, my Civil Service appeal and attendant court cases have been under way for three years and three months.* The legal work done in my behalf so far would have cost at least $100,000 if I had been required to pay for it. Without the American Civil Liberties Union and their volunteer attorneys, my legal fight, with its useful fallout for others, could not have been made.

* EDITORS' NOTE: This paper was written in May of 1973. Ernest Fitzgerald and his attorneys won part of their case in September of 1973 with a Civil Service Commission order that Mr. Fitzgerald be reinstated in his old job with back pay. As of February 1974, the Air Force was still resisting compliance with the order, and the long legal fight was continuing, with ACLU backing. By then, Fitzgerald estimated his legal bill at $250,000 with no end in sight unless he dropped the fight.

The typical whistle-blowing outlaw's most pressing need is an honorable way to earn a living. It seems strange to me that we have well-organized and heavily financed job-placement programs for alcoholics, drug addicts, and former convicts, but there is no plan, at least nothing formal, to aid the most conspicuous victims of our felonious federal bureaucracy.

The help I received in getting work after my difficulties with the military spending coalition should be extended to others. Obviously, though, there is limited potential for useful employment of exiled whistle blowers as Congressional consultants. What is needed is a businesslike employment service to help those thrown out of government for attempting to serve the public interest. I will quickly concede that such a safety-net agency might attract opportunists who would see a little contrived whistle blowing as a passport to a sinecure. However, the problems of screening out undesirable candidates for placement should be no more formidable than in any other professional job-placement agency. The unique need of the safety-net agency would be a group of business clients brave enough to employ competent people excommunicated by that fountainhead of financial blessings, the federal government. Whether sufficient public-spirited businessmen could be found to make the project work is questionable. Nevertheless, I believe the safety-net project should be tried because of its vast possibilities for exposing the most maggotty insides of the federal government to purifying public exposure. From personal acquaintance with many fed-up but fearful government employees, I believe an immense amount of pent-up information useful to citizens would be released if potential whistle blowers had a reasonable chance of avoiding professional and financial ruin.

It is good form to end even the gloomiest appraisal of public affairs problems on a hopeful note. I do so here not only for form but also because I believe the climate for truthful disclosures, by whistle blowing or otherwise, may be improving. In the past, the biggest problem faced by government whistle blowers has been that the great bulk of American people have simply refused to believe their government was as rotten and crooked as pictured by whistle blowers. I found that the typical citizen would accept facts of individual military-procurement fiascos, but preferred to believe each disaster was an abberation. The good people who pay the bills had great difficulty accepting the disturbing notion that they were being deliberately swindled, frightened into authorizing "whatever it took" for so-called defense, then saddled with boondoggles and overcharged for junk hardware. They abhorred the very thought that all those steely eyed generals with the look of eagles, those brilliantly successful businessmen, and those scholarly-looking professors on loan to the Pentagon were stealing. Any troublemaking whistle blower who said so just had to be wrong.

From my standpoint, three things have happened which offer hope. First, President Nixon's overwhelming victory at the polls in 1972 made his subordinates arrogant and overconfident, and they boldly revealed previously unspeakable truths. For example, one Aram Baksian, identified as a White House speech writer, proclaimed to a student club at the University of Maryland on November 14, 1972, that military waste was intentional, and bragged that this policy was well understood by the electorate. He cited the overwhelming defeat of Senator George McGovern as proof of the popularity of limitless military boondoggling.

What seems like confident cleverness in the flush of victory will become just a confession of corruption in the sobering assessment of the costs after the enormity of statements like Mr. Baksian's sink in. In effect, he was saying, Yes, we're stealing. What are you going to do about it? Such arrogant statements enhance the credibility of the worst charges of Pentagon whistle blowers.

The second hopeful sign has been the reaction of liberals to the Southeast Asia war. Until disillusionment with the war set in, this influential group generally defended our all-pervading government and put down dissenters with an enthusiasm rivaling the Nixonian fervor. However, the war gave our intellectual leaders a frightening glimpse of big government's immense capacity for evil, and for the long run, this can only be good.

Again, the acceptance of evil intentions in even part of the government increases the acceptability of the whistle blowers' messages.

Finally, there is Watergate. This astounding scandal has rubbed the collective American nose in the true nature of big-time politics as never before. Senator Proxmire was ridiculed for demanding that the felons in the Pentagon be apprehended. Now, with revelations that the highest officials in government were implicated in burglary, conspiracy, and obstruction of justice, the demands to apprehend the felons in the White House are commonplace.

We whistle blowers might even appear respectable soon.

IV Discussion

MR. PYLE: I would like to confine my remarks to the question of how in-house whistle blowers like Mr. Fitzgerald might be better protected from reprisals. Alumni whistle blowers like myself and Dr. Ellsberg have more options, more latitude, and are less vulnerable than people who speak out while they are inside the bureaucracy.

First, let me say that I am under no illusion about the capacity of Members of Congress or attorneys for the ACLU to save men like Mr. Fitzgerald from losing their jobs. Without powerful allies inside the bureaucracy, the in-house whistle blower soon becomes an alumnus. Having said this, I do believe that it is possible to devise legislation that would make life more difficult for vengeful officials and would ease the transition for the whistle blower from public to private employment. One place to start, as Mr. Fitzgerald has suggested, is to increase the likelihood that officials will be prosecuted for obstructing, intimidating, or punishing candid witnesses before Congress. The best way to proceed, I think, is not to tinker with the laws of evidence, as Senator Nixon would have done with his rebuttable presumption of guilt, but to prod the Justice Department into taking a less benign view of official lawlessness.

There are three ways this could be done. The first would be to grant whistle blowers the right to petition a court to require the Justice Department to show cause why it has not prosecuted his superiors under Title 18, U.S. Code, Section 1505, for obstructing proceedings before a Congressional committee (or an executive board, as the case might be). The Justice Department then would have to justify its inaction by showing the evidence it had collected, the sufficiency of its investigation, and the wisdom of its analysis of that evidence. If not satisfied, the court could order further investigation, the convening of a grand jury, or whatever other relief it might deem appropriate.

This remedy is not without its drawbacks. Prosecutors undoubtedly would oppose it as the opening wedge in a movement to give complainants in all criminal cases the right to question decisions not to prosecute. Thus, it might be better to place this power in the hands of the Congressional committees that normally sponsor whistle blowers.

A third alternative would be to empower the courts to appoint special prosecutors when they find that the Justice Department has failed to prosecute government officials who have harassed whistle blowers.

There are also some civil remedies worth considering. As Mr. Fitzgerald suggests, reprisals against in-house whistle blowers usually take three forms: social pressure, abuse of the security-clearance system, and abuse of personnel rules. There is probably little that can be done through legislation to limit social pressures. In the end, such pressures will probably force most whistle blowers out of government. However, there probably are some ways in which the transition to private employment could be eased.

One of the first reflexes of any government agency that has been stung by criticism is to investigate its critic. It is always easier to attack the critic than answer the argument. Civil servants who have lost their jobs or security clearances as a result of these investigations do have the right to some sort of hearing, but they do not always have the right to confront the witnesses against them or to know their identity. Thus, one way to limit such abuses would be to expand the due-process rights of those who are investigated.

I am not too hopeful that we can expand the First Amendment rights of government employees who expose wrongdoing. The ACLU may be able to protect an occasional schoolteacher who blows the whistle on a school board that has misappropriated funds. However, where the whistle blower is the subordinate of a policy-maker, I think that it would be very difficult to convince the courts that they should protect that subordinate from being fired. The courts will probably continue to find that the need for confidential communications among policy-makers and their subordinates outweighs the need for public disclosure.

However, there is one alternative that might be worth pursuing. That is to grant a whistle blower who has been improperly dismissed the right to bring a civil suit against his superiors and the government for wrongful discharge. Reinstatement probably would not be a feasible remedy in most cases, given the animosities that usually arise, but remedies might include a preferential listing in an agency-wide or government-wide manpower pool, actual and liquidated damages, immediate accrual of *pro rata* pension rights, special retirement benefits, and, of course, legal costs and attorneys' fees.

These seem to me to be remedies which might encourage more whistle blowing without denying policy-makers the right to get rid of disobedient subordinates.

MR. KAHN: I have no doubt about the importance and value of whistle blowing, but I think there is one aspect of this question about which a word should be said. Those of us who were in government in the 1950s remember a time when Senator McCarthy—who always seems to get into every discussion here—announced his belief that there was a widespread network of conspiracy and subversion in the government, whose members protected each other and would not inform on each other. He established what he called the pro-American underground, which was an invitation to federal employees to come to him and inform on fellow employees or superiors whom they believed to be subversive.

What he did was promise anonymity to any employee who came to him with such an accusation. This promise was a guarantee against swift and extreme punishment for civil servants who blow the whistle. Because of the certainty of this punishment, there is a strong temptation on the part of Congressional committees and Congressmen to promise anonymity to whistle blowers. This temptation must be resisted, because it can lead to grave evils. In the McCarthy period, people who were anonymously but falsely accused in this way eventually found it wise to quit.

MR. PHILLIPS: Our subcommittee, as many other investigative subcommittees on the Hill, has a tremendous use of information provided by government employees or former government employees. This is one of the most important leads any investigating committee can have. I have never once had a whistle blower come and ask for anonymity, contrary to what Dr. Kahn has said. The usual pattern is that an individual will come into the office loaded with a briefcase of files, papers, and other information which he feels will prove the accuracy of his whistle-blowing claim against an agency or official who he feels is engaging in corrupt or illegal practice. They are perfectly willing to turn over these records. Meanwhile, we use other sources to try to verify documents that are provided to us in this way.

MR. NEIER: After Ellsberg and others, have you felt any upsurge in this kind of thing recently?

MR. PHILLIPS: Yes, I think this has had a very healthy effect. In many cases, the people who come forward with information end up as witnesses at subcommittee hearings; they are not anonymous. There have been two instances involving our 1971 investigation of black-market activities in Vietnam where we had to hold the hearing in executive session, because the testimony would tend to defame, degrade, or incriminate the individuals involved if it were given in open testimony without that person having an opportunity to reply. This procedure is required by a House rule, the so-called "Joe McCarthy rule," which was adopted eighteen years ago. In each of these hearings, significant information was developed by the witness during testimony given in executive session, on illegal activities involving organized crime. This information was turned over to the appropriate officials in the Justice Department. Data on smuggling was turned over to the Customs Bureau, and so forth.

A second type of whistle blower is the anonymous phone caller. The subcommittee gets quite a few of those too. Some government employee picks up the paper or hears that we are investigating a certain subject, perhaps holding hearings on it, and the call will come in and say, you ought to look into what Mr. So-And-So is doing in such-and-such an office. He is doing something that is wrong and if you have a way to get at certain records—and sometimes specific documents are mentioned—you will learn more. Sometimes these documents are classified. Sometimes the only way that we know of the existence of the information is through an anonymous phone call, which enables us to make a formal request for it. It is then usually provided to us by the federal agency involved.

MR. HALPERIN: One consequence of whistle blowing is that important government decisions are made in small groups: the way to stop whistle blowers is not to tell them anything. This results in a substantial loss of expertise. While it would be nice to know what the State Department experts on China think about what will happen to us if we land in Peking in the middle of the night, if we tell them, it is going to leak, so you don't tell them and you lose the benefit of their expertise.

MR. SCHWARTZ: I would like to dispute that contention that anonymous informants are necessarily bad. Unless an individual who comes forward can feel secure that he may remain anonymous, you are going to lose a tremendous amount of investigative leads. The most important cases which I am familiar with would never have developed had anonymous informants not come forward. Of course, there is a distinction between relying upon an anonymous informant for investigative leads and making charges supported by anonymous informants.

McCarthy has had a devastating effect on thinking in this country. But the fact that the use of anonymous informants, if they existed, was abused by him, is no reason for saying that anonymous informants should never be used. If a low-level individual in government has information that leads to someone right next to the President, he is not going to come forward without a guarantee of confidentiality. Even then there is an overriding loyalty, above and beyond your superiors, or even the White House and its temporary incumbent, which keep people from talking.

MR. EMERSON: There is no doubt that whistle blowing works both ways. Like free speech or other aspects of democratic procedure, it necessarily should work both ways. I don't think one should expect otherwise.

I want to make two comments about the remedy question. One is very far out. Is it possible to conceive of remedies from within the bureaucracy? The way a bureaucracy works is to exact a tremendous loyalty from its members. It begins to have a life of its own. But is it inconceivable that one could build into the idea of a bureaucracy a notion of dissent, that a better bureaucracy is one that has dissenters within it, and, therefore, it is better for the institution to tolerate a certain amount of dissent?

Second, I am somewhat surprised that no one has mentioned the ombudsman, who has traditionally been considered the classic way of dealing with internal abuses in bureaucracy. We have never tried one, particularly in this country, but it does seem to me that the idea has possibilities.

MR. STONE: I think it is important to recognize that the atmosphere set by the President determines exactly what kind of whistle blowing goes on. There is in a bureaucracy an underlying fear of the consequences of dissenting. You might lose your job. Beyond fear of consequences, you have loyalty. Loyalty restrains whistle blowing. Beyond loyalty, there is duty, the notion that you are supposed to do exactly what you are told. One of the things that has to be done is to encourage loyalty to law.

MR. PYLE: To respond to Professor Emerson, I personally see little hope in using ombudsmen, particularly inside the military. The military has an inspector-general system. In my experience, it is quickly captured by the commanders and by the command structure.

MR. KAHN: I agree with Mr. Schwartz that perhaps it is not the anonymity of the informant, but the way in which his information is used that is important.

I want to expand for a moment on what Mr. Halperin said

about one aspect of whistle blowing—that it tends to narrow the group within which decisions are made. It also has a strong tendency to encourage not making a record of what is done and of what decisions were made. The journalists who are asking for a shield law say that their sources will dry up if they don't have a shield law. Journalists speak of people as sources, but scholars and historians use that word to mean documents. There is a strong tendency for the documentary source to dry up if one fears that there is a whistle blower present who might reveal the document. If no record is made, one cannot produce it.

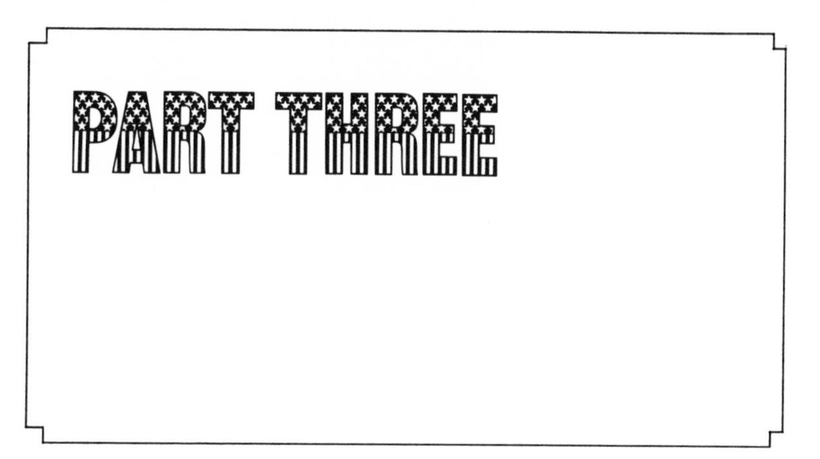

— SPECIAL PROBLEMS

11 The Ellsberg Perspective: A Discussion

MR. ELLSBERG: I had the opportunity to speak before Congress recently on the subject of secrecy.

Until April 1973, we did not know that the Watergate case and my own prosecution were part of the same project by certain officials in government. These cases exhibit the same executive arrogance and contempt for law, the Constitution, and the public which I found in the Pentagon Papers and which I wanted to reveal to the public and to other branches of government. It all came together this morning * as I listened to an honest man named James McCord give testimony that was funny at some points—until you realized it was chilling. For me, it was quite moving because I recognized this man. In a certain sense I recognized myself in him, or my own past in him. He is a little older than I am and has been in government longer, but our careers have been similar in important ways. I, like Mr. McCord, spent a large part—well, really all—of my professional life in the belief that the wishes of the President were the law: the kind of law that really goes beyond the Constitution and the statutes of Congress. At a certain point in my life I discovered that was a mistake, and I acted differently;

* May 18, 1973—*Ed.*

and at a certain point in his life Mr. McCord realized it was a mistake, and he began acting differently. In fact, he used those words at the beginning of his testimony.

Rather than saying, as some other witnesses have, that he did what he did in the sincere and well-founded belief that he was serving the national interest, Mr. McCord simply said he made a mistake and was sorry for it. I have no doubt that the sense of doing wrong was working like an acid on Mr. McCord, eating away the habits of a professional lifetime of lying to the public. What we were hearing was a man finally telling the truth as best he could.

Secrecy has acted like a cancer on democracy over the last generation. It is not mainly a matter of regulations in the executive branch. In fact, most of the dimensions are not written down. It is instead a matter of practice and attitudes—themselves kept secret from the public—of a trained, conspiratorial bureaucracy, a special bureaucracy within a bureaucracy. I hate to use the word conspiratorial, which conveys so strong a sense of conscious illegality and conscious wrongdoing, but I think the word is not misleading here. We are going to hear a lot more about the techniques and the apparatus of conspiracy, involving special communication channels, stamping papers so they don't get into the wrong hands, special safes and procedures, how to make a phone call so you won't be overheard. Mr. McCord was describing his duties using electronic apparatus against the Democrats, but what we heard this morning was how his contact, who presented himself as a White House representative, gave him directions about which pay phones to go to, what code names to use, and so on—all rather low-level conspiratorial tricks, but necessary tricks. If you don't know them, you don't conspire effectively. The word does get into the wrong hands.

The cover story that protects these practices is that there are really no secrets, that everything eventually comes out in *The New York Times*, or even quickly comes out in *The New York Times*. This is untrue. There are secrets. They are kept very effectively. They are not stamped "top secret." As a matter of fact, one could describe the entire overt classification system—"top secret," "secret," "confidential"—as itself a kind of cover, a distraction, to conceal information which may be leaked by low-level officials at their discretion. Officials at the level of deputies, secretaries, assistant secretaries, and White House officials don't hesitate to show "top secret" cables or messages to anyone. "Top secret" is basically a form of news management. It means that the information can only be leaked by a relatively high official. Only he can determine when it gets out, who gets it first, in what context, the accompanying interpretation, and what he wants in return from the person he is leaking it to.

But there are classifications much higher than "top secret." They are not handled routinely, they are not stamped routinely, and those in the know don't play the same games with these. These secrets are kept very well.

Sooner or later, the bureaucracy that was built to carry out secret operations was going to be used to carry out similar operations at home. It could so easily be used for the purpose. And this bureaucracy would bring with it the notion that if the President says something is okay, or if one of the President's men says it—then it is okay.

How did we get into this? My impression is that during World War II, while fighting an enemy who seemed to personify evil and who used conspiratorial techniques, and after the war while fighting another enemy—Stalin—whom we saw in the same way, it seemed necessary to build up a comparable, conspiratorial, covert apparatus. The next step was to use that same apparatus domestically, during the 1950s, to pursue policies that were again seen as being in the national interest, but which the public might not perceive in the same terms because it did not have all the information. It couldn't appreciate the need for a budget for this sort of thing or for certain methods—murders or coups or interventions—and you therefore had to operate conspiratorially, because your conception of the national interest could be trusted more than the public's conception. They did not have the information that you had, and you couldn't give it to them because of the techniques you had used to get it.

The people who were initiated into this system in the 1940s and 1950s were told quite convincingly, whatever their background, that this secrecy, which is much higher than "top secret," is necessary, legitimate, called for by the nation. My initiation with secrets in the Rand Corporation was in the context of the apparent missile gap, in the late 1950s. The first secrets I learned were secrets of the precise vulnerability of the Strategic Air Command. Nobody had to tell me that was a secret I should take very seriously.

Keeping secrets effectively does involve lying. It means that when you are asked if you have certain information, you don't say "No comment," because that is an answer. To protect that secret you have to lie and say, "No, I don't know that." You learn the technique of lying in a way that seems entirely legitimate and essential for national security.

The people with the information act in the best interests of the nation—as they see it. It may differ, they recognize, from the views of lots of other people and parties, but those people don't know what you know. They don't know the President personally, perhaps, and they don't know all this information. They are not fit to judge. You will recognize that I am describing attitudes that are not merely technical. They are attitudes of arrogance and contempt for everyone who does not have the information, attitudes that other people are not fit to participate either in policy-making or in determining who shall run the country. When I say that this is an attitude of arrogance and contempt, I am not speaking of contempt merely for the uninformed who only read *The New York Times*. I mean contempt for U.S. Senators and for others in the bureaucracy who are not in the know.

Nothing could be more directly subversive of democracy. It is hard to see how democracy can survive executive secrecy and attitudes of contempt and arrogance by the executive. What we are seeing is something like an executive coup, which has been building not just since Mr. Nixon took office, but during the last generation. I don't assume that all who take office are corrupt, arrogant, and contemptuous. But the national-security process is an education in contempt for truth, contempt for law, and contempt for any information that does not bear a stamp higher than "top secret."

MR. SALOSCHIN: In describing his career in government or

in the Rand Corporation, Dr. Ellsberg said that at one time he thought that the wishes of the President were the law, over the Constitution and statutes. It seems to me incredible that any educated citizen could be sold on the idea that the wishes of the President were law over the Constitution and statutes. Maybe we need a little more interdisciplinary education for the American populace if that idea has gotten about, because when people get disabused of that idea, apparently it has quite an effect on them emotionally.

MR. LEWIS: Mr. Saloschin, at this very moment, United States planes are bombing Cambodia in the most flagrant, ludicrous violation of what all of us know are the requirements of the Constitution of the United States. There are an awful lot of people in the United States government who are exhibiting, by their execution of that policy, the very same belief that Dr. Ellsberg spoke of.

MR. SALOSCHIN: The Congress of the United States undoubtedly has plenary constitutional power to do quite a number of things about that, and so do the American people through the electoral process.

MR. LEWIS: But the framers of the Constitution did not write in the Constitution that wars shall be legal unless Congress outlaws them. That is not what the Constitution says, and I suggest you read it again.

MR. CLARK: Since our discussion is supposed to be about the legislative branch and secrecy, I wonder if Dr. Ellsberg has any new thoughts on what I understand to have been his efforts to get at least two Senators—Fulbright and McGovern—to release the Pentagon Papers?

DR. ELLSBERG: I had occasion to ask Senator Fulbright just yesterday why he had not put them out. He confirmed the answers I had from staff people—that if he had done so unilaterally, it would have been without the support of the majority of his Committee. But more importantly, it would have given the executive branch an excuse to deny the Senate, and more specifically the Senate Foreign Relations Committee, further documents or testimony stamped secret or top secret. He did request these documents four times from Secretary Laird, in the hope that he would get them formally on a classified basis, and four times was refused without even the invocation of the words "executive privilege." So the judgment I had made at the beginning, which was that the only way he would get those documents was for me to copy them and give them to him, was confirmed.

MR. NEIER: I want to ask Dr. Ellsberg if he now thinks there is any room for a classification system. If you do think so, how would you limit it? If you don't think so, would you favor any other mechanism for maintaining secrecy?

DR. ELLSBERG: The classification system as it now exists and is practiced is unconstitutional. I believe a classification system could be devised to meet the constitutional test of compatibility with the First Amendment, although any system is to some extent an abridgment of the First Amendment interpreted literally. It would have to have characteristics that the present system lacks entirely, characteristics of review within the executive, review by Congress, review by the courts, strict guidelines which would attempt to keep the number of secrets kept out of public discussion very small, plus a process of implementing those guidelines to make sure they were not abused—let's say every other day a review. It would have to involve Congress as well as the executive. It would have to involve appeals to the court, which now practically does not exist.

In short, the question does come down to where do you draw the line, and who should draw it? The line should not be drawn only by executive officials who are thus allowed to determine entirely by themselves what the public shall know about how they are doing their job.

I would like to respond to the earlier statement by the Justice Department representative, Mr. Saloschin. I have been the subject of not only prosecution, but bugging, burglary, and attempted assault by his colleagues. A lecture on constitutional law, which I could have well used as a government official, I do not need from a current member of the Justice Department. I can tell you, sir, that your lectures are very much needed by your colleagues back in your office today, and I think you should not hesitate a moment to go back and lecture them.

MR. SALOSCHIN: Dr. Ellsberg, I don't need and I do not accept any instructions or imputations from you as to who my colleagues are, because I doubt very much if you know who they are. They have included in the past such people in the Justice Department as Mr. Marshall, who was here today. You have undoubtedly been through very strange and emotional experiences in life which other individuals in this world have been through, too, but that does not lend in my eyes any greater weight to your opinions on constitutional law—although your observations are very interesting, as I said earlier.

MR. STONE: These emotional smears, I think, come in very poor taste from a member of the Justice Department. Whether or not you, sir, are involved in it, I think you would do well to have some sense of shame about what has been going on and to avoid smearing others.

MR. SALOSCHIN: If I have engaged in smearing, why, I certainly apologize for that, but I will let the record of this conference show who may have been smearing whom. However, I do feel bound to say on behalf of the people I have known for the last fifteen years in the Department of Justice, that I feel no need to apologize for the performance of most of them.

MR. GOODELL: Having served in the Department of Justice, I agree with that comment. Most of the people there are very upstanding people.

12 The Technology of Secrecy

—*by Alan Westin*

No analysis of government's secrecy in the 1970s would be complete without considering government's growing use of computer systems. In 1972 an inventory of the federal executive establishment counted 6731 computers. Most of these—5815— were installed in the "Big-Three" computer-using agencies: the Defense Department, the Atomic Energy Commission, and the National Aeronautics and Space Administration. But 916 others were distributed among fifty-two more federal agencies and departments. The largest users were the Departments of Transportation; Commerce; Treasury; Agriculture; Health; Education, and Welfare; and the Veterans Administration. Over $2.4 billion were spent on these federal computing activities, with the equivalent of 124,000 full-time employees involved in federal ADP (Automatic Data Processing) work.[1]

This steadily increasing use of computers by federal executive agencies is paralleled by trends in state, county, and municipal government, and in the operations of special governmental authorities, from school districts to water commissions. Especially among larger agencies, so many records have now been converted to machine-readable form and so many client services and administrative operations are being carried on through computerized procedures that the executive branches of American government have become dependent on their computer systems.[2] In this sense, we are not moving into the computer age; we are already deep in it.

As a result, civil libertarians have begun to worry about the effects such heavy reliance on computers may have on the public's right to know. Putting aside science-fiction approaches ("The machines will take over!"), there are fears that computerization may:

— Make it harder for the average citizen, public-interest group, etc., to know what information is in automated files and how it is used, because the specialized procedures of ADP are not yet well known.

— Create delays in furnishing information, as agencies cite data-conversion problems and system "bugs" as reasons why they cannot furnish information in computer storage.

— Make it more difficult for persons to "browse" in public records after these are converted from traditional, eye-readable registers, kept on open shelves, to storage on computer tapes or discs, available only on special call.

— Create large computer data banks whose software for extracting information is geared to what agency directors wish to see produced, making it a costly special effort to produce information sought by public-access groups.

— And lead to significant reliance by government officials on computer-based decision-making aids (models, simulation, etc.), whose use is not made known to the public.

Such concerns about computers and secrecy, unlike similar ones about the effects of computerization on individual privacy, have *not* yet received much serious attention. There have been no empirical investigations of computers and secrecy, no significant treatment of the issue by Congressional committees, and even no exploratory essays on the topic. I believe the public's right to know, in an era of increasing computerization, will suffer badly if we allow this inattention to continue.

To put this inquiry into proper perspective, two pieces of groundwork are needed: 1) the legal and political settings of government secrecy must be understood, in order to compare public access in manual systems with computerized record systems; and 2) the basic patterns of computer usage in those government agencies that are automating and how the computers are actually used.

I The Precomputer Setting of Government Secrecy Issues

The public's right to know (and thereby control) what the executive branch of government is doing is a pivotal element in the American constitutional scheme. The Framers believed that executive affairs were not the private preserve of a President or his agents, in the classic mode of royal households, but an instrument of popular government, to be conducted mainly in public view or subject to public inspection. To carry out this policy, Congress was given power to investigate and oversee the operations of executive agencies (with authority to compel disclosure of information). American courts could compel the production of information by executive agencies whenever necessary to insure a fair trial to defendants in criminal prosecutions or to test the rational basis of government regulatory action involving property rights or personal liberties.

Under a combination of common law and statutory rules, the general public had a right of access to government information. These rules provided that certain records kept by government (for example, tax and land registers) were public documents, open to inspection by anyone. Other records could be inspected by persons with a particular, legitimate interest in seeing them (such as a parent inspecting a child's official school record). Access by the press and by individuals without a specific legal interest would generally depend on the wording of state and federal statutes.[3]

Generally, the courts would balance claims to access by Congress, litigants, and the public against what was usually termed the broad public interest in protecting the integrity of the governmental process. This produced rulings exempting from disclosure such matters as state secrets, investigative files, internal memoranda by agency officials, information obtained from citizens under promise of confidentiality, and certain information protected by a vague but real doctrine called executive privilege. These rulings show that demands to make government information public, central as this is to the citizen's knowledge and control of public affairs, can conflict with two other values of democratic society: the right of privacy of individuals about whom sensitive information is stored in government files (such as census, tax, medical and social-services records), and the need of all formal organizations, governmental or private, for periods of *temporary* privacy, in which to gather confidential information, solicit frank advice, conduct secret negotiations, formulate positions, and reach executive decisions.[4]

In general, statutes and judicial rulings prior to World War II were very generous in accepting government claims that disclosing certain information would jeopardize the orderly and efficient operations of government. But since World War II, there has been increasing government activity in defense and social-welfare areas and strong pressures from the press, Congress, and public-interest groups to make government more responsive. The clear trend has been toward opening up executive-agency files to public access. The single most important step to date was passage of the federal Freedom of Information Act and various state counterparts. The Act has been analyzed in two earlier papers. It is important to recognize, however, that computerization began to spread through the American government establishment at a time when there were disputes over 1) what information should be open to public access under freedom of information laws and 2) what constitutes prompt, complete, and reasonably priced compliance with demands for information to which the public was entitled. Whether computers, adding machines, or 3-by-5 cards are used to manage information is separate from the policy issue. But a basic factual question is whether the move to automated files and procedures has made it easier, harder, or has had no significant effect on compliance with existing law.

II General Patterns of Computer Usage and the Organizational Impact in Government

Although, to the public, a computer is a computer is a computer, patterns of computer usage vary widely in government, from department to department, even from bureau to bureau within a department. In organizational terms, this is because each unit starts with records and files unique to its mission, with distinct functions to perform through its collection and use of information, and with distinct styles of management (including attitudes toward providing information to the public). Furthermore, government officials have a wide range of choices about technology—what kind of computer hardware to adopt and software to buy or develop; which files to automate first; what aids to decision-making or management-reporting to attempt through computer resources. Few centralized controls (either executive or legislative) have yet attempted to set uniform guidelines for computerization at a given level of government. So automation today is largely a process of agency-by agency decision.

Nevertheless, there are some patterns to computerization in government. These help in analyzing computer impact on freedom-of-information problems.

Computer usage enters most organization through payroll and financial applications, then moves into automation of the largest and most frequently used files. In addition, computers are used to produce various management reports and statistical summaries. This is the stage that most agencies are currently at in computerization. Some departments or bureaus, however, have begun to develop multifile applications, merging several files into a data bank in a particular subject area (social services, for example). A few cities and counties are attempting to create a jurisdiction-wide data bank containing files from many different agencies (e.g.,police, tax, welfare, health). In addition, government agencies are using computers to augment data-sharing among government jurisdictions at the same level (police information systems in metropolitan areas) or at different levels (the FBI's National Crime Information Center or the National Drivers Registration system).

A report by the National Academy of Sciences Project on Computer Data Banks, a three-year study into computers and privacy, found that, so far, computer use has reproduced rules and practices of the manual era rather than transforming them. Computer use has not yet led to the collection of more detailed and intrusive information about people, to sharing data with different types of agencies than had been the practice before computerization, or to any lessening of the individual citizen's ability to know and contest the information that was being collected about him or her in a given file. Whatever rules the agency had before computerization (whether respectful of privacy and due process or hostile to them) continue to be reflected in the computerized operations. Where laws or public values have changed secrecy rules, the NAS project found that managers of computerized systems were as able to comply (and were complying) as were managers with manual files. And, highly intrusive new record systems created during the past decade, such as the Army's monitoring of civilian protest groups, were either wholly manual record systems or were being aided only marginally by computers.

The NAS report also showed that there are no fully automated government agencies today. In every department or bureau, some files remain wholly manual. Some decisions are made after examining records or conducting interviews and negotiations. Some reports are prepared and distributed without machine assistance. Even when a file has been automated, there is often a back-up system with the paper or card records that provided the initial entry; or a microfilm or microfiche record is created for archival use in addition to the primary storage on computer tape or discs. The general rule, for reasons of ease and cost in technological usage, is that files which contain the most objective and easily recorded information and which are needed and consulted most frequently will be the first automated.

At the other end of the computerization process, the files *least* likely to be automated are those with extensive narrative material, highly subjective reports, and sensitive information.

The most important results of computerization discovered by the NAS study were more complete and up-to-date files. There was more analysis and use of information already in the files. Automation produces greater accuracy in some areas of record-keeping, but also introduces the possibility (and likelihood) of other errors. Computerization is leading to the creation of larger and more extensive networks of information-sharing groups. Computers are making possible the creation of some very large data banks, which would probably not have been built, or built as rapidly, but for computer resources.

What the NAS study and other studies [5] report is that computerization has not solved certain problems important to privacy and secrecy issues. Computers do not eliminate the power struggles over control of information within an organization or the self-protective manipulation of information among "cooperating" agencies (whether in intelligence, business regulation, or taxation). The competitions and conflicts of the American federal system have been faithfully mirrored in computer usage so that in any given geographic area, separate computer systems will be maintained by municipalities, counties, special authorities, state agencies, and federal bodies covering services to the same population. There has been no amalgamation of different government functions or jurisdictions into a common computer management.

Studies of computer use reveal that, except for funding, legislative bodies have not supervised the way executive agencies have carried out computerization. This lack of oversight extends to privacy impact, impact of public access to information, and provisions for citizen participation.

Finally, several popular notions about how computerization affects government operations should be set aside as red herrings. They confuse questions of public policy with changes in the technological execution of those policies. One is that computers foster the creation of secret files. Government agencies have for centuries been able to maintain secret files about people or transactions so that their existence was unknown to the public. Using index cards, file folders, microfilm, and other precomputer storage media, millions of records were efficiently maintained in these government files. Using the mails, teletype, telephone, and other means of precomputer data communications, some file systems collected and distributed information on a nationwide basis among hundreds of local and regional offices. Computers are not an essential element in the creation of either secret files, or secret national data networks. There is no evidence that computers are making it significantly easier for government to create or manage secret files. Agencies creating secret computerized files still face the problems of hiding fund expenditures from legislative or press view, preventing leaks by defecting employees, and keeping the sources of data secret when reports are produced and used elsewhere in government. The fundamental issues remain: should any secret files be permitted by law? How can the public discover unlawful secret files, whatever the form of data storage and communication?

A second red herring is that computers substantially facilitate government manipulation of information. For centuries, some government officials have lied. For centuries, there have been subordinates who falsified reports about what was happening in the field—in warfare, diplomatic developments, social trends—in order to provide superiors with the reports they demanded. Computers continue the capacity for these deceptions. Inaccurate reports about "safe" villages in South Vietnam, contributed during our pacification policy in the mid-1960s, when into computer systems. These produced the glowing reports of success the Johnson administration wanted to hear. Similarly, false reports sent by base commanders from Cambodia in 1969–1970, about where American bombers were flying their sorties, enabled the Defense Department's computers to print out incorrect data. These were communicated to Congress, in keeping with the policy of secret bombings ordered by President Nixon and Secretary of Defense Laird. Computer systems simply represent another tool officials can use to falsify or distort events or conditions. Computers did not create this capacity, nor do they ease the difficult task of government critics of learning the facts and exposing manipulation of data.

Although computers are not *creating* or inevitably leading to secret files or falsification of information, they do have important physical and administrative consequences that may require new legal rules and supervisory mechanisms to prevent abusive secrecy practices. The goal is to identify these consequences and to frame responsive policies for them.

This brief portrait of computer use by government presents only highlights of the current situation. But it provides a framework for my main question—how computers affect compliance with freedom-of-information laws.

III Computer Impact on Public Access: Reports from the Information-Holders and Information-Seekers

To gather data about computer impact, I sent letters of inquiry and conducted follow-up interviews with two groups: the information-holders and the information-seekers.

I wrote to twenty-eight federal bureaus, agencies, or departments in early 1973, asking them, first, whether their use of computers made it harder or easier to comply with freedom-of-information laws, or had no significant effect. This question was followed with more detailed questions about possible differences with respect to the character of groups seeking access, the type of inquiry, effects on the costs of compliance, and similar matters. Specific examples were requested.

Twenty-three of the twenty-eight agencies sent full replies. Some provided a general report on their computer operations, usually where the agency was a relatively small or single-purpose one or where its computerization was limited.* Other agencies, usually the larger federal departments, concluded that no composite reply could reconcile the differences among various units. These agencies provided individual responses from their units.**

* Agencies furnishing a general reply were the Atomic Energy Commission, Department of Agriculture, Civil Aeronautics Board, Department of Housing and Urban Development, National Labor Relations Board, Federal Communications Commission, Federal Power Commission, and Federal Trade Commission.

** Agencies supplying responses from various constituent units were the *Department of Commerce* (Patent Office, Social and Economic Statistics Administration, Assistant Secretary for Administration, Office of Organization and Management Systems), *Department of Defense* (United States Air Force, Office of the Secretary), *Department of Health, Education, and Welfare* (Social Security Administration, National Institute of Education, Office of Education, National Institutes of Health), *Department of Justice* (Bureau of Narcotics and Dangerous Drugs, Immigration and Naturalization Service, Law Enforcement Assistance Administration, Federal Bureau of Investigation, Assistant Attorney General for Administration), *Department of Labor* (Office of the Secretary, Occupational Safety and Health Administration), *Department of*

In all, there were commentaries from forty-three offices, bureaus, agencies, and departments of the federal government. Of course, these present a manager's view. One does not expect official spokesmen to respond that they are not complying with the law. If computer systems or temporary problems of computer operations were making compliance with access policies slower, more costly, or less complete than under manual procedures, the replies would be likely to repress this. Finally, the replies did not present a set of answers for each major information file maintained by a given bureau or agency. So we do not have a comprehensive picture of practice in each agency.

An attempt to verify managerial views of computer impact on public access would require study of precomputer practices, analysis of procedures in the automated files, and detailed comparisons. This was not possible. Instead, I compensated for the self-protective tendencies in managerial reporting by sending letters and conducting interviews with information-seekers. I wrote to those who regularly battle to pry information from government agencies.

I wrote to spokesmen for five categories of groups. The groups, and the number in each responding with substantive replies, were:

General Counsel to Congressional committees	6
Public-interest law firms and research groups	8
"Guardian groups" (civil rights, civil liberties, consumer interest, women's rights)	10

State (Record Services Division, Agency for International Development), *Department of Transportation* (Office of the Secretary-Director for Management Systems, United States Coast Guard, Federal Aviation Administration, Federal Highway Administration, National Transportation Safety Board, Office of Policy, Plans, and International Affairs, Office for Environment, Safety, and Consumer Affairs, Office of Systems Development and Technology, National Highway Traffic Safety Administration, Office of the General Counsel, Urban Mass Transportation Administration), and *Veterans Administration* (Department of Medicine and Surgery, Department of Veterans Benefits, Information Service, Controller, Department of Data Management).

Freedom-of-information committees of media associations	5
Investigative writers	6

These thirty-five groups were asked whether they found that automation made a difference in efforts to obtain information from executive agencies. I asked for specific instances in which the presence of computerization had made information retrieval easier or harder.

This section contains reports on computerization and public access by spokesman for the two "opposing camps" in the freedom-of-information contest. My main analysis on the developing trends and what needs to be done to advance the cause of public access follows later.

1 *Reports from the federal information-holders.* About a fifth of the agencies report that computerization has not progressed far enough to have an effect on compliance with freedom-of-information laws. They note that computerization has been limited to payroll, financial, and other housekeeping operations not subject to disclosure. Principal files subject to query under freedom-of-information laws remain in manual form. Among those reaching this conclusion were the State Department, the Federal Power Commission, the Federal Trade Commission, the Immigration and Naturalization Service, and the Federal Bureau of Investigation.

The FBI, for example, responded that the Bureau has automated "payroll, fiscal, and some selected FBI personnel data" used only for "internal administrative purposes." "Investigative files, as such, have not been computerized." Legal rules restrict access to wanted-person and stolen-property data in the National Crime Information Center to law-enforcement agencies, state licensing authorities, and certain federally insured banks. Though similar restrictions apply to the summaries of individual criminal histories now being added to NCIC. It is the administrative policy of the NCIC that an individual may "see and challenge the contents of his record . . . subject to reasonable administrative procedures." Because of the small number of criminal-history summaries in NCIC as of February 1973, the FBI reported that no one had yet sought to examine his NCIC record. In conclusion, Acting Director L. Patrick Gray wrote, "computerization is not a significant factor in generating response information" by the FBI to persons and groups seeking access under freedom-of-information laws. Where the records are legally open, he stressed, manual files and procedures are still the basic mechanisms for responses.[6]

A few other agencies report that, although they have automated files that are open under public access rules, computerization has not had any appreciable effect on furnishing information. The U.S. Coast Guard wrote, for example, "We can identify no significant effects of computerization on our ability to release data to the press, public or Congressional groups. As a relatively small organization, we have always been able to quite rapidly derive answers to questions, identify it as releasable data and make prompt releases." [7] A more detailed description of "no appreciable effect," based on the types of requests the agency receives, was supplied by the Federal Highway Administration:

> Computerization has had no effect on this Administration's handling of requests for information under the provisions of the Freedom of Information Act. Most of the requests we receive (approximately 85 per cent) are for copies of our directives, or copies of motor carrier accident investigation reports. Requests for these items are handled promptly (one to three days on the average). Extra copies of our directives are maintained for this purpose, and copies of accident reports are duplicated. We do not believe that computerization would be effective in facilitating our handling of these types of requests.
>
> Most of the other requests we receive are for narrative type information (correspondence, etc.) on specific subject areas. This information is not of the type that would lend itself to computerization. Requests for this kind of material are forwarded directly to the office of primary interest and are normally answered promptly, even when questions arise as to the releasability of the information requested.
>
> We do have extensive statistical data in our computer systems, most of which is available to the public. We provide for the sale of copies of either printouts or tapes in accordance with Departmental regulations. . . . [8]

A few other agencies reported what might be called "mixed effects" on the distribution of information as a result of computer efforts. A particularly frank reply came from the National Labor Relations Board. The NLRB maintains most of its data as case-oriented legal files, kept in manual form. It does not produce over-all statistics about industries, unions, or collective-bargaining trends, except in the "infrequent instances in which such information is offered as evidence in a specific case proceeding." The Board does not have a computer of its own; it purchases computer services. These have been used principally to produce statistics about the Board's own operations and for computer-based photocomposition of NLRB decisions, in bound volumes. As to these, the NLRB reports:

> We would have to conclude that the effect of computers upon our operating statistics (Management Information Systems) has been mixed. A favorable example is that a system recently installed, using terminals connected to a commercial vendor's time-sharing service, has given the Board Members much more information than was ever available before on the performance of their staffs in processing cases and seems to have helped us improve the timeliness of our service to the public. Most of the information from that system is not directly available to the public. In our overall, Agency-wide production of casehandling statistics for purposes of budget review and managerial control, computer processing of reports previously compiled manually and with punch-cards has increased the productivity of our data processing staff. But, as a small agency without a computer of our own, we have encountered nearly chronic shared-computer service problems whose net effect has been that monthly operating reports (some of which are publicly available) are not infrequently issued later than under the prior, non-computerized system. On the other hand, our use of shared time on computers of other agencies has shortened, by nearly half, the number of months which elapse between the end of a fiscal year and the release of the statistics contained in our Annual Report.

On the use of computerized photocomposition of Board decisions, the report concluded, "The technical problems we have encountered thus far have actually impeded the public availability of this large body of information." [9] Over-all, the NLRB felt that its statistical services, photocomposition program, and production of statistics requested by Congress (such as "detailed elapsed time statistics" for NLRB administrative proceedings) would be aided in the future by more effective computer usage. Such improvement "is, of course, our justification for the effort."

A similar response, from an agency with its own computers, came from the Federal Communications Commission. The FCC uses computers to record station reports on political broadcasting (as required by Congress); equal employment opportunities reports; financial and ownership information; technical service studies; radio-operator licenses; license and renewal notices; statistical reports on bureau work; and FCC payroll and personnel files. Though the report noted that "as a regulatory agency, the FCC has an open-door policy on information availability," some of the computerized data it keeps are not available for public access, such as "highly sensitive financial data" and "internal administrative systems." As a whole, the FCC reported, requests for information are met equally well from both the computerized and manual files. The FCC response concluded that "there is no direct correlation here between computerization and access to information" and computerization "may not in itself make for any greater availability of information." [10]

While one fifth of the federal agencies surveyed reported either no-effect or mixed-effects, four fifths of the agencies stated that their computerization of files subject to public access had aided compliance with freedom-of-information laws. In analyzing these replies, it should be noted that my survey had adopted a deliberately broad view of the "public," listing five types of claimants to executive-branch information:

— Individuals or organizations seeking access to their own files or those relating to claims they are pressing.

— Members of the press seeking access for investigative purposes.

— Congressional committees requesting information.

— Scholars doing studies of government policies.

— Officials of business, public-interest, consumer or other

civic groups looking into government policies and programs.

This expansive listing of information-seekers helps explain why four fifths of the agency spokesmen believed they had improved compliance with freedom-of-information laws. Computers were being used to improve internal administrative operations or the agency's public duties. As a result, the agencies were generally able to provide information more easily from large-scale administrative files on clients and subject area. They have more easily retrievable data about their own personnel. They have better management reports about agency operations and decisions. They can produce better statistical summaries about industries, procedures, or services under their jurisdiction.* These improvements in data production and handling were seen by the reporting agencies as producing better distribution of data to each of the five groups about which I had asked:

As to individuals or organizations seeking access to their own files, agencies such as the Veterans Administration and Social Security Administration reported that requests from record-subjects about claims and benefits were being fulfilled much faster and more cheaply than in manual file procedures.[11] This was a direct goal of their computerization efforts. The Veterans Administration noted that veterans seeking access to information in their files generally apply to their local VA regional office. However, faster access is now possi-

* Many of the agency responses featured examples of improvement in the furnishing of information to various groups where the provision of such data was the function of a given unit or bureau within the federal establishment, such as the Patent Office supplying patent information to persons paying the required fees; the National Technical Information Service of the Department of Commerce supplying indexes and copies of government-sponsored research reports; the Office of Education's information system on research into schools and educational problems; the Social and Economic Statistics Administration's preparation of data for general distribution; the Defense Department Documentation Center's On-Line Retrieval System for research reports; or the Atomic Energy Commission's computerized data base of bibliographic citations and indexes to world-wide literature on nuclear science and technology. There is no doubt that the improvement of such services helps the flow of better information to user groups in the public. However, since freedom-of-information issues involve securing data about the policies and practices executive agencies are following, improvement in providing information services per se is not basically relevant to my inquiry here.

ble through various fast-response computer systems "designed to handle veterans/regional office inquiries. This is the computerized Beneficiary Index Records Locator System (BIRLS) at the Austin [Texas] Data Processing Center, which is interconnected with regional office teletype equipment." Another VA system is a computer at the Philadelphia Data Processing Center that generates print-outs to veteran inquiries on their insurance premiums, loans, and dividends. Still a third computerized system generates extracts used to answer inquiries about compensation, pensions, and GI education.[12]

Most of the agencies replied that better statistical data and management reports had improved the quality and quantity of what they were able to provide to the press, either in the form of reports they published or in response to specific requests for information. For example, the Information Service of the Veterans Administration noted that "the wide range of statistics available [to the press] and the currency of such data is largely the result of computerization. The fact that an operating element within [VA] is able to respond to most requests for data, usually statistical, within a period of time that we and the press would characterize as 'reasonable' is evidence enough that computerization has affected the availability of this type of information in a most positive way." [13]

Among groups with legal and political power to obtain information from executive agencies, Congressional committees rank at the top of the list. This was reflected in agency replies. Except in the relatively rare cases where there are issues of executive privilege, Congressional committees make tens of thousands of requests for information yearly to executive agencies (through appropriation and oversight proceedings and in direct inquiries on specific topics). Executive agencies have always spent considerable time answering these requests. The agencies reported that computerization had enabled them to improve these services to Congress, either because of better data and reports available to the agency's management or because computer programming made it possible to extract the information the legislators sought more easily.

For example, Congressional committees and the press have obtained better information about the status of contracts and grants processed by federal agencies as a result of computerized reporting systems employed by many agencies, such as the Law Enforcement Assistance Administration, U.S. Office of Education, and Department of Transportation.[14] The Department of Transportation explained:

> For example, in 1971, an individual who wished to analyze contents and direction of the DOT R & D program would have to communicate and obtain cooperation of perhaps 20 key departmental officials who in turn would have to mount an effort of record identification and processing of some 2000 active R & D work units (contracts), costing anywhere between $20–80K. Most likely, the entire process would have taken three to five months, at which time the requester would have received resumes of R & D contracts or evaluated tabulations. Today, the same individual, whether in DOT or an outsider, is able to get almost 100 percent of the required data at a cost of approximately $1000 and within a week or less. Even this can be improved by those individuals who have access to remote computer typewriters or video consoles by subscribing to TRIS on-line service at an initial cost of $300 (for hook-up and training) and a character of 75¢ per computer minute, they are able to have their questions answered in less than one hour, and at a cost of $20 to $30 per question.[15]

Scholarly research requests are seen by many agencies as an area in which computerization has been particularly helpful. Once a data base has been automated, and assuming that the software programming is adequate for such purposes, a wide variety of special requests can be filled more quickly and at much less expense than before. As the Federal Aviation Administration noted, "studies of Government programs and policies, whether done by scholars, business or civic groups, or others, generally depend upon using information in 'bulk'—hundreds and thousands of cases. These studies are more likely to be economically feasible because of computerization than without." [16]

Many replies gave examples of providing better information to business, public-interest, consumer, and other civic groups looking into government policies and programs when the queries concerned substantive matters (patents, social-science reports, scientific information) as opposed to information on government policies and programs. Other replies addressed this issue and cited improvements in statistical reports, management reports, grant- or contract-information systems, and large-file searches. Frequently, one government agency provided data which regulated or public-interest groups could use to judge the adequacy of policies pursued by other agencies of the federal, state, or local governments. For example, the National Transportation Safety Board has automated files on aircraft accidents and incidents. This provided the data for a study of accident prevention and government safety standards. Citing many special studies and data it has furnished to groups involved in air safety, the Board concluded, "It would be virtually impossible to examine accident files of this magnitude and compile in-depth analyses of this nature without the use of computer technology." [17]

It is noteworthy that the major public-access results of computerization are essentially by-products of the primary goals of improving data services to clients and management. Improving the production of information to other parties, such as the press or public-interest groups investigating government operations, was not a goal of the computerization. Several of the agency replies stated this explicitly.[18] The replies also showed that effects of computerization vary considerably among units within a department. The Department of Transportation, for example, sent responses for eleven of its constituent bureaus, offices, and boards. These ranged from judgments that computerization was having no effect on public access (the U.S. Coast Guard, Federal Highway Administration, and General Counsel's Office) to estimates that it was greatly aiding responses to public requests (Office of the Secretary, Federal Aviation Administration, and Office for Environment, Safety, and Consumer Affairs).[19] Similar diversity was reported in responses from units of the Veterans Administration, Department of Justice, and Department of Health, Education, and Welfare.[20]

Within such units, the effects of computerization also vary according to the kind of information requested (and, therefore, the files to be drawn on for producing replies). The U.S. Office of Education, for example, reported that questions about its policies are "answered without significant recourse to computerized information." Questions about OE personnel, program operations, and agency contracts and grants are answered somewhat more easily as a result of automation of files in those areas. Statistical studies on school populations and programs have been computerized, and "are thus much more quickly available." The area most positively affected, OE reported, is information on educational research projects. OE developed the Educational Resources Information Center (ERIC), an automated system for making data on research results available nationwide.[21] This variation in impact reflects the principle noted earlier: the most cost-effective use of computers is to automate the largest, most frequently used files, often files containing factual and statistical matter. Files containing lengthy narrative texts and those that are not often used (e.g., individual case files in a regulatory or law-enforcement agency; are not prime candidates for computerization and have not generally been automated. Public requests for information from a case-type file (on one individual or about one episode or investigation) were not often affected by computerization. Those would still be filed manually. Requests for large-scale data or for searches of large, automated individual case files to spot patterns or trends are significantly aided by automation.

In terms of the federal Freedom of Information Act, the agency reports offered several important judgments about the effects of automation. Computerization was not significant in making the determination whether a particular record, report, or file was to be supplied to someone outside the executive branch. That remained a legal question, governed by the federal statute, court rulings, and agency regulations. The law does not give any special status to information simply because it is stored in machine-readable rather than eye-readable form. But the agencies did report that computers were enabling them to comply more effectively with the provisions of access laws than had been possible before automation.

Some agencies reported that computers were helping them separate material in a record or file that was available for public access from legally privileged material. The Commerce Department stated: "The use of computer methods unquestionably facilitates the separation and protection of information that is privileged under the stated exceptions under the Act. The suppression techniques available and used by this Department to prevent unwarranted disclosure of privileged information are far more effective than any methods that might be employed in a manual process." [22] Similarly, the Labor Department said that "computerization has improved our capacity in this respect. Data identification and control procedures are more vigorously documented and adhered to as a result of automation." [23]

Several other officials reported that automation was not having such an effect in their agencies. The Federal Aviation Administration commented:

> Computerization seems not to significantly affect our ability to screen out information not available for public inspection such as airmen medical records and detailed FAA personnel records. In both hard copy and computerized files procedural safeguards are necessary. The difference is largely the difference between establishing clerical procedural safeguards and computer program procedural safeguards. Our experience to date is not conclusive but it could be that carefully designed and tested computer screening may be more effective than human screening, subject as it is to human error.[24]

And, the General Counsel of the Transportation Department observed:

> While computerization would make it easier to locate requested records, it would probably not change the capacity or ease with which information items that are available for public inspection can be separated from those that are exempt under the Freedom of Information Act. After a requested record is located, it must still be reviewed and evaluated by persons competent to determine whether the document is exempt, whether it should be disclosed as a matter of policy even though exempt, or whether it should be released with appropriate deletions. Making such a determination as to each document before it is put into a computer system is obviously not feasible.[25]

A second way in which some agencies believe computers have made compliance with the Freedom of Information Act more effective is in the capacity of computer systems to produce special lists, statistical reports, and surveys in direct answer to requests by public groups. These, according to the agencies, could not have been produced with manual files because of the high clerical costs or because the information was scattered in regional offices or because the time needed was longer than the inquiring party could allow.

Finally, improvement in grant, contract, and licensing information is seen as a major step toward greater responsiveness. To whom government agencies award grants, contracts, and licenses is an active public-policy issue. The LEAA's Grant Management Information System, indexing some 30,000 grants and subgrants that have been awarded by LEAA since 1968 has been a boon to Congressional and public-interest groups studying the work of that agency. Furthermore, specialized publications prepared and distributed from the LEAA's automated files—such as a volume with extensive details about each of the automated criminal justice information systems being funded, state by state, through the LEAA—has facilitated analysis by legal, civil liberties, and public-interest groups of the privacy and security aspects of the LEAA grants and the systems they support.[26]

2 *Reports from the information-seekers* The most striking thing about the replies from the five groups of information-seekers is how often they agreed with the estimate of computer impact of federal executive officials, though they start from different interest positions and often make different judgments about how healthy the state of public access currently is.

Congressional committee Counsel replies uniformly corroborated the picture presented by agency reports. Richard Sullivan, from the House Committee on Public Works, wrote: "This Committee and its Subcommittees have not experienced any difficulty in continuing to obtain needed information for the purpose of legislative oversight. The ability of the agencies to furnish detailed statistical information on short notice has been greatly facilitated as a result of the installation of computer systems." [27]

A similar report came from Donald Knapp, Counsel to the House Committee on Veterans' Affairs:

> I am pleased to report that we have experienced no major difficulty with the computerization of Veterans Administration files and records. As a matter of fact, for the most part we have found computerization has expedited the collection of information needed by the Committee to make timely decisions concerning policy matters.
>
> As an example, I am enclosing a copy of House Committee Print #9, 93rd Congress, which was programmed and computerized. In past years, the compilation of this information [relating to the operations of Veterans Administration hospital and medical programs] has required several months. During the past two Congresses, through computerization, we have been able to produce the report in about two weeks.[28]

Lawrence Baskir, Counsel to the Senate Subcommittee on Constitutional Rights, stressed that the central problem in securing access to government data was persuading the department head that he should release the information. If he wanted it released, Baskir said his Subcommittee obtained the data whether it was in manual or computerized storage. The heart of the issue was one of policy, a political question, and "this is not being determined today by the presence or absence of computerization." [29]

The most extensive response from a Congressional Counsel came from L. James Kronfeld. Because the Government Operations Subcommittee of the House Committee on Government Operations, for which he works, regularly investigates complaints from persons who have had difficulties in getting data or have been refused information by executive agencies, its experiences is among the broadest to be found in Congress. Kronfeld wrote:

> What we have found is that the computerization of information does not necessarily have any bearing on its availability. Agencies make their decisions on availability based on

the subject matter of the information rather than its form of storage. Of course, our recent hearings [the Moorhead Committee hearings on revision of the freedom of information law, held during 1972–1973] have shown serious deficiencies in these agency decisions.

The main problem with computerization is the cost to the requester for receipt of the information. For instance, if the information were kept in paper files and a request is made for a specific piece of information which is readily available, it is relatively cheap for the agency to pull the file and make copies of the specific information. However, when a series of files, such as the record of payments under a specific subsidy program, is computerized, the costs assessed by the agencies are quite high, as they are generally related to computer time costs.

As an example, the most common cost for a copy of a tape is $62.00. Agency personnel have told me that it is much easier to supply a complete duplicate tape if a requester wants only a small part of the information on the tape rather than to pull and print that specific information. A duplicate tape, however, is only useful if the requester has print-out facilities. In cases where a print-out of the data is requested, the usual agency practice is to charge a certain amount for the time taken to locate the information on the tape, plus $5.00 per page for the print-out itself. The time charges are generally computed on the basis of the agency costs per hour for use of the computer. . . . Therefore, what would have been a minor charge for pulling and copying a paper file can be an expensive proposition if the material is on tape and a time-use and print-out charge is levied.[30]

However, Mr. Kronfeld went on to note that the computer provided considerable savings when someone wants large bodies of data. "In the case where the requester wants the whole category of computerized information and has the facilities to process the tape, the cost savings can be substantial." Mr. Kronfeld cited the production of computer-generated mailing lists for commercial advertisers and organizations as a prime example.[31]

Most of the other groups of information-seekers reported either no experience with computerized files or no special problems with them. Such replies came from: the Consumer Federation of America and the National Consumers League, from public-interest law firms, such as the Institute for Public Interest Representation and the Citizens Communications Center for Responsive Media; from the National Capital Areas Chapter of the American Civil Liberties Union; from the freedom of information committees of the AP Broadcasters Association and Aviation/Space Writers Association; and from the Washington Office of the League of Women Voters.

However, some of these information-seekers did have experiences with computerization. Among the public-interest law firms the most interesting comments came from two of Ralph Nader's groups, the Center for the Study of Responsive Law and the Public Interest Research Group. Harrison Wellford and Ronald Plesser are the persons with whom I talked.[32] Messrs. Wellford and Plesser said they had had some experiences in which computerization had made it possible to obtain information that would have been difficult if not impossible to get from the previous manual file. Their example was from the Securities and Exchange Commission. An SEC code provision says that anyone who is more than a 10-per-cent owner of shares in a listed corporation must file an ownership form with the SEC. This is a public document. However, it has always been filed under the company name, not the individual's name. When the Nader Congress project was under way in 1972, the researchers wanted to find out what stocks were owned by each Congressman and candidate for Congress in 1972. But, Mr. Plesser noted, "We would have had to go through 10,000 files to get the names."

However, the Nader group learned that the SEC had a name-access program for this ownership file, and asked to have a list compiled of each Congressman and candidate for Congress in 1972. At first, the SEC hesitated, on the ground that it might be an invasion of privacy. It could lead to use of their files for commercial mailings, political solicitations, etc. However, the Nader group persuaded the SEC to supply the list, and it aided the Nader Congress research greatly.

On the other hand, the Nader associates cited several examples where files had been computerized, but the absence of a software program to produce the desired information prevented them from obtaining the data they needed. In one case, litigants in a damage suit against the manufacturer of a helicopter, suing after an air crash, wanted the maintenance background records for a particular ball bearing believed to have been defective, or defectively maintained. The Air Force keeps a computer log of these maintenance records, but its retrieval program is only for major parts, not minor ones like the ball bearing. The Air Force could print out all of the "nonmajor items," but this would provide a print-out 300 sheets long. The issue was whether the Air Force would reprogram their computer system. When asked, they replied that the computer was busy twenty-fours hours a day, seven days a week. Any free time that developed was needed for system repair. Even if there was time available, the cost of reprogramming was estimated at several thousand dollars. *

Another example involved meat-inspection reports and pesticide data. The Center for Responsive Law won the right to inspect these at the Agriculture Department. Some of these data were computerized, but when the Center wanted information on a statewide basis, it was told that it would require costly reprogramming which, Mr. Wellford observed, was "beyond our ability to pay."

The Nader group experience underscores the fact that more information of the kind sought by public-interest groups is potentially available in the computerized files than had been provided in manual records. But where the agency has not provided software programming to extract what these groups want, it is not yet clear under interpretations of the Freedom of Information Act whether a demand can be made that such expensive reprogramming, often interfering with vital computer services, can be required of the government. If so, who must pay for it?

Among the consumer representatives, a typical statement of consumer outlook came from Benjamin Kass, a lawyer for consumer interests and formerly a staff member of two Con-

* A computer expert has said that a tape file copy could have been produced and the desired information retrieved on another system for perhaps $1000.

gressional committees that specialized in supervising government information policies. Mr. Kass observed:

> Whenever my consumer groups or people have ever needed information, we put in a request and get back volumes of microfiche or print-out copies. I don't think computerized information presents a unique problem. If some bureaucrat doesn't want to give information that should be public, it doesn't matter what the nature of the information is—whether it is computerized or not. Generally, it is easier to get information if it is computerized because it is harder to give C information and deny it to A or B. It all boils down to the attitude of the agency bureaucrats. If they don't want to give it out, that's what counts.[33]

Further confirmation that computerized information is often useful but that groups have to fight to get it came from two leaders of women's rights activities. Myra Barrer, of Women Today, related that she had been trying for some time to get access to computer print-out sheets showing the number of women employed in each federal agency at each grade level, at what salary, etc. She pressed for access at the individual agencies, and often got it, "after haggling," but what she really wanted was the collection of agency computer print-out sheets kept by the Civil Service Commission and bound in one volume titled, *Women in Government*. According to Ms. Barrer, this book is "long past due." In terms of its usefulness once it is "pried out of the agency," she commented, "the computer print-outs have the advantage of being a lot easier to use for comparing year-to-year figures. Each agency in the print-out lists the supergrades and the women's names for various years. All the information is in one place." [34]

A similar appraisal of the value of computerized data came from Ko Kimbel of the Women's Training and Resource Corporation, in Portland, Maine. The Corporation applied for a loan from the Small Business Administration but encountered "all kinds of snags and difficulties that we suspected were because we were women. So we decided to find out what percentage of total moneys and services were given to women by the SBA." When they contacted the Director of SBA, he said that the information was not available. By going to Congressman William Hathaway, who asked for these data from SBA, got them, and turned them over to Ms. Kimbel, she was able to secure a computer print-out containing a monthly breakdown of the moneys given as loans to various businesses, and to determine which of these were run by women. It turned out to be less than half of one per cent. SBA officials said that the print-out was not "reliable," but Ms. Kimbel noted that it came from the Reports Management Division of SBA, which "is regarded as a very reliable source." [35] The SBA data was released to the press and various women's groups, and served as highly useful ammunition with which to attack antiwomen policies at SBA.

One response from each of two other categories of information-seeker indicate that these groups have the same reaction as those already discussed.

Sam Archibald, formerly Staff Director of the House Committee on Government Operations and now Washington Director of the Freedom of Information Center wrote these comments:

> It is my impression that computerized records are harder to obtain, although easier to amass. The government collects information in an easily retrievable form but is reluctant to regurgitate that information because it might, just might, contain more facts than the requester asked for or the government administrator wants to divulge.
>
> There have been instances of absurd restrictions placed on the search and retrieval of computerized government records and of absurd search and copying charges levied by government agencies. But I do not have at hand the details of those records. My material, unfortunately, is not computerized.[36]

Mr. Archibald's commentary, it seems to me, coincides with that of the Nader groups in emphasizing the cost factors in obtaining search and print-out access to large computerized data bases.

Finally, let me quote from a letter received from James Ridgeway, a leading investigative writer and book author, now an editor of *Ramparts* magazine: "I have had considerable difficulty obtaining information of a nonsecurity nature from the federal government, but not because of any mechanical reason, such as computers. These reasons all pertain to policy. In certain agencies the government hinders dissemination of information by charging for documents, some of which are computer print-outs." [37]

Following are the two major conclusions suggested by the information-seekers who responded to my inquiry:

1. The strongest agreement that computerization has improved the usefulness and availability of information to be obtained from executive agencies comes from Congressional committee Counsel. The willingness of executive agencies to furnish this without cost to legislative committees, and to suppress arguments about searches taking too much of agency personnel time, help to explain why the legislative Counsel have such a generally untroubled perspective on cost and inconvenience.

2. Among nongovernment information-seekers, computerized records have often been found to be extremely useful, providing material and services that were not previously available. The private seekers agreed with executive-agency officials that the most important issues are ones of policy (is the information open to public inspection or not?) not of the particular form of information storage and retrieval. Antisecrecy forces see agency officials *extending* secrecy-oriented approaches to the computerized files. The private information-seekers pointed to problems of cost in certain requests for information, especially whether agencies are developing access programs that serve public disclosure needs as well as managerial ones

IV An Analysis of the Current Situation

So far, I have reported on and summarized the replies to my survey of information-holders and information-seekers. Now, drawing on these materials but adding my own experiences in studying the effects of computerization in organizations, let me present my analysis of what has been happening, and what it means to public access.

First, computerization has unfolded as a process in which organizational managers decide what they want to do with this new technology to carry out their missions more efficiently. It is in pursuit of this organizational efficiency goal that decisions have been made whether computers should be installed, which files to automate, what "better services" to pursue through software programming, what program evaluation data or policy-planning data to seek from the computerized data bases, and what reports should be generated to management. Legislative, public, and judicial pressures in the past few years have elevated the issues of privacy to the level where they now command some executive attention in computerization plans and procedures, and there has been some legislative examination of the cost-justifications and cost-effectiveness for agency automation. But virtually no attention has been paid by the managers of organizations to the *public-access issues* in their computer decisions, nor have these issues been put before the managers by the usual public-interest and legislative-watchdog forces. No Congressional hearings have yet focused on these matters, no Nader group has taken up this question as its prime concern, no group of computer professionals has accepted this as an obligation of their civic and professional duties, and no judicial rulings have dealt with the issues of access presented by computerization. In short, the major decisions about the use of computer technology, in terms of whose interests are to be served by the development of this powerful new tool, have been entirely in the hands of executive-agency officials.

Second, even though the reports of agency officials and the experiences of many information-seekers indicate that there have been some increases in availability and usefulness of information as a result of computerization, these have been basically serendipitous effects. That is, they have been fall-outs from better control and utilization of information. To the extent that these techniques, designed to help agencies use information for their own purposes, have helped information-seekers, it has not been because the agencies have set out to provide better services to the press, scholars, public-interest groups, or government critics. This point needs to be understood, not because it brands the officials of agencies as deliberate culprits but because it indicates that the forces seeking to improve the public's access to information have not begun to appreciate what computer technology might do—with the proper inputs to agency computerization plans and procedures—if public-interest spokesmen had some say in how the public's money is spent on this costly technology.

Third, this failure to realize what is at stake, to force the development of new laws, procedures, and institutions to bring public-interest groups into the computerization process, to insure better public access to government data, has taken place at a distressingly critical time in the expansion of computer technology in government. In the late 1960s and early 1970s, third-generation computer systems have been installed in the major government agencies and departments. Basic decisions about the architecture of the systems have been made, money has been allotted for the vital software programming that will control how the files are used, new networks for information exchange and dissemination have been created, and the technical priesthood to manage these systems has been assembled and invested with important authority to control the machines. While computerization is basically an ongoing process, and many things can be done to modify or alter the systems, it is very difficult, very costly, and very disruptive of organizational functions to attempt major changes once they have been designed and programmed in a particular way.

Furthermore, developments in computer technology unfolding in the 1970s threatens to make the problem more acute. For example, the proliferation of mini-computers means that government agencies will be able to place many "small" files of information on relatively inexpensive machines. This will make it harder to keep track of where information is stored and how it is used.

In the first fifteen years of computerization in government, I do not believe the record reveals a significant *lessening* of public access to government information as a result of automation. What it does reveal is a case of *lost opportunities* and of *potentially great danger* in the future. We have not appreciated how to bring public participation into the computerization decisions, and we have failed to develop the standards and procedures that will prevent computerization from upsetting the desired balances between public access and government secrecy.

V Recommendations for Action

I see four main objectives for public-access spokesmen in the effort to bring computer technology under greater public control:

1. Create a public right to effective participation in the decisions of government agencies regarding computerization. It is also necessary to develop the groups, institutions, and procedures that are able to take advantage of this right and to provide the financial support needed.

2. Legislate a right of access by the individual to records kept about him in government agencies. This right would cover all but a small group of government files. It would include provisions for giving citizens an easily obtainable guide to the individually identified records kept by government agencies. There would also be a right to challenge the continued retention of inaccurate, incomplete, or misleading information. These rights are essential if the right of the public to know what government is doing extends beyond access only by representative groups. It must also be secured for millions of individuals who have lost confidence that government agencies—in social services, taxation, health, law enforcement, etc.—always collect proper and accurate information. For these citizens, only a direct and personal right of inspection in their own record will satisfy the access principle in an age of large-scale data banks.[38]

3. Identify and develop techniques to make computer systems help the cause of public information as well as agency operations, such as requiring publicly available indexes to file content and software programs, instituting requirements to develop the software necessary to produce information that is in a data base but is not retrievable, and requiring audit-trails that record the uses made of information in files. Again, providing the funds to finance such operations is critical.

4. Pay attention to the effect of antisecrecy actions on the

rights of personal privacy of persons and groups about whom there is sensitive information in files. Develop the exceptions and special procedures that will not make these civil-liberty interests the victim of the need for public disclosure. Protection of the government's need for temporary privacy for its decision-making processes should be incorporated in the new policies and procedures.

I am sure it will take a great many legislative hearings, organizational conferences, scholarly studies, and public debates before all the elements of such a program will be properly defined and put into law and practice. But long journeys do have to begin somewhere, and in this spirit of a beginning, let me cite some of the steps we might take.

First, we dare not let the current process of revising the Freedom of Information Act be concluded without getting the issue of computerization and access on the Congressional agenda. Hearings should be held, perhaps by adding this topic to the series on "Federal Use and Development of Advanced Information Technology" which have been initiated by the House Foreign Operations and Government Information Subcommittee.[39] The basic measure that should emerge from such hearings is statutory language doing two things. The first is to create a duty in executive agencies to give specific consideration to the improvement of public access in their plans for and operations of automatic data processing (ADP), with a review of the adequacy of their compliance vested in a legislative committee or legislatively responsible agency or commission.

An excellent model for this provision can be found in a bill sponsored by Senator Lee Metcalf, S. 770, to establish an Intergovernmental Office of Consumers' Counsel. One purpose of the Metcalf bill is "to improve methods for obtaining and disseminating information with respect to the operations of regulated companies of interest to the Federal Government and other consumers. . . ." To make sure that this purpose is served, the Metcalf bill provides:

> Sec. 301 *Automatic Data Processing*
>
> (a) Federal agencies are hereby authorized and directed to make full use of automatic data processing in preparing the

> information required under this Act and other Acts to which they are subject, to the end that the Counsel, the Congress, and the public shall receive information in a timely and understandable manner. Federal agencies are hereby directed to include, in their annual reports, accounts of their progress toward full use of automatic data processing.
> (b) The Comptroller General of the United States shall review the activities of the Federal agencies in compliance with this section, and shall report to the Congress the results of such compliance, and where full use of automatic data processing is not being made in the preparation of such information he shall recommend those actions which should be taken to achieve such full use of automatic data processing techniques and equipment.[40]

While the Metcalf-suggested provision is there to create a particular office affecting consumers, I see no reason why such a provision should not be written directly into the amendments to the Freedom of Information Act. It would need Congressional funds expressly authorized for its implementation, perhaps a set percentage of the cost of each computer system (5 per cent) assigned to public-access facilities.

The second legislative action needed is the requirement of a public proceeding whenever a new computer system is installed by a government agency or a major expansion of an existing system is contemplated. Notice of these hearings should be published in the *Federal Register* and opportunities for submissions and appearances should be available to interested parties or groups. The agency would have to present, in addition to other items, detailed privacy-impact and public-access impact statements. The record of the hearing and an official response to objections and protests submitted by the head of the agency should be filed with an appropriate Congressional committee, perhaps the committee with subject-matter authority or appropriation authority over the agency's function, or perhaps a committee like Government Operations.

This underscores a dilemma that deserves far more sustained attention than it has received from civil libertarians and democrats: to deal effectively with issues of computers, privacy, and public access means creating working groups of persons with legal, technological, and social-science skills, to provide the blend of expertise needed to examine the computerization proposals of executive agencies and to inspect their actual operations. While there have been some still-born early efforts—like the attempt by Ralph Nader to enlist volunteers from the Washington area Association for Computing Machinery in projects to use computer resources to get consumer information directly to shoppers, and to distribute consumer-agency violation data on business establishments directly to buyers—these have been few and have not had much of an influence. There are many groups that could be enlisted, if the proper organizational format and funding could be supplied. For example, a public interest group of lawyers, computer specialists, social scientists, and journalists could be set up to work on "Computers and Democratic Government." Or the American Civil Liberties Union's new Surveillance Project in Washington, D.C., might undertake this operation, drawing on the necessary specialists. A group like Common Cause or the Freedom of Information Center might be the catalyst and organizer.

Again, there exists precedent to draw on for this idea. The Federal Power Commission, in April 1972, issued a notice that it proposed to create a "Fully Automated Computer Regulatory Information System," as an aid in the FPC's basic responsibilities under the Federal Power Act. The general plan for the system was described, in considerable detail, and interested parties were apprised of their opportunity to appear and comment on the proposed system. The proposal has not yet been implemented, and various parties have filed letters, briefs, and comments with the FPC. When I examined the docket entries indicating who had filed such comments, I found a long parade of power companies, oil companies, and state public-service commissions, but no public-interest laws firms, spokesmen for the press, or other guardian groups for public access. This suggests that the excellent procedure that the FPC is following will not do much for public access (or for privacy) if there are no organizations, financially and technically capable, ready to speak for these values.[41]

VI A Concluding Note

Thomas Jefferson, the leading apostle of a free press and open government, was also a devoted enthusiast of science and technology. While he was drafting the First Amendment, composing Virginia's statute on religious liberty, and fighting Chief Justice John Marshall's use of judicial power to enhance the rights of property holders, Jefferson was also involved in what eighteenth-century writers called "useful invention," the application of science to liberate mankind from enslavement to nature and endless physical labor. He mastered architecture and designed and built Monticello. He invented what he called the "polygraph," an instrument that attached one pen to another, so that a written copy could be made automatically by a person when writing a letter or document. For Jefferson, science was not an enemy of liberty; it was an ally, and even though he had read deeply about the uses of science to develop new instruments of warfare, he rested his faith in the belief that the rational spirit, in science as well as in republican government, offered man his best chance for progress.

We need the Jeffersonian spirit today, more than ever. Technology has grown increasingly powerful, and the struggle over who will control and use it more intense. Were a Jefferson to return to the United States today, I believe he would be fascinated by computers, by the way that automation of clerical functions had replaced armies of petty clerks and minor officialdom. But after his wonder had subsided, he would ask: For whose benefit are these new tools being used? Who controls them? Are they on the side of civil liberty or of arbitrary authority? We owe it to the Jeffersonian heritage to develop the necessary technical information and skills to be able to monitor this new technology, within the tradition of open government and protection of personal privacy that Jefferson would have insisted upon for the preservation of a free society. The skilled and persuasive advocates for the values of computers for organizational goals have, so far, enjoyed a monopoly of serious discussion. It is time that those concerned with access to data, by the individual and by representatives of an informed public, also be heard—in the kind of adversary process from which wise public policies have traditionally emerged.

VII Discussion

DR. WIESNER: Does modern technology make legitimate and illegitimate access to information more difficult to control? On the one hand, we are obviously concerned about privacy, the rights of the individual; and on the other, computers and modern communication techniques can increase the difficulty of monitoring the performance of government and discovering the data government has. The use of modern technology does not automatically guarantee access to information.

The legitimate and illegitimate use of modern technology does endanger the rights of the citizens in many ways. Probably the greatest danger comes from the opportunity for accumulation, centralization, and processing of information. We have the acquisition of data by the Army on people who attend war-protest meetings. This was followed by an attempt to check this data against files on credit ratings. Then there are computer personality profiles, designed for experimental purposes, but used to make predictions about social or criminal behavior patterns of citizens.

It is a Kafkaesque use of technology, not only information technology but a variety of other scientific pursuits, all of which seem to me to be used to frighten and intimidate the people. One can't be sure the results will always be so unimpressive or that the people using new technologies will remain incompetent. We do need, I think, a stronger guarantee against misuse of these burgeoning technologies. It is very clear that the power of the computer to accumulate data and to model hypothetical situations is going to grow as is our ability to coordinate information from all over the world. One of the things that people keep hoping is that there are technical solutions to these problems, and in fact there probably are some technical aids. For example, I think you could program computer memories to fade, if you wanted to, in six months or one year or ten years, the way human memories fade. You could program computers not to accept certain kinds of data. One can dream of a whole variety of technical safeguards that one can build into the system, but it seems to me that anything that a designer could put into such a system could be overcome by somebody in a position of authority, who could give instructions to circumvent the devices. It seems unlikely that society is going to get protection from the technicians. It may get some help, but by and large I view this as a social and legal problem and it has got to be faced.

MR. KRONFELD: Under the Administrative Procedure Act, regulations which an agency intends to make which affect the public have to be published in the Federal Register, with a thirty-day period for public comment, and the comment must be taken into consideration prior to drafting the final regulation.

I wonder if that vehicle might be used to get public feedback on decisions to go to data processing.

MR. PLESSER: The Freedom of Information Act guarantees access to certain Securities and Exchange Commission forms filed pursuant to rule 16B of the SEC. The computer makes it easier to use these forms. The SEC made a decision that they would allow us to use the easier access. That was great. But I am not sure that that is a principle created in the law. You might have access to information, but do you have a right to use a computer for easier access? That question has to be dealt with.

But the computer can also make it harder. You can walk into the Department of Agriculture, walk up to the file room, and look at whatever you want. What happens when they start to computerize those records, reduce them to magnetic tapes, and put them in the data bank? There is no question that the information is public information, but who has the burden of paying the computer time? Who has the burden of paying for running that computer to get that information out?

MR. SCHWARTZ: I want to emphasize my own personal appreciation for the broader approach of Dr. Wiesner and Professor Westin. It is vital to realize, as Dr. Wiesner so well pointed out, that the problem we are concerned with, executive governmental secrecy, is really part of a much broader problem—the problem of how the law and government institutions will cope with the kind of society we are going into. For the first time in our history, we are finding a problem, a crisis, confronting the society, a domestic crisis which the legal mind and legal techniques and attitudes may not be sufficient to resolve. If you go back over our history, what were the great crises before? Setting up the nation, tearing apart the nation in the Civil War, expansion of the society and the economy. We were able to frame all these in legal terms, but now we are confronted with a new technology in a postindustrial society. For the first time, perhaps, we are confronted with the possibility of an awesome reality.

If we try to deal with this problem in purely legal terms as we are wont to do, I wonder if it would be adequate. The legal mind, with all its advantages, is a very narrow mind. It emphasizes techniques and technicalities. It is restricted in its reasoning and response. How is the individual to remain an individual in this new kind of society? We ought to start asking the questions. We ought to start combining law, technology, the legal mind, the political scientist, and others, or the brave new world that we are going into will surely turn into 1984.

MR. WESTIN: Before we allow agencies automatically to computerize the information they held previously, and become national holders or regional holders of such information, we need to ask whether we don't want instead some independent holders. A good example is the FBI's National Crime Information Center.

In 1971 Attorney General John Mitchell made the decision to give management of the National Crime Information Center to the FBI. He rejected two alternate proposals to let it be run either by an independent agency under LEAA or the Justice Department directly or by state law-enforcement officials. We have allowed a line investigative agency, the FBI, to manage this system. It should not be in a line agency, but an-independent agency, without prosecutors or investigators or a probation function, so we are assured that the computer is not abused.

DR. WIESNER: One of the things that has become evident in the last decade is that we pass laws to control things we don't understand, and then we get into trouble of all kinds.

This has been true in the environmental field and in a number of other fields. We have sometimes confused the goals and the process—the goals are clear but the process may not exist. We pass the laws nonetheless, and then hope that either technologists or lawyers or political scientists or educators will invent the process. Much of our current turmoil is a consequence of the gap between the goals we continue to articulate and our inability to develop the process to achieve them. In many instances, the time to develop the processes is longer than the time we are willing to allow. We don't understand these things and we become very impatient.

So I see the need for public-interest groups to study and understand the many problems that arise from the interaction of society and technology.

MR. STONE: I wanted to raise the "measure countermeasure game" in the secrecy area.

The FBI invented the trash cover a few years ago. They go around and pick up the trash of people they have under surveillance. This probably led to the paper shredder.

Similarly, the government can subpoena telephone records to find out whom you talk to. This has led to the "sterile" phone number. It leaves no record of calls made to it. Howard Hunt wanted one.

Since telephone records can be subpoenaed, people can be kept under surveillance even without tapping their telephones. By subpoenaing records to find out how often one person called another, you can make a map of who knows whom. I don't know how long these records are kept, but it seems to me they pose a real threat. If someone starts following me around, checking on whom I have talked to each day, even if they don't hear the conversations, they could learn a lot about me. Would I have a remedy against that?

MR. GOODELL: This is often used in criminal investigations.

MR. STONE: I met an old lady who had been called on by the FBI agents. They didn't even know who she was, but they knew she had talked to somebody else in whom they were interested. Some restraint should be put on this process of mapping out personal relationships.

MR. SCHWARTZ: This is one of the most important investigative techniques. It is used not only by the FBI, but by investigators on the Hill. You can use telephone calls to break very important cases.

MR. SHATTUCK: There is a new federal statute, the Bank Secrecy Act, which requires banks to photocopy all bank checks on microfilm and keep them for five years. The bank records of an individual are even more revealing than telephone records. It has not been sufficiently emphasized that the investigative tools of the government are greatly enhanced by the technology of record-keeping.

MR. CALLEN: The fight against crime is going to provide the major push that will bring technology to bear on individual privacy. There is a tremendous desire to stop crime; technology is being studied extensively as a tool in that fight. It is difficult for one foot patrolman to walk the streets and cover everything. There are studies around the country to have scanning television cameras up and down the street. One man can sit in an office and look at a whole bank of television cameras and follow everything that goes on for a number of blocks. The time may well come where it will be impossible to walk the streets without having somebody sitting in a police station watching you as you walk along, perhaps recording you on video tape. A parabolic microphone could be aimed to pick up what you say to somebody as you walk down the street. As another example, remote, Doppler-shift sonic lie detectors are now being developed. They sense the breathing rate of subjects without their knowing that they're taking lie-detector tests. All those things will be used as weapons against crime, but they are also threats to the privacy of the individual.

13 Government Secrecy in the United Kingdom

—by J. A. G. Griffith

It is commonly believed by those who have dealings with the departments of state in the government of the United Kingdom that that government is obsessed with secrecy and by nature and habit withholds information unless forced to disclose it. Frequently, unfavorable comparisons are made with systems of government operating in other parts of Western Europe and in North America. Scandinavian countries—and Sweden in particular—are for this, as for some other less political purposes, displayed as splendid examples of a better way of life which we should strive to imitate. Without wishing to denigrate the democratic achievements of those (or any other) countries, there is a suspicion in all this of the grass being greener on the other side of the sea. Skepticism is not diminished when, talking to nationals of other countries, we find that they assume things are probably better ordered (in this matter of political accountability) in the United Kingdom than in their own benighted nations.

My own experience of West European countries suggests that while the United Kingdom is not on fortune's cap the very button, she is not the sole of her shoe either. (I prefer, in these days of the new puritanism, which we are struggling to withstand, not to pursue Shakespeare's metaphor lest I be done in for obscenity.)

Nevertheless, I am one of those who believes that the citizens of countries which have a bill of rights written into a constitution are in a happier position than those who labor under the well-known advantages of a flexible, unwritten, pragmatic, sophisticated, what you will, constitution. So in any account of governmental practice and legal provision in the United Kingdom, we must remember yet again that governments no less than individuals are in the United Kingdom equal before the law whereas there is a case for saying that governments should, in the exercise of their great powers, be rather less than equal. And that there should be special principles binding governments which do not bind individuals.

I Secrecy in the Political Process

I do not intend to write a truly comparative analysis but rather to set down some aspects of the problems surrounding government secrecy as they appear in the United Kingdom today. This is because I do not believe that institutions are comparable, especially when they are in different countries. Of course, this does not mean that one country cannot learn from another. But, when divorced from politics, the comparison of one country's laws with the laws of another country leads primarily to confusion rather than enlightenment. As the Franks Committee [1] put it:

> In each of the four overseas countries which we visited, as in this country, there is a variety of factors affecting openness, Constitutional arrangements, political tradition, and national character, habits and ways of thought, all have their influence. Our examination of the position in five countries, differing from each other in all these respects but each within the broad tradition of western democracy, has confirmed that the law is by no means the most important influence on openness. In some countries it is not even a major one. A particular national law cannot in any event be sensibly assessed apart from the whole national context.[2]

We may look first at the kinds of information which the government of the United Kingdom is reluctant to part with, although neither the national interest nor national security is involved. Immediately we are deep in the political process and in the party political process. Perhaps it is not wholly unsurprising that politicians do not wish to air their thought processes in public while those processes are actually in movement. We are told little about the government's struggles to arrive at a decision, what is taken into account, what treated as irrelevant. "Ongoing policy formation" is conducted in private. To this there are exceptions. Recently, administrations have been publishing Green Papers which are meant to be discussion documents, showing the state of the administration's mind at the time of publication and inviting comment. The reorganization of the national health service was thus discussed. So also was the reform of local government finance though in this latter instance the Green Paper seemed designed less for instruction and the stimulation of debate and more for setting up the whole range of possibilities and then knocking down all but one of them in an excessive display of selective Aunt Sally-ing. There has also been more information in relation to the Budget and generally a greater willingness, as a result of parliamentary pressure, to make public the administration's forecasts of public expenditure over the ensuing five years. Similarly, there has been a change not only in the amount of statistical material collected by government departments and by the Central Statistical Office but also in the amount of its publication.

The weakness in the machinery of government which flowed from the paucity of statistical material is being progressively removed. So also the development of recent years of select committees of the House of Commons concerned with the activities of particular government departments and with particular subjects which embrace the activities of two or more departments has meant that more information has been extracted from Departments.[3]

But politicians are also reluctant to display the thought processes they had in the past which led them to arrive at decisions long since put into effect and superseded by other decisions. This is close to the reluctance of politicians to define precisely what their policies are—quite apart from how those policies are arrived at. This reluctance seems to be based on the principle that no politician should ever admit that he has made a mistake, and this purity is more easily maintained if there is some obscurity cast over what it was he was trying to achieve. In the United Kingdom, policies about the control of land-use are often remarkable for their lack of precision. Before accusing governments of undue secrecy about their policies, it is necessary (to be fair) to establish that they had policies to conceal. And that is by no means straightforward.

That governments may become agitated by leakages which have nothing to do with national security and everything to do with party politics is evidenced by a curious and still obscure occurrence in late 1972. *The Sunday Times* newspaper published an article which said that the administration was considering a plan which would reduce rail services by a further 40 per cent. At the end of November, many weeks after the publication, the police searched the offices of the *Railway Gazette*, a monthly publication with a circulation of some 12,000. They appeared to believe that they would find there some information which would explain how the "plan" had come into the hands of *The Sunday Times* but in this they appear to have been unsuccessful. Subsequently it was stated that the search had been authorized by the Director of Public Prosecutions, who presumably was contemplating legal action against someone or other. The information was said to be classified as secret. On this occasion, the House of Commons proved, perhaps not surprisingly in this type of case, to be of little use to those who wished to discover what was going on. The editor of the *Railway Gazette* complained that his telephone was being tapped, and one of his employees complained that he had been threatened by detectives with the exposure of his private life. Eventually the story, never very strong, ran into the sand. But it seemed to show to some people an alarming willingness on the part of the authorities to turn out newspaper files.

The power of the Crown to withhold documents from production in litigation before the courts has a long and, until recently, an unhappy history. In a series of decisions, the courts upheld this privilege of the Crown which was claimed (and could not be controverted) on the ground that production of a document would be injurious to the public interest. But in *Conway* v. *Rimmer* [4] the House of Lords held that the courts had a duty to weigh the conflicting interests of the public (as claimed by the Crown) and the administration of justice; and that the courts were empowered to go against the Crown's affidavit and order production of documents for which privilege was claimed. It is not easy to assess the practical importance of this change (which brought the law of England into conformity with the law of Scotland) partly because the cases have never been numerous. But certainly there has been a drying up of claims of privilege and it may well be that the effect of the decision in *Conway* v. *Rimmer* is more subterranean and preventive and none the less effective for that. But it is also likely that courts will be most reluctant to go against the administration's view where privilege is claimed. The real result of *Conway* v. *Rimmer* may prove to be the abandonment by the Crown of the claim of privilege in all cases except those where the documents touch national security or the inner workings of government departments.

In the United Kingdom, a rule now operates for preserving from general disclosure for thirty years public documents, including files and notes and correspondence from the departments of state. Although some information is excluded from the thirty-year rule and protected for longer periods, what can be seen is often fascinating and occasionally illuminating. But any light shining from the early 1940s is necessarily somewhat dimmed as it seeks to penetrate the mists of time.

Public servants in the United Kingdom also prefer to operate behind closed doors. But it does not seem to me that this is something for which they can properly be criticized. Their job is to achieve certain ends. They are professionals for certain particular purposes. I do not mean here to involve myself in the arguments about whether they rather than their political masters "really govern the country." I mean that their function is to run an efficient defense system, a social-security system, or to improve the balance of payments or whatever. Of course it may be that a particular job is more efficiently done—that is, the public servants will more completely effect what they purpose—if there is a considerable measure of public participation. But this is not necessarily so. The achievements, for example, of a foreign policy may depend on secrecy. Are they to be blamed for that secrecy in those circumstances? I think not.

This raises a fundamental question. Governments may be regarded as special institutions not comparable in the last resort with other large organizations. Their difference is said to lie in the nature of their relationship with the public. I believe it is part of the constitutional theory of government in the United States to view the people as sovereign and governments as repositories of power delegated from the people. On that basis, governments owe duties to the people to whom they are responsible and accountable. Secrecy then becomes a denial in part of that responsibility and that accountability only tolerable to the extent that the people recognize the necessity or desirability of this partial denial of their sovereignty.

But there is another view which owes nothing to such notions of theoretical obligation. Historically, sovereignty in the United Kingdom is an attribute of the sovereign which meant the monarch and has come, under political pressure, to mean the servants of the Crown, being both ministers and public servants. On this view there is no theoretical obligation but only a political relationship which is shaped and determined by political forces, by the positives of power. If therefore "the people" or any group of people wish to make government less secret and more open, they cannot call on any general principle, they cannot found themselves on some premise. All they can do is to seek to shift the distribution of political power so that those in executive authority have a smaller share and the people have a greater share.

This is to say that the government of a country is not in the last resort distinguishable from any other large organization. It is strictly comparable in all important respects with Imperial Chemical Industries or the Ford Motor Company. It is different indeed, seeking different ends. But its relationship to the people—to the consumer—is not special. The shareholders of a large company have about as much or as little control over the activities of the board of the company as the people have over governments. So we should not be surprised or shocked or distressed if a public servant acts secretly. It is said that Voltaire's last words were "*Le bon dieu me pardonnera. C'est son métier.*" For a public servant, secrecy may be seen by him to be a necessary part of his trade also. We may want to change all that. But it is not a moral question.

Legislative secrecy in the United Kingdom points up this matter quite neatly. The most important stage in the legislative process is that which precedes the presentation of a bill to Parliament. The idea for legislation may have come from many sources: from departmental committees, from electoral promises, from Royal Commissions, or merely from defects in the existing administrative machinery. Memoranda will begin to flow within the department and between departments. The Treasury will be involved. Cabinet committees will decide on the justification for a bill like this at this time. Very many and very considerable consultations are likely to take place between public servants in the department and outside interests likely to be affected by what is proposed. Far more than in the United States (as I understand it) the bill will be conceived, born, and spend the early months of its life in the department. All this will be as secret as can be—and certainly little information leaks out, even by way of the consulted interests, to the general public. Moreover, the bargains that are struck between the department and those interests will be regarded by Ministers as binding on them; and sometimes, Ministers are greatly embarrassed (when the details of the bill are known and debated) by the terms of those secret arrangements which have been come to.

After the bill has been presented to one or other House of Parliament by the responsible Minister, it will typically be considered in detail and at length in a standing committee. If the bill is controversial, that consideration will be hostile, as the Opposition members seek to expose its iniquities and its inequities. Very commonly, a large part of the examination to which the bill is subjected will have as its aim the uncovering of the intention of the government and the background, often the statistical information on which the bill is based. Here is, if not a peculiarity, at least a characteristic of the legislative process in the United Kingdom. For the Minister will not put before the committee more than a small part of the information in his possession and on which the bill is based. Much of this information has to be prised out of the department in an operation which the department clearly considers to be painful and so resists.

We have recently had a particular example of this. The government introduced a Housing Finance Bill which altered the basis on which the rents of publicly owned houses and apartments—of which there are in the United Kingdom a considerable number—were to be assessed. The result was to be an appreciable increase in the rents of those properties. The increases would vary from town to town, from region to region. And it was obvious that detailed financial estimates must have been made by the department on the likely effects of this bill in different places. None of this information was at first provided. What was eventually obtained was essential to the critical function of the Opposition. And it was only obtained after many long struggles in committee.

This sort of secrecy does genuinely inhibit the Opposition. And that is why the secrecy continues. It has the political purpose of making life more difficult for political opponents. It has often no other justification. If we are seeking to improve the critical function of Parliament, such secrecy is a stumbling block and should be done away with. But it should not be supposed that Opposition spokesmen are continuously calling for this reform in the procedures and practices of Parliament. For they see themselves as the next Ministers and they do not wish to be, in their turn, toads under that harrow.

Select Committees of the House of Commons—not concerned with legislative but with the administrative process—are more free of the constraining effects of the party political struggles. In February 1971 Mr. Docksey, a former general manager of British Petroleum Ltd., was appointed to conduct an independent inquiry. In December 1971 he made his report under the title "The Government rôle in developing and exploiting inventions." Throughout 1972 the Select Committee on Science and Technology pressed for the publication of the report. On July 19, 1972, Mr. Docksey gave evidence to the Select Committee and said that he saw no reason why his report should not be published in an edited form. On July 24, the Committee made a formal request for the production of the report. On September 13, the Committee received copies of the report from the government. On December 6, the Committee published the report in its edited form.[5] The Committee said they were concerned at the reason given in May 1972 by the government for nonpublication. The Minister had said then: "I think the Government needs to consider very carefully how far the recommendations of that report are compatible with its broad approach to research and development generally speaking. I think that the Government will not wish to publish the report until they have finished that consideration, and perhaps not to publish it at all if they were to reach the conclusion that it was incompatible with the Government's broad approach to research and develop."

The Committee commented:

> We do not take this view. Too often Governments seek to avoid being questioned on aspects of policy by appointing an enquiry, then refusing to make any comment on the subject until the enquiry has reported. This device is made doubly objectionable if the Government then decide not to publish the report.
>
> We consider it essential that Select Committees should be given unobstructed access to reports which have a direct bearing on their work. It is inevitable that Ministers receive much confidential advice—and we accept that this should be so—but we think that reports of enquiries commissioned by the Government should be made available unless there are unusually compelling reasons to prevent it. It is only in this way that advice given to the Government can be subject to critical evaluation by the House, and "open government" made a reality.

The Chairman of the Select Committee said there was no case for shrouding in secrecy reports with conclusions with which a government department disagreed. He said that the government had a right to withhold secret information involving national security and to exercise discretion on information of commercial importance but that neither consideration applied to this particular case. He thought that this report would not have been published had the Committee acted as they did. It was the first case of a select committee calling for a report and then publishing it itself.

What does it mean to say, as did the Minister in this case, that the government might withhold publication if the report were "incompatible" with the government's broad approach? Can it mean anything except that the findings (factual and other) in the report failed to give support to the policy which the government intended to pursue? And so, once again, we see operating that reason for government secrecy which is that of not giving information which might be politically damaging, even where the information has been publicly called for by the government.

The powers of the House of Commons to require Ministers, as Members of the House, to appear as witnesses before committees of the House, and to produce documents, are considerable but are also embedded in the party political process. When a select committee is appointed, it is usually given power by the House to send for "persons, papers and records." Under this authority, witnesses may be summoned, by an order signed by the chairman of the committee, to attend the committee and to bring with them all such documents as they are informed will be required for the use of the committee. If a witness fails to appear, the House (not the committee) [6] may order him to attend at the bar of the House. If, in the meantime, he appears before the committee, the order for his attendance is usually discharged. If he persists in his nonattendance, he is in contempt of the House, and he may, after a hearing before the Committee of Privileges, in the last resort be imprisoned. These rules apply both to Members and to non-Members.

Normally, select committees begin by inviting witnesses to appear and, almost without exception, the invitation is willingly accepted. "In extending such invitations to government departments," says Erskine May, "the committee will usually rely on departmental cooperation in the selection of witnesses and will not normally summon individual officers. Nevertheless, the power of a select committee to send for persons is unqualified."[7]

In fact, there has been no instance of a Member (nor, it is believed, of any public servant) persisting in a refusal to give evidence. If, to take the extreme but also the most important instance, a Minister refused to attend to give evidence to a committee of the House, and the committee reported this to the House with a view to an order being made by the House requiring his attendance, it is likely that a minor constitutional crisis would arise. The committee would have had a governmental majority in its membership so it is probable that some government supporters on the committee had agreed to the report. If the reason for the nonappearance of the Minister was political in origin, the whips would be put on and the House would refuse to make the order. But it is possible (though difficult) to imagine a situation in which the refusal was more in the nature of a personal aberration on the part of the Minister and, conceivably, the House might order the Minister to attend.

The power to call for papers is limited to subjects that are of a public or official character. And one consequence of this is that the House and its committees can call for departmental papers which represent the end product of decision-making but are not empowered to call for such papers as departmental files, representing the internal stages in the decision-making process. But the Parliamentary Commissioner for Administration (the "ombudsman") is empowered by statute "to require any Minister, officer or member of the department or authority concerned or any other person who in his opinion is able to furnish information or produce documents relevant to the investigation to furnish any such information or produce any such document" with the exception of Cabinet papers.

The function of the press and of television and radio reporting is obviously crucial. They—and often only they—have the skills to penetrate the veil of secrecy and the means to publicize what they have found on a scale that may cause pain and embarrassment to politicians and public servants. There was recently a case where a medically qualified man who was later discovered to be a paranoid schizophrenic killed three babies in a hospital. The Minister said that the circumstances were so special that there were, in effect, no lessons to be learned, and so he refused a public inquiry. The British Broadcasting Corporation, through one of its current affairs teams, investigated the matter. It subsequently reported in a television program which produced persuasive evidence to suggest that, at least, the system which operated, or failed to operate, for checking references to see whether a person to be appointed was fit to be appointed, was extremely faulty; and that there were lessons to be learned; and, by inference, that a public inquiry should be held. This is the *kind* of case which makes the public believe that the refusal to inquire (which is the other side of the coin of secrecy) is inspired by a desire not to know or not to reveal.

We have also in recent months been watching with fascination the disclosures at a bankruptcy hearing of the affairs of a nationally and internationally known architect who seems to have made a practice of giving gifts of various kinds to many public persons who were in a position to help him. In this case, as in other cases, the magazine *Private Eye* has provided information or drawn attention to events which the national press has failed to record. More and more we are coming to rely on fewer and fewer people for this sort of investigation and publication. I find truly frightening how tenuous is the hold we in the United Kingdom have on the means of exposure. If any government were ever so minded, it could silence the exposé type of political criticism by the removal of a handful of people and the suppression of a tiny number of publications. Perhaps it has ever been thus. More likely is it that we happen to be living in a period—I would say at the beginning of a period—when corruption amongst politicians and public servants is on the increase. History records such increases and declines. It seems to me that we are fast approaching that danger point when the suppression of criticism becomes unimportant because no one is surprised or made angry by disclosures of corruption. For, in a paradox, the more secrecy we have, the more hope there is—at least where the secrecy is imposed for fear of the consequences to the individual of facts being known. When no one is impressed by exposure, because of a feeling of cynicism or of helplessness, then secrecy can be progressively abandoned and corruption become open.

II The Official Secrets Act

So far I have been speaking mostly of secrecy in the broadly political sphere. I must now turn to legal provisions in the United Kingdom.

Spying is dealt with by Section 1 of the Official Secrets Act 1911 and Section 2 of the Official Secrets Act 1920.[8] Section 1(1) of the Act of 1911 provides that a person shall be guilty of an offense if he for any purpose prejudicial to the safety or interests of the state a) approaches or enters any prohibited place; b) makes any sketch which is calculated to be or might be or is intended to be directly or indirectly useful to an enemy or potential enemy; c) obtains or communicates any information which is calculated to be directly or indirectly useful to an enemy or potential enemy.

Thus the action must be intended to be prejudicial and must involve either a prohibited place or material calculated, etc. Section 1(2) provides that the inference as to intention may be drawn from the circumstances, or from the defendant's conduct, or from his known character. And if the information relates to a prohibited place or a secret official code or pass word, the defendant is deemed to have the prejudicial intention unless he proves the contrary. Section 2 of 1920 Act provides that in a prosecution under Section 1 of the 1911 Act the fact that the defendant has been in touch with a foreign agent shall be evidence that he has, for a purpose prejudicial to the safety or interests of the state, obtained information which is calculated to be or might be or is intended to be useful to an enemy.

Since 1946, there have been twenty prosecutions under Section 1 of the 1911 Act. In eighteen cases the defendants were convicted for passing information to a foreign power—to Russia (fourteen), to Czechoslovakia (twice), to Poland and to Iraq.[9] In one other case, two defendants were convicted of conspiracy to commit a breach of Section 1 by obtaining information on behalf of Russians and one of the defendants was also convicted of an offense against Section 1. In all these nineteen cases, sentences of imprisonment were imposed ranging from forty-two years down to three years. In another case, the defendant was acquitted. And in another, six defendants were convicted on charges of conspiracy under Section 1 by entering a prohibited place as part of a nuclear-disarmament demonstration; five were sentenced to eighteen months' and one to twelve months' imprisonment.

Espionage is a part of international politics. There has been little argument in the United Kingdom about the law and practice. This may be because when actions are brought they are almost always successful, the evidence is generally conclusive, and public opinion is little moved, even by the imposition of extremely long sentences.

The debate in the United Kingdom has centered instead on Section 2 of the Official Secrets Act 1911, and I have already referred to the report of the departmental Committee, set up under the chairmanship of Lord Franks, of September 1972.[10]

The report of this Committee opens with some general considerations in the manner of such bodies. The committee sees the "wider context" of secrecy to be its relation with democratic control and advances some views in the general field of political philosophy which clearly they regard as no more than self-evident truths but which in truth beg some of the more fundamental questions. I mean statements like: "It is . . . the concern of democratic governments to see that information is widely diffused, for this enables citizens to play a part in controlling their common affairs." I have already said enough to indicate that I am doubtful whether governments see the wide diffusion of information as a part of their concern. Or, rather, that they see it as a part of their concern only so far as it does not impede other parts of their concern, like the prevention of political criticism by their opponents. Politicians do not, I think, much take "the people" into account, not because they are, in any ordinary sense, anti-populist or undemocratic but because to them "the people" are palpable and visible only so far as they manifest themselves as individuals or groups with definable grievances or interests.

Whatever governments may say, they do not act like men and women who feel driven, in the name of democratic theory, to tell more than they need. The Committee itemizes factors which have "increased the pull towards secrecy": the greater sophistication of the processes of government; the vital importance of a government's "economic" maneuvers; advances in science; rapid changes in society. It is not altogether obvious why these lead to greater secrecy but the Committee also refers to the fact that more and more information about the private affairs of citizens comes into the possession of governments.

Now this last point has some validity. On the other hand, it is a strictly limited point. I doubt whether the government knows so much more about the private affairs of individual working-class men than they knew fifty years ago. Their bosses almost certainly know less than they did a hundred years ago. The statement about government knowledge is far more true if taken to apply to the trading and manufacturing middle class and to the financial and other activities of the larger registered companies. "There is a feeling," says the Committee, "that the Government should safeguard the confidences of the citizen almost as strictly as it guards information of use to an enemy." That may well be the feeling of those who are required to part with information they would sooner keep to themselves. But it may not be the feeling of others who consider far more should be known about activities which closely affect the lives and livelihood of those affected as employees or whatever. I can well believe that Lord Franks, Sir Patrick Dean, the Rt. Hon. William Deedes, M.P., Lord Glendevon, Sir Harold Kent, Lord Ogmore, and some others amongst the thirteen members of the Committee could easily subscribe to this "feeling."

The usual chat, under the guise of statements of unimpeachable principle, is continued "more simply" when the Committee speaking of the general issues underlying their work says: "Even a democratic government requires a measure of secrecy for some of its functions, as a means whereby it can better carry out its duties on behalf of the people." But such a government "needs the trust of the governed." Now all this is, in moderation, true enough. But the whole argument as put forward by the Committee reeks of a kind of sanctimoniousness about the working of an industrial democracy that makes suspect even its simple truths. If the Committee had chosen to talk about power and where it lies in our society and the extent to which secrecy is a consequence of power, its premises would have been founded more securely than they are on the principle of nineteenth-century liberalism they espoused.

Section 2 of the Official Secrets Act 1911 is entitled "Wrongful communication etc. of information." The words of the section which found the principal offense are "(1) If any person having in his possession . . . any . . . information . . . which he has obtained . . . owing to his position as a person who holds . . . office under Her Majesty or as a person who holds . . . a contract . . . made on behalf of Her Majesty . . . (a) communicates the . . . information to any person, other than a person to whom he is authorized to communicate it" that person shall be guilty of an offense. The section is therefore primarily concerned with a Crown servant [11] or a government contractor. But by virtue of other words a person who is neither a Crown servant or a government contractor also commits an offense if he makes an unauthorized communication of official information that has been entrusted to him in confidence by a Crown servant. And other words suggest that any recipient of official information wrongly communicated to him commits an offense if he passes it on.

Section 2 is often referred to as a catch-all section. It covers all official documents and information, with no distinctions of kind or of degree.[12] And it covers all Crown servants irrespective of status, as well as some other persons. But an offense is committed only if the information is disclosed by one person to someone other than "a person to whom he is authorized to communicate it" or "a person to whom it is in the interest of the State his duty to communicate it." Of these words the Committee says:

> We found that they were commonly supposed, by persons outside the Government, to imply a fairly formal process of express authorisation. Actual practice within the Govern-

ment rests heavily on a doctrine of implied authorisation, flowing from the nature of each Crown servant's job. In the words of the Home Office, "the communication of official information is proper if such communication can be fairly regarded as part of the job of the officer concerned". Ministers are, in effect, self-authorising. They decide for themselves what to reveal. Senior civil servants exercise a considerable degree of personal judgement in deciding what disclosures of official information they may properly make, and to whom. More junior civil servants, and those whose duties do not involve contact with members of the public, may have a very limited discretion, or none at all.

Furthermore, other words make the mere receipt of official information if the recipient knew, or had reasonable grounds to believe, that the information was communicated to him in contravention of the Acts, illegal. Apart from this provision, *mens rea* is not explicitly made a necessary part of any offense. There are conflicting judicial decisions on whether *mens rea* by implication is necessary.

Prosecutions under the Acts can be brought only with the consent of the Attorney General or, in Scotland, of the Lord Advocate.

From 1945 to 1971, twenty-three prosecutions were brought under Section 2 of the Act of 1911, involving thirty-four defendants, of whom twenty-seven were convicted. About two thirds of the defendants were Crown servants or former Crown servants. In only two cases were professional journalists prosecuted. Over one third of the cases involved information relating to matters of defense, national security, or intelligence; one third concerned police or prison information. One famous recent case was summarized in the report of the Committee thus: "This case involved four defendants, who were charged under section 2 in connection with the communication and receipt of a confidential assessment of the situation in Nigeria written by the Defence Adviser at the British High Commission in Lagos. A copy of this report passed through a number of hands and eventually came to the Sunday *Telegraph*, which published it. As a result, the newspaper, its editor, and two of those along the chain of communication, were prosecuted. In February 1971 all four defendants were acquitted." [13]

The judge in this case criticized the operation of the Acts and suggested they should be replaced by new provisions which would enable people like the four defendants to determine without great difficulty in what circumstances the communication of official information would put them in peril of prosecution.

The width and generality of the provisions of Section 2 evoked much comment, both because it involved the press and because it concerned matters deep in political controversy. The Committee saw their task as being to consider what part *the criminal law* should play in the protection of official information.

Some witnesses told the Committee that the threat of prosecution was used regularly to prevent the publication of official information which had come into the hands of the press or other media. Some Crown servants and former Crown servants said that their attention had on occasion been drawn to the possibility of prosecution and so had been used or believed to have been used to keep the matter secret when, in their opinion, it should have been made public. Other witnesses said that Section 2 was frequently broken or disregarded with impunity by Crown servants and journalists. But the Committee thought this was based on a misunderstanding about self-authorization and implicit authorization. The Committee said that many witnesses apparently assumed that when a Crown servant specified that official information which he disclosed was nonattributable (that is, the source was not to be identified) or was given as background (that is, not intended for general disclosure) or when he talked informally about his work, he was technically in breach of Section 2. But this, thought the Committee, was based on a misconception and the Crown servant was, in one way or another, "authorised" to say what he said.

The Committee heard views on Section 2 which ranged "from almost unqualified approval to total rejection".[14] The evidence from a number of government departments fell into the first category. That from the editorial and proprietorial sides of newspapers and periodicals fell into the second. The distinction was commonly drawn between espionage and leakage and journalists objected to being placed in peril of prosecution alongside spies and traitors. A not dissimilar distinction was drawn by witnesses between the interests of the nation and the interests of the government. For these and like considerations the Committee concluded that the Official Secrets Acts "would be better limited to spying and related matters" and that "the main justification, though not the only one, for the use of criminal sanctions to protect official information from harmful leakage is to guard the security of the nation and the safety of the people." [15]

Before proceeding to their conclusions, the Committee considered the other safeguards for official information. In particular it noted, very properly, that public servants take care not to make unauthorized disclosures because their reputation is at stake and their chances of promotion depend on their being known as reliable, as having good judgment and as exercising discretion. Then there is the internal discipline which applies within the departments to public servants. This brought the Committee to consider security classification. The four levels of classification are related to the degree of damage which disclosure might lead to. They are Top Secret (exceptionally grave damage to the nation); Secret (serious injury to the interests of the nation); Confidential (prejudicial to the interests of the nation); Restricted (undesirable in the interests of the nation).

The first decision which faced the Committee was whether the catch-all quality of Section 2 should be retained. It was generally agreed, even by government departments, that not all the various kinds of official information required the protection of the criminal law. But it was perhaps predictable that many of the most important witnesses felt sorrowfully obliged to argue for the retention of a catch-all provision:

> Sir Peter Rawlinson, the Attorney General, told us that his personal reaction to section 2, as a lawyer, was one of gross distaste, because it involved the criminal law in matters which the criminal law should not be involved in. . . . Sir Peter went on to say that nevertheless, because of the great

difficulties in the way of identifying and defining with certainty those kinds of official information which should be covered, and because the control over prosecutions under section 2 exercised by Attorneys General ensured that in practice the section operated in a reasonable way, he thought it preferable on balance to retain a catch-all section, together with the Attorney's control over prosecutions, as the lesser of two evils.

Mr. James Callaghan (a former Home Secretary) summarized his viewpoint as "different does not necessarily mean better" and he thought Section 2 should be retained, possibly with a new defense that publication was in the public interest. Lord Brooke of Cumnor (another former Home Secretary) "stressed the difficulties of devising a satisfactory alternative" and, with a soaring imaginative leap, found a parallel in the failure to discover a "half-way house" between retention and abolition of capital punishment. Lord Parker (the former Lord Chief Justice) thought the difficulties surrounding any satisfactory revision of the law so great that he preferred the *status quo*, with the possibility of some reinforcement of the arrangements for controlling prosecutions.[16]

Despite—or possibly because of—the antiquity of these reasons for doing nothing, the Committee decided Section 2 should go and be replaced by an Official Information Act.

The Committee proposed ways in which the catch-all quality of Section 2 could be abandoned and by which specific provisions would limit the area of *criminal* liability. The information to which the new Act would apply was to be limited to specified areas. First, it would include defense and internal security; foreign relations; and currency and reserves. The Act would apply to such information if it had been classified as secret on the ground that its unauthorized disclosure would cause *serious* injury to the interests of the nation. When a prosecution was pending, the responsible Minister should review the classification and the prosecution should proceed only if the Minister was satisfied that the classification was proper. Secondly, the new Act would apply to certain information under the heading of maintenance of law and order; and to all Cabinet documents. Thirdly, the new Act would make it an offense for a Crown servant to use official information for the purpose of obtaining private gain for himself or any other person. Fourthly, the main provision to cover those other than Crown servants made it an offense for anyone knowing or having reasonable ground to believe that information he received had been disclosed in contravention of the Act to communicate that information to some other person.

In requiring the Minister to review the classification, the Committee presumably hoped to prevent the evasion of the new Act which could otherwise be effected by the wholesale classifying of documents as secret. But they leaned far over in the opposite direction when they made the Minister's certificate *conclusive* evidence both of the fact that the document was so classified and of the propriety of the classification in the case before the court.

In effect the Committee left with the government the power and duty of defining what was "serious" and so proper for criminal proceedings. Some would regard this as inevitable. But others would prefer that the courts should be enabled to review this making of definitions in ways similar to those now accepted in cases where the government claims Crown privilege for the nondisclosure of documents in litigation.

It would be idle to pretend that even the modest proposals of the Franks Committee are likely to be adopted by this or any other government. The powers of the security establishment in Britain are very great and their influence is no less so. We shall, doubtless for a considerable period, probably forever, continue to carry the provisions of the Official Secrets Acts and to hear time and again that we are protected by the discretion of the Attorney General. It is a highly flimsy protection. Whatever may be the tradition in this matter, however strong may be the intention of successive Attorneys General that when exercising this discretion they will make an independent legal judgment, they are appointed by the Prime Minister, belong to his political party, and hope for political preferment. In the future we may find that this safeguard is no safeguard. And then it will be too late.

III In the Balance

In general conclusion, one or two final points may be made without expecting them to attract universal agreement.

I believe that, in the United Kingdom and perhaps elsewhere, those of us who are concerned about the protection and extension of civil liberties rely too much on the expression of liberal sentiments and the expression of our sense of outrage and indignation. I have already suggested that such expression is a fast-wasting asset, and that soon we shall find little or no response. Publicity is still our chief weapon, but it relies on what we disclose being *news.* Of course we must continue to protest at corruption. And secrecy is often the handmaid of corruption. But we need to be more sophisticated politically and more astute politically than is suggested by the public wringing of hands. I suspect that this criticism can more justifiably be made of those of us in the United Kingdom than of you in the United States.

But we do need to have a clear view of society and of the reforms necessary to promote the kind of society we want. To give one example of what I mean: in the United Kingdom and no doubt in every other country in the world, there are economic and financial interests who make it an important part of their activity to uncover what it is that governments are considering and then seeking to insure either that government action is made to serve their interests or that government action is prevented or frustrated. In such a case, government secrecy may be something we wish to support. In other words, openness to me is not a value which self-evidently must be striven for. First I must know for what purpose secrecy is being maintained. Only then can I say whether I am for it or against it. And I will come to that decision by reference to political aims and purposes which partake more of absolutes.

What I want to defeat or to promote may be a far wider concept of evil or good than is reflected in the notion and practice of secrecy. The ideas which civil liberties evoke for me involve the changing of our society—not today, nor tomorrow, but sometime. And in that sense, government secrecy is in the end a contingent and ambivalent question.

Notes

CHAPTER 1 —*by Norman Dorsen and John Shattuck*

1 *The New York Times,* July 24, 1973, p. 19.

2 *Ibid.*

3 *Ibid.*

4 *Ibid.*

5 *Congressional Record,* April 22, 1948, p. 4783.

6 "The Present Limits of Executive Privilege" (study prepared by the Government and General Research Division of the Library of Congress), *Congressional Record,* pp. H2243–H2246, March 28, 1973.

7 *Congressional Record,* p. H5817, April 4, 1963.

8 *Congressional Record,* p. H2245, March 28, 1973. See also *The Washington Post,* December 19, 1972.

9 Statement of Richard G. Kleindienst, Attorney General of the United States, on S. 858 and S.J. Res. 72, "Executive Privilege," before the Separation of Powers Subcommittee of the Committee on the Judiciary, and the Intergovernmental Relations Subcommittee on Government Operations, United States Senate, April 10, 1973.

10 Attorney General Opinion, "Position of the Executive Department Regarding Investigative Reports," Robert H. Jackson, 40 Op. A.G. 45 (April 30, 1941). See also "Executive Privilege: The Withholding of Information by the Executive, Hearings on S. 1125 before the Subcommittee on Separation of Powers of the Committee on the Judiciary, United States Senate," 92nd Con-

gress, 1st Session (July 27–29 and August 4–5, 1971) (hereafter, Hearings on S. 1125 Concerning Executive Privilege), p. 576.

11 "Special Senate Investigation on Charges and Countercharges Involving: Secretary of the Army Robert J. Stevens, John G. Adams, H. Struve Hensel and Senator Joe McCarthy, Roy M. Cohn, and Francis P. Carr," Hearings before Special Subcommittee on Investigations Committee on Government Operations, United States Senate, 83rd Congress, 2nd Session (1954), pp. 1169–72.

12 William Rogers, "Constitutional Law: the Papers of the Executive Branch," 44 *American Bar Association Journal* 941 (1958).

13 *Ibid.*, p. 942.

14 See generally Raoul Berger, "Executive Privilege v. Congressional Inquiry" (Part I), 12 *UCLA Law Review* 1043, 1078–1111 (1965) (hereafter, Berger).

15 Quoted in "Power of the President to Withhold Information from Congress," Memorandum of Attorney General Rogers submitted to Subcommittee on Constitutional Rights of the Committee on the Judiciary, United States Senate, 85th Congress, 2nd Session (1958), p. 6. See also Berger, p. 1093.

16 *Howard* v. *Gossett*, 10 Queen's Bench 359, 379–380 (1845).

17 Quoted in *Chandler, History and Proceedings of the Third Parliament of King George II* (1743), p. 172. See also Berger, p. 1058.

18 Quoted in Wolkinson, "Demands of Congressional Committees for Executive Papers," 10 *Federal Bar Journal* 103, 128 (1949) (emphasis supplied). See also Berger, p. 1059.

19 1 Stat. 65–66 (1789) (now 5 U.S. Code, Section 242).

20 Quoted in Schwartz, "Executive Privilege and Congressional Investigatory Power," 47 *California Law Review* 3, 23 (1959).

21 354 U.S. 178, 187 (1957).

22 *Myers* v. *United States*, 272 U.S. 52, 177 (1926).

23 343 U.S. at 637 (Jackson concurring).

24 Joseph Bishop, "The Executive's Right of Privacy: An Unresolved Constitutional Question," 66 *Yale Law Journal* 477, 488 (1957) (hereafter, Bishop).

25 Statement of Philip B. Kurland, Hearings on S. 1125 Concerning Executive Privilege, p. 539.

26 Quoted in Philip B. Kurland, "Comment on Separation of Power," occasional paper from the Law School, University of Chicago, p. 8.

27 "Congress and the President: Executive Privilege in Past and Present," speech by Roger C. Cramton, Dean Elect, Cornell Law School and former Assistant Attorney General, Office of Legal Counsel, Department of Justice, at Cornell Law School, March 14, 1973.

28 *The New York Times*, April 19, 1973, p. 1.

29 See, e.g., testimony of Dean Acheson, former Secretary of State,

in Hearings on S. 1125 Concerning Executive Privilege, July 28, 1971, pp. 259–72.

30 *Powell* v. *McCormack,* 395 U.S. 486, 549 (1969), quoting *McPherson* v. *Blacker,* 146 U.S. 1, 24 (1892).

31 *Baker* v. *Carr,* 369 U.S. 186, 217, 226 (1962).

32 *Gravel* v. *United States,* 408 U.S. 606 (1972); *United States* v. *Brewster,* 408 U.S. 501 (1972).

33 *Environmental Protection Agency* v. *Mink* 410 U.S. 73, 83 (1973).

34 *United States* v. *Reynolds,* 345. U.S. 1, 7 (1953).

35 5 U.S. Code, Section 552(b) (b), (7).

36 Letter of May 17, 1954, to Secretary of Defense Charles Wilson, 100 *Congressional Record* 6621 (1954).

37 Bishop, *loc. cit.,* p. 488.

38 Testimony of Professor Alan C. Swan, Hearings on S. 1125 Concerning Executive Privilege, p. 249.

39 See note 32, *supra.*

40 Nathan Lewin, "The Cloak of Immunity," *The New Republic,* July 28 and August 4, 1973, pp. 17–18.

41 *In re Subpoena to Nixon,* 360 F. Supp. 1 (D.C.C.), aff'd sub nom. *Nixon* v. *Sirica,*——F.2'd——, 42 L.W. 2211 (D.C. Cir. 1973). The parallel suit filed by the Senate Select Committee on Campaign Activities was initially dismissed for lack of jurisdiction, but was reinstated following the enactment of a statute authorizing the suit.

CHAPTER 2 —*by William G. Phillips*

1 37 *Federal Register* 5200 (March 10, 1972).

2 18 U.S. Code 793–98; 50 U.S. Code 781.

3 H.R. 6046; S. 1400, Section 1124.

4 National Archives, "Origin of Defense Information Markings in the Army and Former War Department," prepared by Dallas Irvine, December 23, 1964 (revised 1972), p. 24. Most of the historical examples cited below are taken from this study.

5 Now codified as 5 U.S. Code 301. Public Law 85–619, enacted in 1958, eliminated from the ancient "housekeeping" statute authority to withhold information from the public on that basis.

6 5 *Federal Register* 1145 (March 26, 1940).

7 Office of War Information Regulation No. 4, issued September 28, 1942.

8 50 U.S. Code 401.

9 15 *Federal Register* 597 (February 1, 1950).

10 16 *Federal Register* 9795 (September 27, 1951).

11 18 *Federal Register* 7049 (November 9, 1953).

12 Section 142 of the Atomic Energy Act of 1954, as amended (42 U.S. Code 2162).

13 26 *Federal Register* 8932 (September 20, 1961).

14 Hearings, U.S. House of Representatives, Foreign Operations and Government Information Subcommittee, Committee on Government Operations, "U.S. Government Information Policies and Practices—Security Classification Problems Involving Subsection (b) (1) of the Freedom of Information Act," (hereinafter cited as 1972 hearings), Part 7, p. 2309. See also H. Rept. 93–221, 93rd Congress (May 22, 1973), based on the Subcommittee's 1971 and 1972 Hearings on Classification.

15 Hearings, U.S. Congress, House of Representatives, Special Government Information Subcommittee, Committee on Government Operations, "Availability of Information from Federal Departments and Agencies," 17 Parts, 84th and 85th Congresses (1956–1957). See also H. Rept. 2947 (84th Congress), H. Rept. 1619, H. Rept. 1884, H. Rept. 2578 (85th Congress).

16 A full report by the Subcommittee on the work of the Coolidge Committee is contained in H. Rept. 1884 (June 16, 1958), pp. 20–37. The Wright Commission was created by Public Law 304, 84th Congress, 1955.

17 H. Rept. 1884, 85th Congress, pp. 23–24.

18 *Ibid.*, pp. 107–116.

19 *Report of the Commission on Government Security*, June 21, 1957. Government Printing Office. See "Document Classification Program" description and recommendations section, pp. 151–184.

20 H. Rept. 1884, 85th Congress, pp. 15–16.

21 *Ibid.*, p. 152.

22 H. Rept. 1257, 87th Congress (September 22, 1961), p. 57.

23 Hearings, U.S. House of Representatives, Foreign Operations and Government Information Subcommittee, Committee on Government Operations, "U.S. Government Information Policies and Practices—The Pentagon Papers" (hereinafter cited as 1971 hearings), Parts 1, 2 and 3.

24 1972 hearings, *op. cit.*, p. 2309.

25 *Ibid.*, pp. 2283–2284.

26 See *ibid.*, pp. 2604–2605; pp. 2471–2472; also 1971 hearings, *op. cit.*, Part 1, p. 97; Part 3, pp. 905–906.

27 1972 hearings, p. 2935.

28 1971 hearings, Part 1, p. 98; p. 104.

29 1972 hearings, p. 2313.

30 Progress Report of the Interagency Classification Review Committee, Memorandum for the President, April 17, 1973.

31 1971 hearings, Part 3, p. 975.

32 *Ibid.*, Part 1, p. 97.

33 1972 hearings, pp. 2909–2910.

34 *Ibid.*, pp. 2286–2293.

35 *Ibid.*, pp. 2656–2657.

36 1972 hearings, p. 2310.

37 *Ibid.*, p. 2827.

38 *Ibid.*, p. 2312.

39 H. Rept. 93–221, 93rd Congress (May 22, 1973), p. 30.

40 Hearings, U.S. House of Representatives, Foreign Operations and Government Information Subcommittee, Government Operations Committee, "Amendments to the Freedom of Information Act—H.R. 4960 and H.R. 5425."

41 1972 hearings; p. 2850.

42 H. Rept. 93–221, *op. cit.*, pp. 80–83; pp. 102–103.

43 *Ibid.*, pp. 83–87.

44 For the most recent conclusions and recommendation for reform of the classification system see pp. 100–104, H. Rept. 93–221, unanimously adopted by the House Government Operations Committee, May 22, 1973.

45 Muskie bill, S. 2965 (92nd Congress), December 7, 1971; Moorhead bill, H.R. 15172 (92nd Congress), May 24, 1972; Gravel bill, S. 1726 (93rd Congress), May 7, 1973.

CHAPTER 3 —*By Stanley Futterman*

1 5 U.S. Code Section 552 (b) (1).

2 H. Arendt, *Crises of the Republic* (New York, 1972), p. 85.

3 One of those tapped thinks even this explanation, grudgingly conceded by administration officials, too kind to the administration. He contends the real reason was to test the political attitudes of White House staffers. See M. Halperin, "Leaks and Bugging: an Unlikely Link," *The Washington Post*, June 11, 1973, p. 1.

4 Statement by President Nixon, "Scope of U.S. Involvement in Laos," issued at Key Biscayne, Florida, March 6, 1970, in *Six Weekly Compilations of Presidential Documents* 322 (1970).

5 Sheehan, *et al.*, *The Pentagon Papers* (paperback ed., 1971), pp. 238–40, 258–61.

6 Wise and Ross, *The Invisible Government* (paperback ed., 1971), p. 101.

7 With respect to secret agreements, it is possible to take the view that military commitments not concurred in by the Congress do not obligate the United States to take or support military actions. This is the view taken by the National Commitment Resolution, Senate Resolution 85, agreed to on June 25, 1969. If secret agreements then can amount only to indications of intent by the executive, a status not far removed from the forming of an intent, the argument for compelling disclosure may be weakened.

8 93 S. Ct. 827 (1973).

9 5 U.S. Code Section 552 (b) (5).

10 403 U.S. 713 (1971).

11 The composition of the Court had changed somewhat between the two cases, with Justices Black and Harlan being replaced by Justices Powell and Rehnquist.

12 For what it is worth, possession cuts two ways with respect to criminal sanctions. Since "the cat is out of the bag," see Wise, *infra*, p. 235, the element of possession favors a restrictive attitude toward the application of the criminal law. On the other hand, the criminal sanction as it might be applied to former employees and contractors is an important deterrent in keeping the cat in the bag.

13 466 F. 2d 1309 (1972), cert den. 93 S. Ct. 553 (December 11, 1972). Three members of the Supreme Court—Brennan, Douglas, and Stewart—expressly indicated they would grant certiorari. It is rare for Justices to dissent from a denial of certiorari and rarer still for three of them to feel deeply enough about the issue to do so and yet not be able to gather the fourth vote necessary for the grant of certiorari.

14 283 U.S. 697 (1931).

15 Executive Order 11652, "Classification and Declassification of National Security Information and Material," appeared March 8, 1972, 37 Fed. Reg. 5209, March 10, 1972. The order specifies just plain "damage" for the classification "Confidential," "serious damage" for the higher classification "Secret," and "grave damage" for the highest classification "Top Secret." These gradations affect such matters as the kind of safe in which the material may be stored as well as the normal length of time it will remain classified.

CHAPTER 6 —*by M. L. Stein*

1 *Grassroots Editor*, March–April, 1972, p. 14.

2 Gary Cooke, "Brown Act Violations Common," *California Publisher*, October 1969, p. 6.

3 *California Publisher*, November 1966, p. 6.

4 *Harvard Law Review*, Vol. 75 (April 1962), p. 1221.

5 *Des Moines Register*, April 6, 1972.

6 *Editor & Publisher*, April 17, 1971.

7 Report of the 1972 Sigma Delta Chi Advancement of Freedom of Information Committee, p. 22.

8 *Virginia Publisher*, June 1971, p. 7.

9 *North Dakota Publisher*, April 1972, p. 5.

10 *The New York Times*, November 2, 1972.

11 *Editor & Publisher*, February 10, 1973, p. 9.

12 *Publishers' Auxiliary*, May 25, 1972.

13 *St. Louis Globe Democrat*, September 17, 1968.

14 *Editor & Publisher*, April 15, 1972.

15 *Philadelphia Inquirer*, December 10, 1971.

16 *The New York Times*, February 24, 1971.
17 *The Washington Post*, June 2, 1972.
18 *San Francisco Chronicle*, March 25, 1972.
19 *American Society of Newspaper Editors Bulletin*, March 1972.

CHAPTER 8 —*by Harrison Wellford*

1 U.S. Senate, Committee on the Judiciary, "Clarifying and Protecting the Right of the Public to Information," S. Rep. No. 813, 89th Congress, 1st Session, Page 3 (1967).
2 "Attorney General's Memorandum on the Public Information Section of the Administrative Procedure Act," 20 *Administrative Law Review* 263 (1968).
3 Charles H. Koch, Jr., "The Freedom of Information Act: Suggestions for Making Information Available to the Public," *Maryland Law Review*, Vol. 32, No. 3 (1972).
4 Preamble to "Attorney General's Memorandum," *op. cit.*
5 Following is a summary of the nine exemptions from disclosure described by the Freedom of Information Act: 1) matters specifically required by Executive Order to be kept secret in the interest of the national defense or foreign policy; 2) matters related solely to the internal personnel rules and practices of an agency; 3) matters specifically exempted by statute; 4) trade secrets and commercial or financial information obtained from a person and privileged or confidential; 5) inter-agency or intra-agency memorandums . . . ; 6) personnel and medical files, the disclosure of which would constitute a clearly unwarranted invasion of personal privacy; 7) investigatory files compiled for law-enforcement purposes; 8) matters contained in or related to examination, operation, or condition reports prepared by, on behalf of, or for the use of an agency responsible for the regulation or supervision of financial institutions; and 9) geological and geophysical information and data.
6 Statement of Ronald Plesser on H.R. 5425 and H.R. 4960 before the Subcommittee on Foreign Operations and Government Information, House Committee on Government Operations, May 16, 1973.
7 House Committee on Government Operations, *Administration of the Freedom of Information Act*, H. Rept. No. 92–1419, 92nd Congress, 2nd Session, 8 (1972).
8 "Attorney General's Memorandum."
9 *Ibid.*, p. 55*f.*
10 Hearings, before the House Subcommittee on Foreign Operations and Government Information, "U.S. Government Information Policies and Practices—Administration and Operation of the Freedom of Information Act (Part 4)," 92nd Congress, 2nd Session (1972), p. 1218.
11 Plesser, *op. cit.*

12 *Ackerly* v. *Ley*, 420 F. 2d 1336, 1341 (D.C. Cir. 1969).

13 Kenneth Culp Davis, *Discretionary Justice* (Baton Rouge, La., 1969).

14 *Consumers Union* v. *Veterans Administration*, 301 F. Supp. 796 (S.D.N.Y., 1969), *appeal dismissed*, 436 F. 2d 1363 (2d Cir. 1971).

15 *Bristol-Myers Co.* v. *FTC*, 424 F. 2d 935 (D.C. Cir. 1970), cert. den., 400 U.S. 824 (1970).

16 Statement of Ralph Nader on S. 1142 before the Senate Subcommittee on Administrative Practices and Procedures, Separation of Powers and Intergovernmental Relations, April 12, 1973.

17 Koch, *op. cit.*, p. 214.

18 *Wellford* v. *Hardin*, 444 F. 2d 21 (4th Cir., 1971). See also *Bristol-Myers Co.* v. *FTC*, 424 F. 2d 935 (D.C. Cir. 1970).

19 *Ditlow* v. *Volpe*, Civil Action No. 2370–72 June 12, 1973.

20 *Wellford* v. *Hardin*, *supra* note 18, p. 24.

21 *Administration of the Freedom of Information Act*, *Supra* note 7, p. 38.

22 448 F. 2d 1067, 2 ERC 1626 (D.C. Cir., 1971).

23 Peter Hutt, "Public Information and Public Participation in the Food and Drug Administration," speech to Association of Food and Drug officials of the United States, Monticello, New York, June 21, 1972.

24 See comments of David Parson, Chairman of the Committee on Government Information of the Federal Bar Association, in "Administration of the Freedom of Information Act," p. 39.

25 See Harrison Wellford, *Sowing the Wind* (New York, 1972), pp. 96–97.

26 *Ibid.*, p. 165.

27 Robert Fellmeth, "The Regulatory Industrial Complex," in B. Wasserstein and M. Green, *With Justice for Some* (Boston, 1970), p. 244.

28 See Plesser, *supra*, note 6.

29 *Ibid.*

CHAPTER 9 —*by David Wise*

1 It is interesting to note that E. Howard Hunt, Jr., the former CIA operative whom Colson had brought to the White House as a "consultant," thought otherwise. In his plea for leniency to Judge John Sirica on March 23, 1973, Hunt said the Watergate case proved that "political offenses are not to be tolerated by our society within our democratic system."

2 *New York Times Co.* v. *United States*, 403 U.S. 713 (1971).

3 The Supreme Court in *Red Lion Broadcasting Company, Inc.* v. *Federal Communications Commission*, 395 U.S. 367 (1969) held that broadcasters do not possess "an unabridgeable First Amend-

ment right to broadcast comparable to the right of every individual to speak, write, or publish." On the other hand, the Court in *Rosenbloom* v. *Metromedia, Inc.*, 403 U.S. 29 (1971), ruled that George Rosenbloom, a distributor of nudist magazines in Philadelphia, could not successfully sue a local radio station for libel for reporting his arrest. Here the Court extended its dictum in *New York Times* v. *Sullivan*, 376 U.S. 254 (1964), to apply to private persons involved in public events. In *Rosenbloom*, the Court seemed to be saying that broadcasters did, after all, enjoy First Amendment protection.

4 *Near* v. *Minnesota*, 283 U.S. 697 (1931).

5 Departmental Committee on Section 2 of the Official Secrets Act 1911, Report of the Committee, Vol. I (London, September 1972), p. 29.

6 *Gorin* v. *United States*, 312 U.S. 19.

7 David Wise, *The Politics of Living: Government Deception, Secrecy, and Power* (New York, 1973), p. 98.

8 From a brief filed by Professor Emerson and Representative Bob Eckhardt of Texas in the Pentagon Papers case, cited in the *New York Times* v. *United States: A Documentary History* (New York, 1971), II, 1057–58.

9 *Branzburg* v. *Hayes, In the Matter of Paul Pappas, United States* v. *Caldwell*, all 408 U.S. 665 (1972).

CHAPTER 12 —*by Alan Westin*

1 *Inventory and Summary of Federal ADP Activities for Fiscal 1972*, General Services Administration, Automated Data and Telecommunications Service, 1973, pp. 2, 5, 12, and 36.

2 See Alan F. Westin and Michael A. Baker, *Data Banks in a Free Society* (New York, 1972).

3 For articles recounting the development of public-access laws, see the bibliography, "Availability of Information from Federal Departments and Agencies," House Committee on Government Operations, January 1964.

4 Westin and Baker, *op. cit.*

5 Alan F. Westin "Information Technology and Public Decision-Making," in *The Harvard University Program on Technology and Society, 1964–1972, A Final Review* (Cambridge, 1972) pp. 59–67; Anthony G. Oettinger, "Compunications [*sic*] in the National Decision-Making Process," in Martin Greenberger (ed.), *Computers, Communications, and the Public Interest* (Baltimore, 1971); *Information Technology: Some Critical Implications for Decision-Makers*, The Conference Board (New York, 1972). See also Alan F. Westin (ed.), *Information Technology in a Democracy* (Cambridge, Mass. 1971).

6 Letter from L. Patrick Gray III, Acting Director, Federal Bureau of Investigation, February 23, 1973.

7 Memorandum from T. McDonald, Chief, Public Affairs Division,

U.S. Coast Guard, March 26, 1973, enclosed in letter from John L. McGruder, Director of Management Systems, Department of Transportation, June 13, 1973.

8 Memorandum from John R. Provan, Associate Administrator for Administration, Federal Highway Administration, March 30, 1973, enclosed in letter from John L. McGruder, *op. cit.*

9 Letter from Lee D. Vincent, Chief, Organization and Methods Branch, National Labor Relations Board, March 2, 1973.

10 Letter from Leonard Wienles, Chief, Office of Information, Federal Communications Commission, April 11, 1973.

11 Letter from Louis Zawatzky, Acting Assistant Commissioner for Administration, Social Security Administration, March 21, 1973; letter from John J. Corcoran, General Counsel, Veterans Administration, June 21, 1973.

12 Memorandum from Department of Data Management (no author or date), enclosed in letter from John J. Corcoran, *op. cit.*

13 Memorandum from Information Service, Veterans Administration (no author or date), enclosed in letter from John J. Corcoran, *op. cit.*

14 Memorandum from Dean St. Dennis, Public Information Office, Law Enforcement Assistance Administration, enclosed in letter from Robert G. Dixon, Jr., Assistant Attorney General, Office of Legal Counsel, Department of Justice, July 6, 1973; letter from Patricia L. Cahn, Assistant Commissioner for Public Affairs, Office of Education, March 1, 1973; memorandum from Robert E. Parsons, Director, Office of R & D Plans and Resources, Department of Transportation, April 5, 1973, enclosed in letter from John L. McGruder, *op. cit.*

15 Memorandum from Robert E. Parsons, *op. cit.*

16 Letter from J. Meisel, Director of Management Systems, Federal Aviation Administration, April 2, 1973.

17 Memorandum from Richard L. Spears, General Manager, National Transportation Safety Board, March 30, 1973, enclosed in letter from John L. McGruder, *op. cit.*

18 The Veterans Administration wrote: "As can readily be understood, the primary purpose of accumulating and storing data in our computer-based systems is for the internal processing and operation of the many systems of benefits available to veterans and their beneficiaries," letter from John J. Corcoran, *op. cit.* See also letter from W. Fletcher Lutz, Director, Bureau of Accounts and Statistics, Civil Aeronautics Board, March 21, 1973.

19 The full replies are contained with the letter from John L. McGruder, *op. cit.*

20 Letter from Robert G. Dixon, Jr., *op. cit.;* letter from John J. Corcoran, *op. cit.;* letter of Patricia L. Cahn, *op. cit.;* letter of Louis Zawatzky, *op. cit.;* and letter of John F. Sherman, Acting Director, Public Health Service, National Institutes of Health, Department of Health, Education, and Welfare, April 18, 1973.

21 Letter from Patricia L. Cahn, *op. cit.*

22 Letter from Joseph O. Smiroldo, Acting Director, Office of Organization and Management Systems, Department of Commerce, March 30, 1973.

23 Letter from Frank S. Johnson, Jr., Director, Public Affairs, Department of Labor, March 28, 1973.

24 Letter from J. Meisel, *op. cit.*

25 Memorandum from John W. Barnum, General Counsel, April 2, 1973, enclosed in letter from John L. McGruder, *op. cit.*

26 See booklet on the *Grant Management Information System*, Law Enforcement Assistance Administration, Information Systems Division, Office of Operations Support, April 13, 1972.

27 Letter from Richard J. Sullivan, Chief Counsel, House Committee on Public Works, April 30, 1973.

28 Letter from Donald C. Knapp, Counsel, House Committee on Veterans' Affairs, May 3, 1973.

29 Telephone interview with Lawrence Baskir, Counsel, Senate Subcommittee on Constitutional Rights, May 8, 1973. Some of the telephone interviews conducted with information-seekers were made by my research assistant, Ms. Caryn Leland, whose help I gratefully acknowledge.

30 Letter from L. James Kronfeld, Special Counsel, Subcommittee on Foreign Operations and Government Information, January 16, 1973.

31 For a detailed presentation of the additional capacities that computers give federal agencies to produce special lists from their computerized base files, see Hearings before a Subcommittee of the Committee on Government Operations, "Sale or Distribution of Mailing Lists By Federal Agencies," 92nd Congress, 2nd Session, House of Representatives, June 13 and 15, 1972.

32 Letter from Harrison Wellford, January [no date] 1973; telephone interviews with Wellford and Ronald Plesser, March 1973.

33 Telephone interview with Benjamin L. Kass, April 26, 1973.

34 Telephone interview with Myra Barrer, April 20, 1973.

35 Telephone interview with Ko Kimbel, April 20, 1973.

36 Letter from Samuel J. Archibald, February 21, 1973.

37 Letter from James Ridgeway, December 23, 1972.

38 A full discussion of the need to create a Citizen's Guide to Files at each level of American government, and to establish a legal right of access for the individual appears in the testimony of Alan F. Westin before the Subcommittee on Government Information of the House Committee on Government Operations, in "Hearings on Records Maintained by Government Agencies," 92nd Congress, 2nd Session, June 22 and 27, 1972; and *Data Banks in a Free Society*, pp. 355–372. Such a proposal is presently before the Congress in bills sponsored by Representative Edward Koch and Senator Birch Bayh.

39 For an announcement and outline of these hearings, see *Congressional Record*, April 2, 1973, pp. H2373–74.

40 The Metcalf bill is reprinted in *Congressional Record,* February 6, 1973, pp. S2112–16, with the ADP provision p. 2115.

41 For the FPC notice, see Docket No. R–438, "Development of a Fully Automated Computer Regulatory System—Revisions in Title 18, Code of Federal Regulations, "Notice of a Proposed Rulemaking and Request for Comments," April 13, 1972; letter from William L. Webb, Director of Public Information, FPC, March 2, 1973; Docket Entries for No. R–438, through April 16, 1973.

CHAPTER 13 —*J. A. G. Griffith*

1 Departmental Committee on Section 2 of the Official Secrets Act 1911 (Cmnd. 5104, September 1972).

2 Paragraph 81.

3 For a somewhat overstated and eulogistic account of these and other improvements in publication, see *Information and the Public Interest* (Cmnd. 4089), published in June 1969 by the Labour Government.

4 [1968] A.C. 910.

5 H. C. 43 of 1972–1973.

6 Pursuant to a resolution of March 16, 1688: "If any Member of the House refuse, upon being sent to, to come to give evidence or information as a witness to a committee, the committee ought to acquaint the House therewith, and not summon such Member to attend the committee."

7 Erskine May, *Parliamentary Practice* (18th ed.) p. 630; see also Chapters IX, X, p. 250, and pp. 666–70.

8 See Cmnd. 5104 App. 1.

9 *Ibid.*, App. II.

10 Cmnd. 5104.

11 This includes Ministers, members of the judiciary, public servants employed in central government departments, police officers, and others.

12 Cmnd. 5104, paragraph 17.

13 *Ibid.*, paragraph 8.

14 *Ibid.*, paragraph 40.

15 *Ibid.*, paragraph 54.

16 *Ibid.*, paragraphs 91, 93.